Indian Ocean Community

Uniting Nations on path of progress

Borobudur. Stone relief of an Indonesian trade ship.

S. Kalyanaraman

Sarasvati Research Center

2012

Library of Congress Control Number 2012921968

Printed in the USA.

First paperback printing: November 2012

ISBN 13: 978-0-9828971-5-7

ISBN: 0982897154

Indian Ocean Community

Uniting Nations on path of progress

Let us seize the historic moment to realize the civilizational declaration pronounced by our ancestors, *sadhabas*, the ancient mariners, the *sādhyas* who accomplished an extraordinary cultural tradition in their navigational path, sealane of the *Rāṣṭram* along the Indian Ocean rim.

S. Kalyanaraman October 23, 2012 Sarasvati Puja.

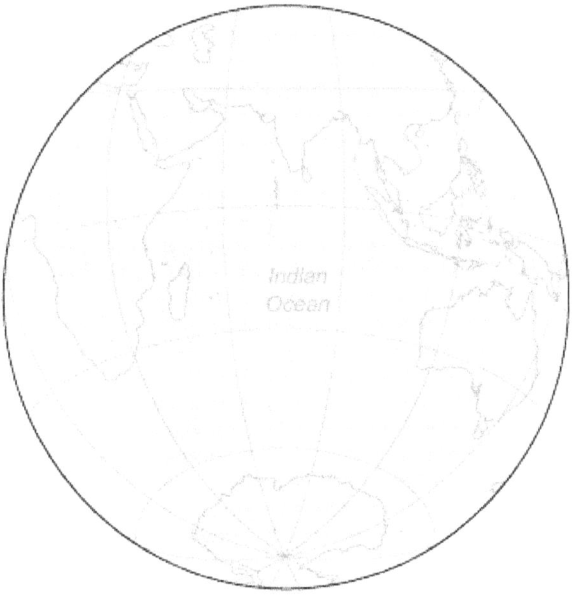

Rāṣṭram is Indian Ocean Community. Nations along the rim of the Ocean of 63,000 miles should together constitute a socio-economic powerhouse to resolve the global financial crisis. As a counterpoise to European Community, the Indian Ocean Community can bring new developmental opportunities for over a third of humanity and contribute to setting up an equitable and just global order.

The Indian Ocean is the warmest ocean in the world. North of 20° south latitude the minimum surface temperature is 22 °C (72 °F), exceeding 28 °C (82 °F) to the east.

Monsoon controls the ocean currents. It is the only ocean with an asymmetric and, in the north, semiannually reversing surface circulation.Two large circular currents, one in the northern hemisphere flowing clockwise and one south of the equator moving anticlockwise, constitute the dominant flow pattern. During the winter monsoon, however, currents in the north are reversed. These churning currents have a dominant structural control over rare earth mineral placer deposits along the rim of the Ocean. The minerals include ilmenite (a mixture of iron and titanium oxide), tin, monazite (a rare earth), zircon, and chromite, all of which are found in nearshore sand bodies. The shallow waters of the tropical zone are characterized by numerous corals and other organisms capable of building, together with calcareous red algae, reefs and coral islands. These coralline structures shelter a thriving marine fauna consisting of sponges, worms, crabs, mollusks, sea urchins, brittle stars, starfish, and small but exceedingly brightly coloured reef fish… Despite great fishery potentials, however, most commercial fishing is done by small-scale fishermen at lower depths, while deep-sea resources (with the exception of tuna) remain poorly fished.[1]

Ancient Sanskrit literature calls Indian Ocean *ratnākara* '*ratna – ākara* = mine of jewels, precious stones and gems' and in Indian languages, the

Indian Ocean is known as *Hindu Mahāsāgar* (Hindu Great Ocean), a clear indication that the word Hindu referred to the people of India.

On 26 December 2004, countries surrounding the Indian Ocean were hit by a tsunami caused by the 2004 Indian Ocean earthquake and resulting in more than 226,000 deaths. Over 1 million people were rendered homeless.[2]

The climate north of the equator is affected by a monsoon climate. Strong north-east winds blow from October until April; from May until October south and west winds prevail. In the Arabian Sea the violent Monsoon brings rain to the Indian subcontinent. In the southern hemisphere the winds are generally milder, but summer storms near Mauritius can be severe. When the monsoon winds change, cyclones sometimes strike the shores of the Arabian Sea and the Bay of Bengal.

Indian Ocean, third largest of ocean divisions covers, on the surface of Planet Earth, about 20% of the water, bounded on the north by Asia, including India after which the ocean is named. The northernmost extent of the Indian Ocean is approximately 30° north in the Persian Gulf. Archipelago of Indonesia borders the ocean on the east.Bounded on the west by Africa, on the east by Australia, and on the south by by Antarctica, there are many island nations within the ocean: Madagascar, Comoros, Seychelles, Maldives, Mauritius and Sri Lanka.

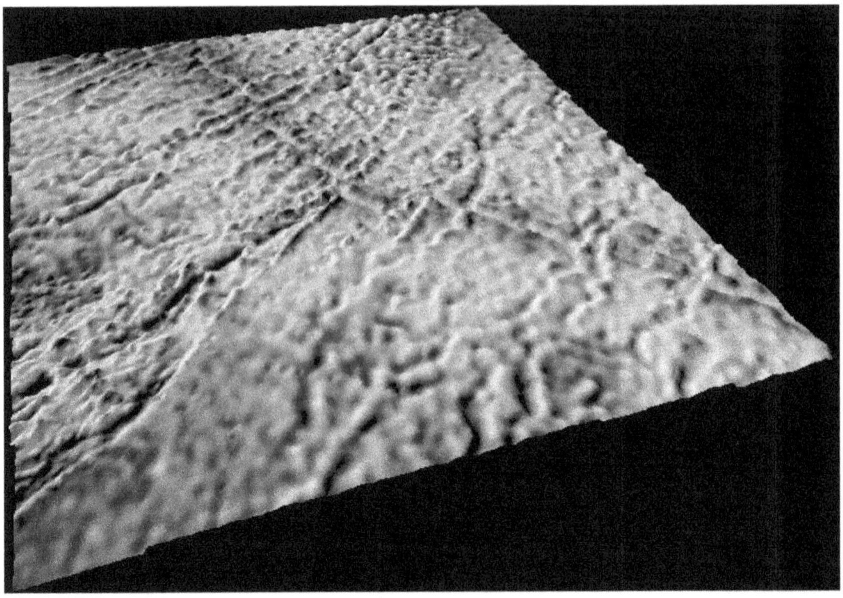

Rodrigues Triple Point[3] – a geologic triple junction in southern Indian Ocean of three plates: African Plate, Indo-Australian Plate and Antarctic Plate.

Left 65E, right 75E, back to front = 1100 kms[4].

Average depth of the ocean is 3,890 m with the deepest point called Diamantina Deep at 8,047 m

Marginal Seas, Gulfs, Bays and Straits of Indian Ocean are : 1. Arabian Sea 2. Persian Gulf 3. Red Sea Gulf of Aden 4. Gulf of Oman 5. Strait of Bab-el-Mandeb connecting Arabian Sea 6. Gulf of Kutch 7. Gulf of Khambat 8. Palk Strait connecting Arabian Sea and Bay of Bengal 9. Bay of Bengal 10. Andman Sea Laccadive Sea 11. Malacca Strait 12. Madagascar Strait 13. Great Australian Bight 14. Gulf of Mannar. Mozambique Channel.

Ports: Port of Singapore, Mumbai Port, Nhava Sheva (Mumbai). Marmugao Port, Panambur (New Mangalore Port), Kochi Port, Chittagong Port, Colombo Port, Hambantota Port, Galle Port, Kolkata Port, Visakhaptnam Port, Paradip Port, Chennai Port, Ennore Port, Tuticorin Port, Nagapattinam Port, Karachi Port, Aden Port, Mombasa Port, Dar es Salam Port, Zanzibar Port, Durban Port, East London Port, Richard's Bay Port, Beira Port, Port Louis, Muscat Port, Yagon Port, Jakarta Port, Medan Port, Perth Port, Dubai Port.[5]

Mediterranean Sea is accessible through the Suez Canal via the Red Sea.

An estimated 40% of the world's offshore oil production comes from the Indian Ocean.[6]

Indian Ocean sea routes connect the Middle East, Africa and East Asia with Europe and the Americas, carrying heavy traffic of fossil petroleum fuels from the oil fields of the Persian Gulf and Indonesia. Offshore area of Saudi Arabia, Iran, India and Western Australia have large reserves of hydrocarbons. Choke points include Bab el Mandeb, Strait

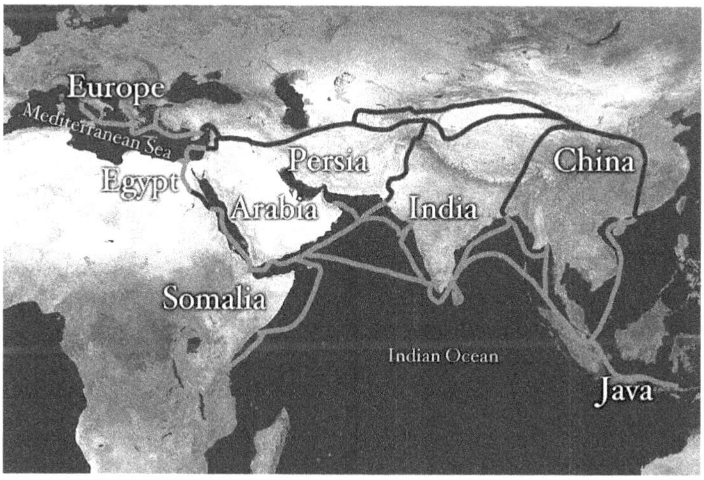

of Hormuz, Lombok Strait, Strait of Malacca and Palk Strait with threats of piracy off the Somali coast since the second phase of the Somali Civil War in the early 21st century.[7]

Fishing fleets of many nations exploit the Indian Ocean for shrimp and tuna. Endangered marine species include dugong, seals, turtles and whales.

Silk route and sea route[8] encompass the Indian Ocean Maritime/Trade Community

Indian Ocean is home to the world's earliest civilizations in Mesopotamia (beginning with Sumer), ancient Egypt and the Hindu civilization (also called Indus Valley civilization).

The civilizations began along the Tigris-Euphrates, Nile, Indus and Sarasvati rivers and all developed around the Indian Ocean. Civilizations arose in Persia (starting with Elam) and I Southeast Asia (starting with Funan). First dynasty (c. 3000 BCE) sailors of Egypt journeyed to Punt (which could be present-day Somalia or west coast of Konkan in India) and brought gold and myrrh in returning ships.

The earliest known maritime trade occurred between Mesopotamian and Hindu civilizations (c. 2500 BCE) and was conducted along the Indian Ocean. An area for research is if Phoenicians of the late 3rd millennium BCE entered the area.

Powerful monsoons enabled ships to sail west early in the season, wait a few months and return eastwards. These also enabled Indonesian peoples to cross the Indian Ocean to settle in Madagascar.

Eudoxus of Cyzicus of Greece crossed the Indian Ocean (c. 2nd or 1st century BCE). Hippalus perhaps discovered the direct route from Arabia to India at this time. 1st and 2nd centuries CE saw trade relations develop between Roman Egypt and Tamil kingdoms of Cheras, Cholas and Pandyas in southern India. Use of monsoon to cross the ocean by western sailors is described in the sea route and trade routes (c. 70 CE) in *Periplus of the Erythrean Sea* (unknown author). Fleets of the Ming Dynasty led by Admiral Zheng He (1405 to 1433 CE) made several voyages to the Indian Ocean reaching the coastal country of East Africa. After Vasco da Gama rounted the Cape of Good Hope in 1497, Portugal dominated trade and discovery along the east coasts of Africa and Asia until the mid 17th century. Dutch East India Company (1602-1798) and later trade companies of France and Britain sought control of maritime trade across the Indian Ocean. Spain's major trading operation was in the Philippines and the Pacific. By 1815, Britain became the principal power in the Indian Ocean. End of World War II saw the end of colonial regimes in the Indian Ocean Rim states, starting with the independence and partitioning of India in 1947.

Bordering countries and territories

Heading roughly clockwise, the states and territories (in italics) with a coastline on the Indian Ocean (including the Red Sea and Persian Gulf) are[9]:

Africa

South Africa, Mozambique, Madagascar, *French Southern and Antarctic Lands*, France (Réunion, Mayotte), Mauritius,

Comoros, Tanzania, Seychelles, Kenya, Somalia, Djibouti, Eritrea, Sudan, Egypt

Asia

Egypt (Sinai Peninsula), Israel, Jordan, Saudi Arabia, Yemen, Oman, United Arab Emirates, Qatar, Bahrain, Kuwait, Iraq, Iran, Pakistan, India, Maldives, *British Indian Ocean Territory*, Sri Lanka, Bangladesh, Burma (Myanmar), Thailand, Malaysia, Indonesia, *Cocos (Keeling) Islands*, *Christmas Island*

Australasia

Ashmore and Cartier Islands, Indonesia, Timor-Leste, Australia

Southern Indian Ocean

Heard Island and McDonald Islands, *French Southern and Antarctic Lands*

Solemn Dharma-Dhamma declaration for Indian Ocean Community

On 22 September 2012, 450 scholars gathered in an international Dharma-Dhamma conference declared their resolve to form an Indian Ocean Community to further socio-cultural-religious dialogues, Ocean economic integration, and development for Indian Ocean nations.

Preamble

Founded on Dharma-dhamma continuum, the imperative of Indian Ocean Community calls for new developments to meet the dangers of the world economic crisis and to realize the responsibilities, wishes and aspirations of the democratic people of Indian Ocean.

Peoples' Parliament

We resolve to constitute Indian Ocean Peoples' Parliament by universal suffrage, as an expression of Indian Ocean Community as a republic.

Fundamental responsibilities

We are determined to stay together to promote democracy, fundamental responsibilities and rights, freedom, equality and justice.

Convinced that, in order to resolve the world economic problems, Indian Ocean Community must strengthen its commitment to the civilization dynamism of the Community and intensify multi-disciplinary efforts to launch developmental projects for *abhyudayam* (general welfare) and creation of an ecologically sustainable Indian Ocean Order while coping with natural hazards of continental drift, volcanic eruptions and dynamics of tectonics of the Indian Ocean Region.

The whole complex of relations among 59 nations of Indian Ocean Community will transform their states into an Indian Ocean Union speaking with a single voice in foreign policy and common currency of Mudra, dictated by a common, coherent socio-political approach venerating the ancestors who have provided the firm roots of the civilizational continuum of the Indian Ocean and in celebration of the Rāṣṭram as a union of federating states, further strengthened by common bonds of dharma-dhamma faith and myriad heritage sites as *tirthasthana*, pilgrimage islands and sacred places which the Buddha and ancient sages walked and navigated.

We resolve to strengthen and expand the role and objectives of multi-lateral, regional institutions by fusing them together under the umbrella of the Indian Ocean Community to realize the common destiny of the community and Indian Ocean identity. To further this goal, Indian Ocean Council of Heads of State or Governments of the Indian Ocean Community will deliberate upon and further the construction of Indian Ocean as a reservoir of wisdom and wealth, improve promotion of knowledge systems, approximation of laws working towards the constitution of an Indian Ocean Court of Justice, spiritual values of Dharma-Dhamma, safeguar and protection of the Region's cultural heritage, cooperation and exchanges of talent particularly among young people, a harmonization of social security systems, for peace and security in the globe.

Outline of the book

Indian Ocean Community inspired by setubandha

Declare Nobel Peace Prize for Indian Ocean Community

Sanchi Declaration: Indic-Bauddha studies

Making a vision a reality

Rāṣṭram is dharma-dhamma in action.Dharma-Dhamma is the ordering principle.

Theravada faith and dhamma-s

Rāṣṭram is the path for movement, progress

Social Stabilityand Rāṣṭram

Rashtradā Rāṣṭram me datta svāhā, Rāṣṭradā Rāṣṭramumuṣmai datta svāhā (Vājasneyi Samhitā)

Attributes of Vedic Rāṣṭram

Rāṣṭram in Śukla Yajurveda points to the unity and wealth achieved in waters

Epistemological[10] underpinnings of *rāṣṭram* -- a connotation wider than a 'nation'

Indian Ocean Community as cultural identity

Dharman, satya, ṛta

Milestones of Bauddha Dhamma

Bauddham in Sri Lanka

Pravṛtti-Nivṛtti: Social action, Personal knowledge

Greater Indian Ocean Region: cultural and historical vignettes

Formation of Rastram, a federating comity of nations

Golden threads of friendship that existed between India and Indian Ocean Region

Indian Ocean Community as a geographical identity

Economic history of two millennia

Indian Ocean Community can help avoid a global financial meltdown

Śreṇi dharma
Rāṣṭram -State-Panchayat structure for a dharma-dhamma constitution

Dharma-dhamma is this that is indicated in the Vedas as driving to the biggest good.

Peoples' Parliament

Law of the Sea and Freedom-of-the-seas doctrine

Developmental projects for Indian Ocean Community: New Law of the Sea extending Economic Zone to 200 kms. beyond territorial waters

Developmental projects for Indian Ocean Community: Trans-Asian Railway (TAR) Network

Maritime claims among nations and conflict zones

Powerplay vs. Regional cooperation

Indian Ocean Community, *setubandha*, Rama's bridge connecting India and Sri Lanka

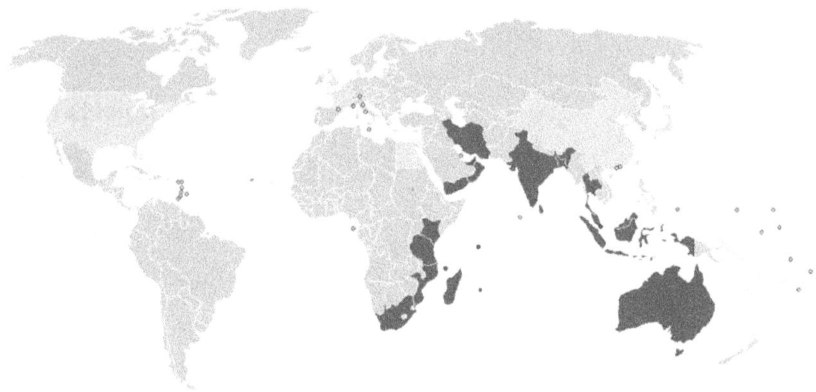

Setubandha[11]: आ सेतु हिमाचलम् From Setu to Himachalam defines the sovereign Indian Ocean Community.

Sri Rama on the edge of the Indian Ocean debating setubandha with Samudrarājā. (Raja Raviverma's painting in Mysore Palace narrating an episode from *Rāmāyaṇa*). Sri Rama is the role model for values of dharma-dhamma cherished by Indian Ocean people, for integrity and stability of the Rāṣṭram.

- Skanda Purana (III.1.2.1-114), Vishnu Purana (IV.4.40-49), Agni Purana (V-XI), Brahma Purana (138.1-40) refer to the **construction of Rama Setu**. Skanda Purana (VI.101.1-44) describes the installation of three Shiva linga at the end, middle and beginning of Rama Setu and **making the same bridge submerged and thereby creating Setu-Teertham**. This is also related in Kurma Purana (21.10-61). Garuda Purana (1.81.1-22) lists sacred places including Setubandh and Rameswar. Narada Purana (Uttara Bhag 76.1-20) extols the greatness of Rama-Setu.

Maritime trade

Maritime trade dates back to the days of Hindu civilization which flourished on the Sarasvati-Sindhu (Indus) river basins

Archaeologists have found evidence for the presence of black-slipped jars common in the Persian Gulf, represented by hundreds of sherds from individual archaeological sites: Amlah, Baat, Hilli 8, Ras Ghanadha 1, Ras al-Hadd-1, Ras al-Junayz, RJ-2. Samples of this ware were found at Harappa (a site of Sarasvati civilization) in a potter's workshop. The blac-slipped jars inevitably hav a short Indus script inscription scratched on the shoulder of the pot after firing. These storage/shipping jars are uniquely shaped with a deep, narrow base.[12]

Clearly, there was a significant maritime activity in the Mediterranean and Arabian Seas.

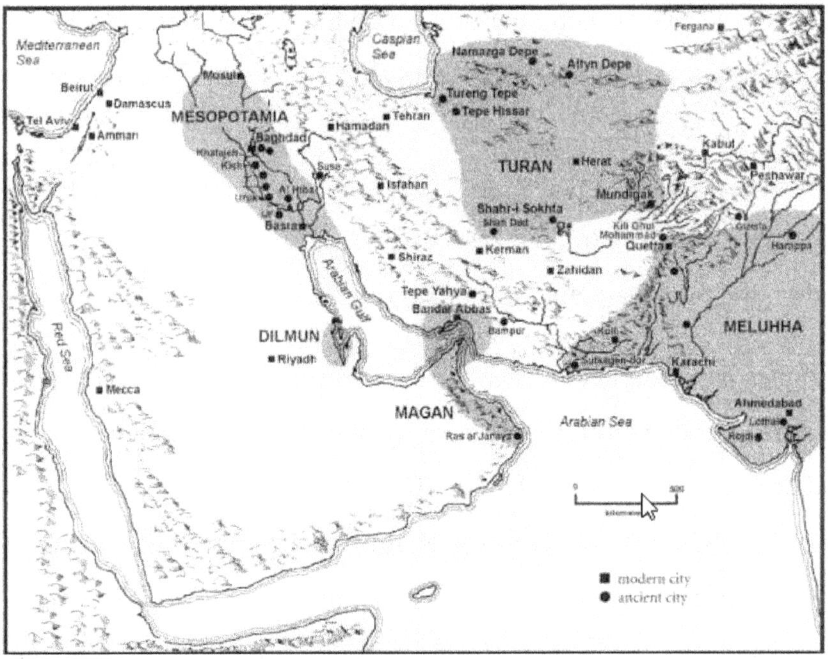

Areas of the Middle Asian Interaction Sphere [13]

Indus-type seals with script have been found in the Gulf sites such as Tell Umma, Ur, Tepe Gawra, Tell Asmar, Kish, Tell Suleimeh, Tello, Lagash, Hamma, Nippur, Susa, Sahdad.

Tello. 3rd millennium BCE. During Caspers 1973 (Fig. 12.18)Tell Suleimeh. 3rd millennium BCE. Collon 1996, fig. 8b (Fig. 12.17)

Seal from Hamma. C. 2000-1750 BCE. Ingholt 1940: 62, pl. XIX (Fig. 12.19)

Seal from Nippur. Kassite (c. fourteenth century BCE). Gibson 1977 (Fig. 12.20)

Bronze female figurine from Shahr-i-Sokhta (after Tosi 1983)(Fig. 12.30) "The figurine is of a woman with a

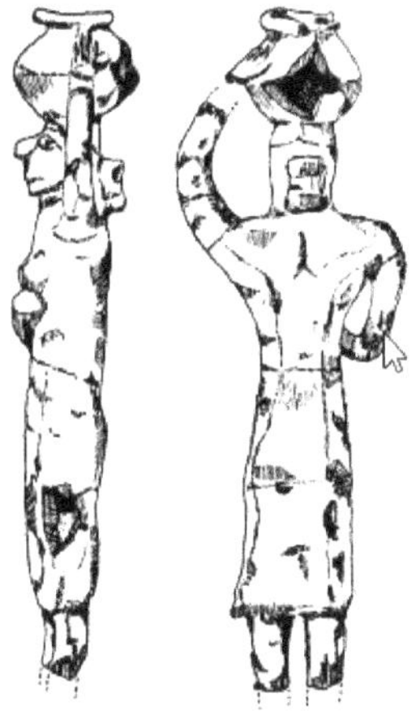

prominent nose and almond-shaped eyes. Her hair is in a large bun at the back of her head. She is shown carrying a basket or a pot on her head. Her left arm is raised, balancing this object, as though she is walking. Her right arm lays across her low chest, just below the breasts. The pose of this woman is one with clear Mesopotamian parallels associated with building activity, especially foundation deposits. Such figurines have a long chronology in Mesopotamia from the early third millennium into the second, so the Shahr-i-Sokhta figurine is not out of plae in this regard. It is interesting, but not out of place, to think that on the eastern end of the Iranian Plateau there may have been people who incorporated ideological aspects of Mesopotamian building practices into their structures."[14]

An extraordinary reconstruction of the seafaring in the days of Magan, historical Oman was demonstrated by archeologists. Professor Maurizio Tosi, Prehistoric Archaeologist from the University of Bologna notes that the conquest of the seas was a human feat of tremendous significance.

"The conquest of the ocean was the first step forward into a murch larger universe…It was an incredible adventure, an enormous challenge…to go out to sea knowing death is waiting for you behind the waves. The ocean was an enemy, but humans would not surrender. They were dreaming, looking into the horizon for more and more interesting places…we humans have to conquer the universe."[15] Two of his colleagues were Professor Serge Cleuziou from the Sorbonne at the University of Paris and Dr. Tom Vosmer from Curtin University of Western Australia.

Magan was a land bridge between the two seas, the Gulf and the Indian Ocean.

Ancient bitumen slab fragments, with imprints of ropes, bound reeds or woven mats on one side and the remains of barnacles on the other were momentous discoveries in Oman, the United Arab Emirates, Kuwait and

Iraq. Bitumen was used to seal boats made of reed, wood and rope from 5th millennium BCE. Magan people built these reed boats. Dr. Tom Vosmer analysed how the boats were built. His team constructed an ancient bitumen boat of Magan which weighed four and a half tones and could carry seven tones of goods and a crew of nine.

This was followed by a sail boat called Jewel of Muscat which was a sewn-plank ship which began its journey from Muscat on February 16, 2010 and arrived in Singapore on July 3, 2010 completing a historic five-month voyage on the Indian Ocean via India, Sri Lanka and Malaysia. The 60-foot-long vessel took after a 9th century wreck of a ship which carrying more than 60,000 pices of Chinese ceramics, silver and gold artefacts, spices and other commodities, now known as the Tang Treasure discovered in 1998 in Indonesian waters. The ship used a compass called Al Kamal, a small piece of wood tied to the body in such a way as to hep calculate the latitude.[16]

A boat shown on a three-sided moulded tablet with Indus script ca. 2500 BCE. A flat bottomed boat with a central hut that has leafy fronds at the top of two poles. Two birds sit on the deck and a large double rudder extends from the rear of the boat, used to navigate the Persian Gulf from Sarasvati-Indus (Sindhu) river basins and Gulf of Kutch.

LANDING OF VIJAYA IN CEYLON (ABOUT 543 B.C.)

From Ajanta Frescoes

Ships Landing of Prince Vijaya in Sri Lanka - 543 BCE from Ajanta Frescos. Ajanta painting of a later date depict horses and elephants aboard the ship which carried Prince Vijaya to Sri Lanka.

(source: India Through the ages - By K. M. Panikkar).

Royal Barge of Angkor (Hansa headed barge) Relief found at Borobudur temple (9th century) in the Indonesian island, Java

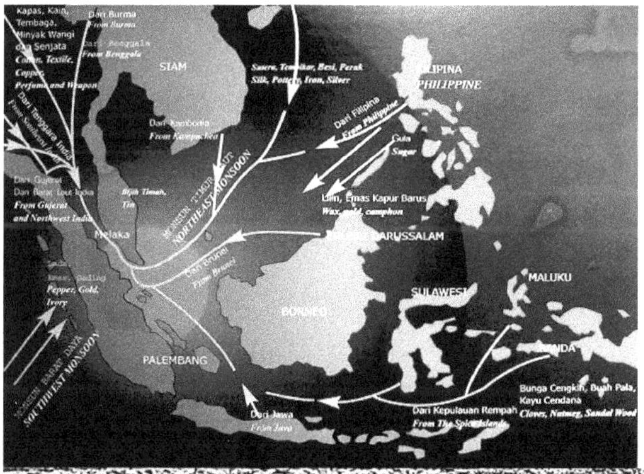

Model of the Chola ship, rebuilt by the Archaeological Survey of India. Seen in the Naval Muesum in Tirunelveli.

Large four-masted ships possessed by the Indians who navigated to Java.[17]

The picture is that of a Polynesian Catamaran. [18]The word catamaran comes from the Tamil language, in which the word kattumaram means "logs bound together". The catamaran was the invention of the paravas, an aristocratic fishing community in the southern coast of Tamilnadu, India. Catamarans were used by the ancient Tamil Chola dynasty as early as 5th century CE for moving their fleets to conquer such south-east Asian regions as Burma, Indonesia and Malaysia.

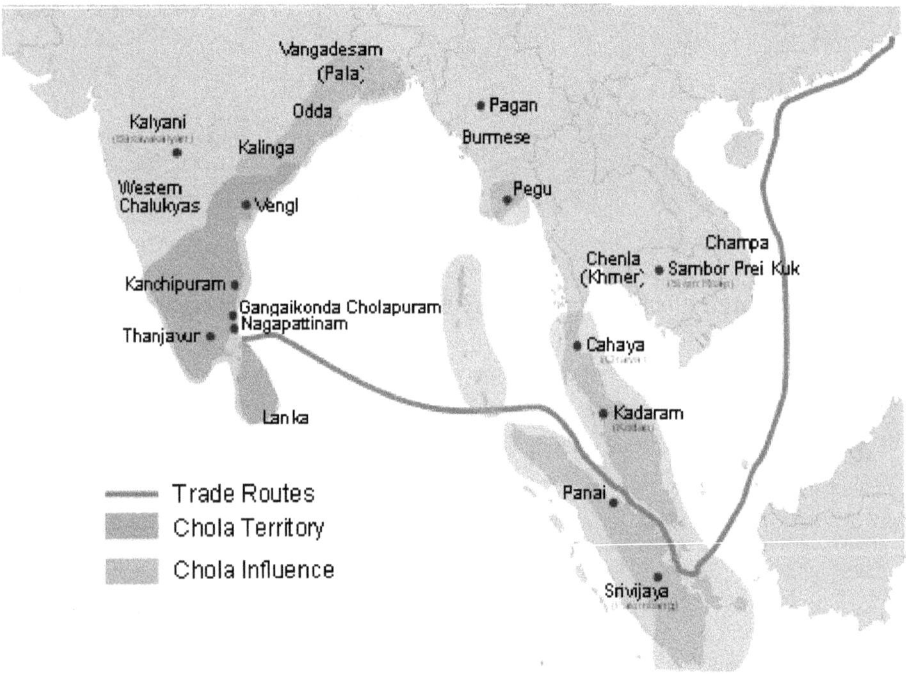

Indian vessel as shown in the Fra Mauro map (1460). Chola territories during Rajendra Chola I, c. 1030 CE.

Image of Calicut, India from Georg Braun and Frans Hogenberg's atlas *Civitates orbis terrarum*, 1572.

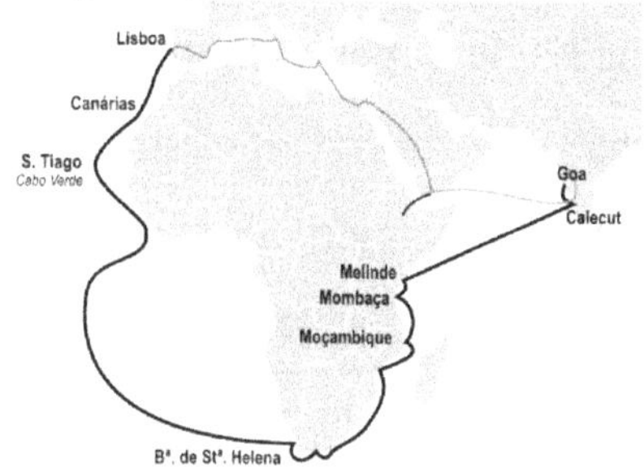

This figure illustrates the path of Vasco da Gama's course to India (black), the first to go around Africa. Voyages of Pêro da Covilhã (Calicut-Saudi Arabia) and Afonso de Paiva (across Suez canal) are also shown with common routes marked in green.

“In Rajavalliya, the ship in which Prince Vijaya and his followers were sent away by King Sinhala of Bengal, was large enough to accommodate seven hundred passengers. The ship in which Prince Vijaya’s bride was conveyed to Sri Lanka, was big enough to accommodate eight hundred people of the bride’s party. The ship which took Prince Sinhala to Sri Lanka contained five hundred merchants besides the Prince himself. The Janaka Jataka mentions a ship-wreck of seven hundred passengers. The ship by which was effected the rescue of the Brahmin mentioned in Sankha Jataka was 800 cubits in length, 600 cubits in width, 20 fathoms deep, and had three masts. The ship mentioned in the Samuddha Vanija Jataka was big enough to transport a village full of absconding carpenters, numbering a thousand, who had failed to deliver goods paid for in advance…Sutras of Panini describe various types of small river craft were in use, and their names were utsagna, udupa, udyata, utputa, pitaka etc. A large boat was called Udavahana or udakavahana. Of special interest is the distinction made between the cargoes coming from an island near the coast and those coming from mid-ocean islands: the former were called dvaipya, and the latter dvaipa or dvaipaka. Certain other sutras speak of ferry chages, cargoes, marine trade and the like of those days… Kautilya Arthasastra, of about 320 B.C. devotes a full chapter to waterways under a Navadhyaksha 'Superintendent of ships'. His duties included the examination of accounts relating to navigation, not only on oceans and mouths of rivers, but also on lakes, natural or artificial, and rivers. Fisheries, pearl fisheries, customs on ports, passengers and mercantile shipping, control and safety of ships and similar other affairs all came under his charge. Jaina scriptures, Buddhist Jatakas and Avadanas, as well as classical Sanskrit literature, abound in references to sea-voyages. They acquaint us with many interesting details as to the sizes and shapes of ships, their furniture, and decorations, articles of import and export, names of seaports and islands, in short, everything connected with navigation."[19]

Rāma, *vigrahavān dharmah* (dharma personified) says Valmiki.

The centrality of role of elders is to declare dharma, pitṛ-s, is mentioned in a passage of Mahābhārata: *na sa sabhā yatra na santi vrddhā, nate vrddhā ye na vadanti dharmam.* Trans. That ain't no Assembly where there are no elders; those are not elders who do not declare dharma. Purohita were Rāṣṭragopa (protectors of the realm).[20]

Declare Nobel Peace Prize for Indian Ocean Community

Dharmo rakṣati rakṣitah, dharma protects the protector. It is our responsibility to protect dharma by constituting the Indian Ocean Community.

The roots for this remarkable statement by Manu have to be traced in the perceptions of the rishi-s from the days of the R.gveda.yato dharmah tato jayah (success goes hand in hand with righteousness) (MBh. 6.65.18)

dharma eva hato hanti dharmo rakṣati rakṣitah tasmādharmo na hantavyo mā no dharmo hatovadhīt (Manu 8.15)

Dharma protects those who protect it. Those who destroy Dharma get destroyed. Therefore, Dharma should not be destroyed so that we may not be destroyed as a consequence thereof.

Dharma is an ordering principle which is independent of one's faith or methods of worship or what is understood by the term 'religion', thus providing for total freedom in the path chosen or ethical norms employed, in an eternal journey from being to becoming. Hence, it is truly universal, sanatana dharma, the ordering principle eternal. Since it is an ordering principle, the word is applied across many facets of life, for example to rajadharma as an ordering principle for governance, svadharma as an ordering principle of one's spiritual quest or life in society or as'ramadharma denoting responsibilities associated with one's station in life's progress from childhood, through studentship, marital life and to old age. Dharma is elaborated with the use of terms such as satyam, rita, rinam, vrata to defining ethical responsibility performed in relation to social and natural phenomena. Dharma can be the defining paradigm for a world as a family, vasudhaiva kutumbakam. Aano bhadraah kratavo yantu vis'vatah. Let noble thoughts flow to us from all sides. These thoughts from Vedic times are as relevant today as they have been over millennia of pilgrims' progress and exemplified by the progress and abiding continuum of Indian Ocean civilizations, Jaina ariya dhamma, Bauddha dhamma, Khalsa Pantha and other Dharma-Dhammapanthas. In such an ordering, dharma-dhamma becomes a veritable celebration of freedom, freedom in moving from being to becoming.

A 21st century example celebrating and consolidating a Community was the award of the 2012 Nobel Peace Prize to the European Union which has a common currency called the Euro. The Nobel award was intended as a catalyst to the member countries of the European Community[21] to jointly overcome the serious financial crises faced by some member states. Preceding the European Union was a successful cooperative enterprise called the European Coal and Steel Community. Before the European Community gained its form, shape and content, an institution called *Organization for European Cooperation and Development (OECD)* was set up to provide the framework of trade, investment and development projects in various socio-economic sectors.

Despite the historical background of two world wars fought on European soil, during the 20th century, a key reason for the successful formation of European Community was economic. European Coal and Steel Community created a common market for coal and steel among European countries. European Atomic Energy Community created shared market for supply of electricity to European countries.

I suggest that the Nobel Peace Prize should go to the *Indian Ocean Community (IOC)*, an imperative for *abhyudayam* (general welfare) of about 2 billion people in the Community.

The time has come for making the idea of *Indian Ocean Community (IOC)* a reality. The key reason for the formation of the Indian Ocean Community will be cultural-economic.

Sanchi Declaration: Indic-Bauddha studies

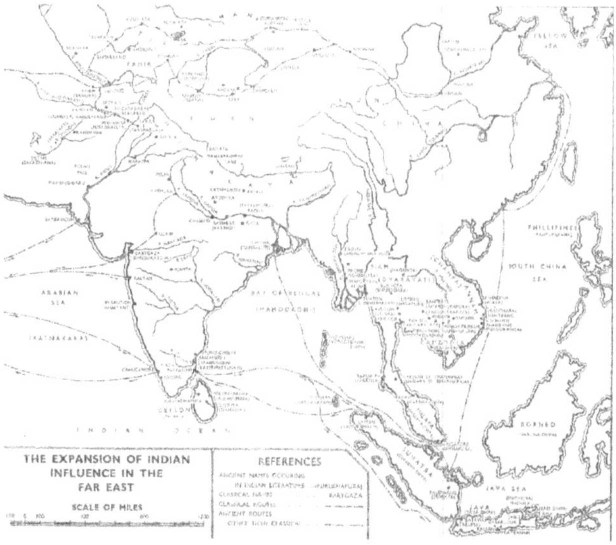

What could turn out to be a historic moment occurred in Bhopal on September 22, 2012, when *Sanchi Declaration*[22] was announced by over 450 scholars from 20 nations who assembled in a conference on Dharma-Dhamma. The Sanchi Declaration launched flagship vision of Indian Ocean Community as a development powerhouse for over 2 billion people. The Declaration coincided with the the occasion of the Foundation Laying Ceremony of Sanchi University of Buddhist-Indic Studies. The framework was built by Prof. Kapil Kapoor, who was felicitated in the Conference. The Conference was jointly sponsored by the Centre for Study of Religion and Society and the Mahabodhi Society.

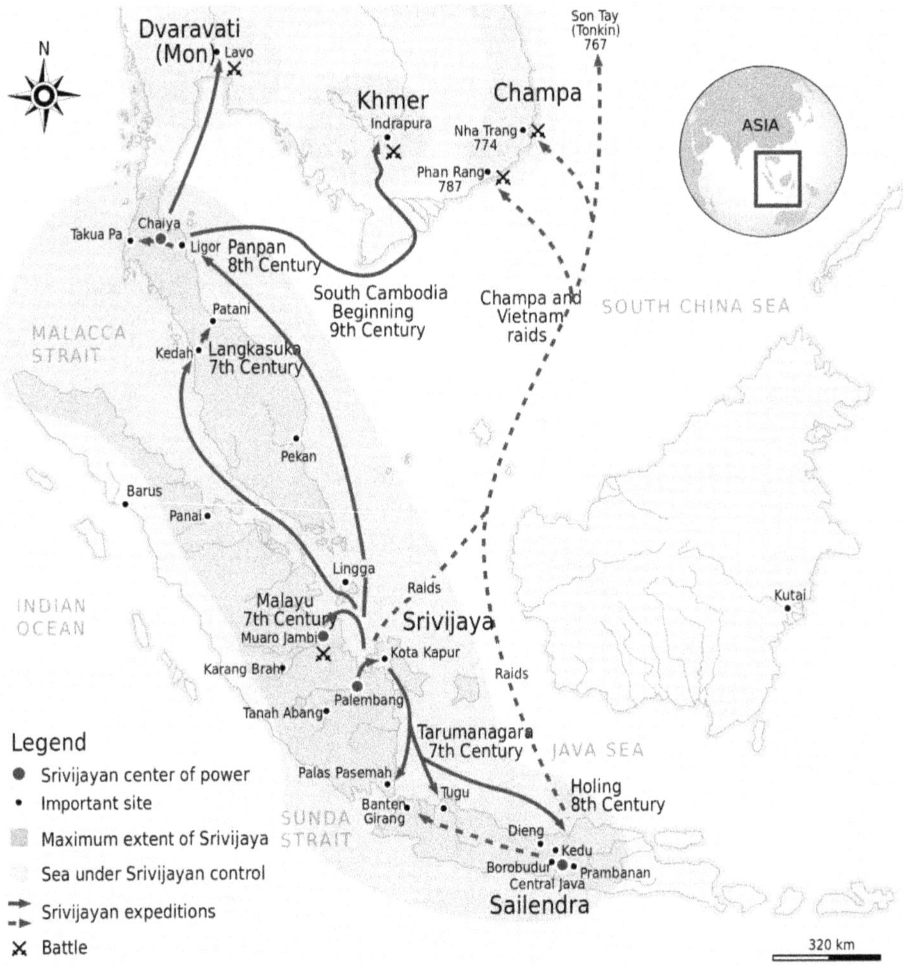

According to Coedès Indian merchants were the founders of the states Srivijaya (7th to 13th cent.), Majapahit (1293 to 1500) and Khmer empire

(802 to 1431), some assign the founding of the kingdoms to Southeast Asian rulers as founding them while importing Hindu pundits as advisers on rajadharma (ethics of kingship).

The extent of Srivijaya Empire in 10th to 11th century AD, according to Chinese source and Srivijayan inscriptions. (Source: Gunawan Kartapranata, based on "Atlas Sejarah Indonesia dan Dunia" (Indonesian and World Historical Atlas) page 32, Drs. Achmad Jamil, Yulia Darmawaty, S.Pd, Sri Wachyuni, S.Pd, Mastara, Jakarta 2004). Arun Bhattacharjee, in *Greater India*, explains: thus: "That culture can advance without political motives, that trade can proceed without imperialist designs, settlements can take place without colonial excesses and that literature, religion and language can be transported without xenophobia, jingoism and race complexes are amply evidenced from the history of India's contact with her neighbours...Thus, although a considerable part of central and south-eastern Asia became flourishing centres of Indian culture, they were seldom subjects to the regime of any Indian king or conquerors and hardly witnessed the horrors and havocs of any Indian military campaign. They were perfectly free, politically and economically and their people representing an integration of Indian and indigenous elements had no links with any Indian state and looked upon India as a holy land..."

Lauding Pancharatna, proposed five schools of thought, the declaration was dedicated at the feet of Bharat Mata, on the Sacred, Hallowed Land the Buddha and Dharma-Dhamma sages walked.

1. Buddhist philosophy

2. Sanatana dharma and indic studies

3. International Buddhist studies

4. Comparative Religion

5. Language, literature and arts in Bauddham and Sanatana Dharma

Making a vision a reality

The Sanchi Declaration may look like a small step by a gathering of scholars. But it is a giant leap for realizing the Indian Ocean Community. Like the Pipal tree sapling planted to found the Sanchi University of Indic-Buddhist studies, the Community will rise.

The Sanchi Declaration resolved 1) to promote co-operation and unity among peoples of the world who cherish the eternal , universal dharma-dhamma traditions as cardinal instruments of peace, harmony and socio-cultural-economic advancemen and 2) to promote the formation of Indian Ocean Community as a comity of nations celebrating Dharma-Dhamma traditions.

The formation of Indian Ocean Community is a visionary movement.[23] Respectfully recollecting the words of Gautama, the Buddha, "One who is virtuous and wise shines forth like a blazing fire," President Mahinda Rajapaksa of Sri Lanka who laid the foundation stone for the

Sanchi University of Indic-Buddhist Studies invoked the blessings of the Noble Triple Gem: Buddha, Dhamma and Sangha..

The movement for Indian Ocean Community imperative has to learn from the experience of formation of European Community. An Organization for Economic Cooperation and Development for Indian Ocean nations may have to be constituted, as a building block, to collect, archive socio-economic data and developmental statistics and programmes in the Indian Ocean Rim countries (59 of them from Madagascar to Tasmania). Scholars have to meet to deliberate upon many topics of common interest:

1. Indic and Bauddha cultures in Indian Ocean Community
2. Contacts and debates of India and Bauddha civilizations in global communities
3. Indian Ocean Studies to celebrate maritime traditions and sea-lane security starting with Bali yatra
4. Temple architecture and cultural Bauddham-Indic traditions of worship Deliberations to provide impetus to daily worship in Angkor Wat, the largest vishnu temple of the world and similar tourist temples.

Rāṣṭram is dharma-dhamma in action.Dharma-Dhamma is the ordering principle

Dharma-dhamma continuum unites the Indian Ocean Communityto realize a *rāṣṭram*.

Rāṣṭram is the cultural pathway. Dharma-dhamma is the journey along the pathway.

Indian Ocean Community as a *rāṣṭram* is a twin identity. First, it is a cultural entity with common and shared values which bind the people together. Second, it is a geographical entity bonded by *āsetu himācalam* – from the Indian Ocean to the Himalayas.

Moving away from legitimizing a 'nation' as a 'political rule', let us begin with the Veda, an ancient human document, celebrated for millennia in Indian Ocean civilizational history.

Vedic concept of *rāṣṭram* is elucidated in the context of dharman and ṛta.

asṛgam indavah pathā dharman ṛtasya siśriyah (Trans. With the support of and along ṛta, the principle of truth and order, flow soma essences; dharman stands parallel to pathā, 'path' (RV 9.7.1)[24]

Veda uses the word '*rāṣṭram*'.

What is this path? The answer is provided by the derivation of the word, '*rāṣṭram*'. The root could also be raj,[25] 'to be resplendent, shine'. Soma and Varuna are *rājā,* 'guidance'. (RV 10.49.4).

Theravada faith and dhamma-s

Human existence is a privileged state, because only as a human being can a bodhisattva become a buddha. Moreover, according to Theravada, human beings can choose to do good works (which will result in a good rebirth) or bad works (which result in a bad rebirth); above all, they have the capacity to become perfected saints. All these capacities are accounted for in terms of a carefully enumerated series of *dhammas* (Sanskrit: *dharmas*), the elements' impermanent existence. In continual motion, these changing states appear, age, and disappear…

Dhammas are divided and subdivided into many groups. Those that are essential to psychophysical existence are the 5 components (Sanskrit: *skandhas*; Pali: *khandhas*), the 12 bases (Pali and Sanskrit: *ayatanas*), and the 18 sensory elements (Pali and Sanskrit: *dhatus*). The 5 *skandhas* are *rupa* (Pali and Sanskrit), materiality, or form;*vedana*, feelings of pleasure or pain or the absence of either; *sanna* (Pali), cognitive perception; *sankhara* (Pali and Sanskrit), the forces that condition the psychic activity of an individual; and *vinnana* (Sanskrit: *vijnana*), consciousness. The 12 *ayatanas* comprise the five sense organs (eyes, ears, nose, tongue, and body) and the mind (*manas*), as well as the five related sense fields (sights, sounds, odours, tastes, and tangibles) and objects of cognition—that is, objects as they are reflected in mental perception. The 18 elements, or *dhatus*, include the five sense organs and the *mano-dhatu* (Pali and Sanskrit: "mind element"), their six correlated objects, and the consciousnesses (Pali: *vinnana*) of the sense organs and *manas*.

The Theravada system of *dhammas* (Pali) is not only an analysis of empirical reality but a delineation of the psychosomatic components of the human personality. Moreover, Theravadins believe that an awareness of the interrelation and operation of these components, as well as the ability to manipulate them, is necessary for an individual to attain the exalted state of an arhat (Pali: *arahant*, "worthy one"). Through the classification of*dhammas*, a person is defined as an aggregate of many interrelated elements governed by the law of karma—thus destined to suffer good or bad consequences. All of this presupposes that there is no eternal metaphysical entity such as an "I," or atman (Pali: *attan*), but that there is a psychosomatic aggregate situated in time. This aggregate has freedom of choice and can perform acts that may generate consequences…

Two basic forms of meditation (Pali: *jhana*; Sanskrit: *dhyana*) have been practiced in the Theravada tradition. Closely related to a Hindu tradition of yoga, the first of these involves a process of moral and intellectual purification…

Theravadins maintain that the ideal Buddhist is the "one who is worthy" (Sanskrit: arhat; Pali: *arahant*), the perfected person who attains nirvana through his own efforts. Although the Theravadin arhat "takes refuge in the Buddha," his focus is on the practice of the Buddha's *dhamma* (Pali)…

The Buddha has been given many other names, the most common of which are Arahant and Tathagata ("He Who Has Thus Attained"). According to Theravada scriptures, previous buddhas (mostly those who met Gotama in one of his past lives) are recognized by name, and there is a single mention of the future buddha Metteyya (Sanskrit: Maitreya). The Theravadins came to believe that Metteyya is presently in the Tusita heaven and will come into the world in the distant future to reestablish the religion.[26]

***Rāṣṭram* is the path for movement, progress**

The feminine form of the word is used early in Rgveda: Goddess Sarasvati or Vak or Vaghambrini says : "I am the *rāṣṭrī* and I move people towards their welfare (abhyudayam)". Welfare is understood both as material prosperity and spiritual/religious enlightenment.This philosophy or world view animated all of history of India and the countries of what is called Greater India.[27]

Derivation: *rāj dīptau sthā gatinivṛttau*, 'when the path is lost, the *rāṣṭram* provides the light.' (*rāj*, *rāijita,* 'shine , glitter'). *rāj* (Vedic also *rāṣṭi*) 'anything the best or chief of its kind' as in: *śankharāj* 'best *śankhā* (*turbinella pyrum*) conch'. *ṛj* 'to go ; to stand or be firm ; to obtain , acquire ; to be strong or healthy.' This is why *Vāk* Devi says: *aham rāṣṭrī samgamanī* 'I am the *rāṣṭram.*' (RV 10.125: I am the sovereign queen, the collectress of treasures, cognizant (of the Supreme Being), the chief of objects of worship; as such the gods have put me in many places, abiding in manifold conditions, entering into numerous (forms.). She 'moves in splendor'. She is the mover in the path for people to create wealth (*vasūnām*). She, *rāṣṭrī,* constitutes the stability for a group of people and phenomena. She moves firmly and resolutely; she is śakti.
There cannot be a more emphatic and precise definition of the *rāṣṭram* which was founded on dharma, the global ethic. *rāṣṭram vai aśvamedhah*, trans. 'building up of the nation is *aśvamedha*, the effort to consolidate the path of nation'. The exhortation is to build the nation with valour (*aśva*) and intellect (*medha*). [*Śatapatha brāhmaṇa* (13.1.6.3)]

Social Stabilityand Rāṣṭram

dhruvám̥ te rājā váruṇo

dhruvám̥ devó bŕ̥haspátiḥ

dhruvám̥ ta índraś cāgníś ca

rāṣṭrám̥ dhārayatām̥ dhruvám (RV 10.173.5)

Trans.

Steadfast, may Varuṇa, the Rājā, steadfast, the Divine Bṛhaspati

Steadfast, may Indra, steadfast too, may Agni keep they steadfast Rāṣṭram.

In this Rgvedic statement, Rāṣṭram is emphasized as the epitome of 'steadfastness'.

It is this Rāṣṭram referred to in *ātmastuti* by Devi: *aham rashtrī samgamanī vasūnām* (RV 10.125).

It is this Rāṣṭram that binds people together mentioned in RV 7.84.2: *yuvó rāṣṭarám bṛhád invati dyaúr yaú setŕ̥bhir arajjúbhiḥ sinītháḥ pári no héḷo váruṇasya vr̥jyā urúm̥ na índraḥ kr̥ṇavad ulokám*

This Vedic word *rāṣṭram* can provide the framework for Indian Ocean Community as One Nation, a common path to achieve general welfare of the people in the Community.

Rāṣṭram as a supranational foundation to remove vestiges of colonial loot, to make such a loot unthinkable and materially impossible and reinforce democracy of all nations along the IOC rim as janapada(peoples' republics) for peoples' welfare (abhyudayam) governed by the inexorable traditional ethic dharma-dhamma

Rāṣṭram is etymologically explained as a firm, enlightened path for welfare of a community. The word is derived as a combination of two roots: ras'mi 'the sun' and sṭha 'firm, placed in'. This leads to an extraordinary evocation in the Vedas: *Rāṣṭram me datta* (Give me, in exchange (for prayer), that lighted path).

Thus *rāṣṭram* is a wider connotation than what is denoted by the word, 'nation'. It is certainly distinct from 'state' which is just an institutional framework for governance. *Rāṣṭram* is the path to achieve a fundamental component of dharma: abhyudayam (general welfare).

Other lexical entries:

राष्ट्र in Manu means 'one of the 5 प्रकृतिs of the state(Mn. vii , 157), realm , empire , dominion , district , country (RV)'

राष्ट्रिः *f.,* **-ष्ट्री 1** A female ruler or sovereign. **-2** Proprietress.

राष्ट्रिकः 1 An inhabitant of a kingdom or country, a subject; राष्ट्रिकैः सह तद्राष्ट्रं क्षिप्रमेव विनश्यति Ms.1.61. **-2** The ruler of a kingdom, governor. राष्ट्रिय राष्ट्रीय *a.* [राष्ट्रे भवः घ] Belonging to a king- dom. **-यः 1** The ruler of a kingdom, king; as in राष्ट्रिय- श्यालः Mk.9. **-2** The brother-in-law of a king (queen's brother); श्रुतं राष्ट्रियमुखाद् यावदङ्गुलीयकदर्शनम् Ś.6. **-3** An heir-apparent. **-4** An officer in the kingdom; ततः संप्रेषयेद् राष्ट्रे राष्ट्रीयाय च दर्शयेत्

Mb.12.85.12.राष्ट्रम् [राज्-ष्ट्रन् Uṇ.4.167] **1** A kingdom, realm, empire; राष्ट्रदुर्गबलानि च Ak; सामदण्डौ प्रशंसन्ति नित्यं राष्ट्राभि-वृद्धये Ms.7.19;1.61. **-2** A district, territory, country, region; as in महाराष्ट्र; नगराणि च राष्ट्राणि धनधान्य- युतानि च Rām.1.1.93; स्वराष्ट्रे न्यायवृत्तः स्यात् Ms.7.32. **-3** The people, nation, subjects; तस्य प्रक्षुभ्यते राष्ट्रम् Ms. 9.254. **-ष्ट्रः, -ष्ट्रम्** Any national or public calamity. **-Comp. -अभिवृद्धिः** increase of a kingdom. -**कर्षणम्** distressing a kingdom; तथा राज्ञामपि प्राणाः क्षीयन्ते राष्ट्रकर्षणात् Ms.7.112. **-तन्त्रम्** administration. **-पतिः, -पालः** a sovereign. **-भेदः** division of a kingdom. राष्ट्रकः = राष्ट्रिकः q. v.; निरीक्ष्य तावुत्तमपूरुषौ जना मञ्चस्थिता नागरराष्ट्रका नृप Bhāg.1.43.2.अधिराज्यम् adhirājyam ष्ट्रम् ṣṭram अधिराज्यम् ष्ट्रम् [अधिकृतं राज्यं **राष्ट्रम्** अत्र] Imperial or sovereign sway, supremacy, sole sovereignty, impe- rial dignity, an empire.

Rāṣṭradā Rāṣṭram me datta svāhā, Rāṣṭradā Rāṣṭramumuṣmai datta svāhā (Vājasneyi Samhitā)

Trans. I pray to Devi, seeking in exchange, resplendedent crucibled protecting Rāṣṭram

Rāṣṭradā Rāṣṭram me datta svāhā, Rāṣṭradā Rāṣṭramumuṣmai datta svāhā (cf. Vājasneyi Samhitā 10.2-4) is the refrain, an invocation to purifying, protecting Devi, the personification of the four vedas, seeking in exchange, (expressing) a desire for a ravishing, captivating, dazzling, excellent Rāṣṭram.

Rāṣṭradā is the rashtra desired for protection (of janam, bhāratam janam).

Rāṣṭra is Devi's anugraham.

राष्ट्रदा राष्ट्रम्मे स्वाहा

राष्ट्रदा राष्ट्रममुष्मै राष्ट्रममुष्मै दत्त स्वाहा

स्व्-ाहा svaahaa is an invocation of Devi, daughter of Dakṣa, personification of the four Vedas.

> *f.* an oblation (offered to अग्नि, इन्द्र &c) or Oblation personified (as a daughter of दक्ष and wife of अग्नि; she is thought to preside over burnt-offerings; her body is said to consist of the four वेदs , and her limbs are the six अङ्गs or members of the वेद; she is represented also as a wife of the रुद्र पशु-पति)

दा *f.* (√ दे) , protection , defence; *mfn.* ifc. " giving , granting "; **दा** *f.* (√ दस्) cleansing , purifying; Rashtradā means 'rashtrī (devi) who purifies, protects'.

Rāṣṭram me datta 'Rastram presented to me in exchange (for invocation)'.

मे *cl.1 A1.* (Dhatup. xxii , 65)

> मयते (ep. also *P.* मयति ; pf. मन्मे Gr. ; aor. अमास्त ib. ; fut. माता , मास्यतेib. ; ind.p. - मित्य or -माय ib.) . to exchange , barter (cf. अप-. and नि-
>
> √मे): Caus. मापयति ib. : Desid.मित्सते ib. : Intens. मेमीयत्च् , मामेति , मामाति ib.

दत्त *mfn.* (√ दे) protected *mfn.* (√1. दा) given , granted , presented

RV. i f. , viii , x

मुष् to ravish , captivate , enrapture (the eyes or the heart) MBh. Ka1v. ;

to blind , dazzle (the eyes); surpassing, excelling Megh. Ka1d. Ba1lar.

mumuṣ 'wishing to dazzle, surpass, excel' *muṣā, mūṣī* 'crucible'; mūṣīkaraṇa ' melting in a crucible'.

In grammar, a **desiderative** (abbreviated desid.) form is one that has the meaning of "wanting to X".

Hence, Desid. मुमुषिषति means 'wanting to (obtain, crucibled) captivating, dazzling Rāṣṭram'.

This derivation is consistent with the derivation of the word Rāṣṭram from the root:

Rāj dīptau shthā gatinivṛttau ('shining, resplendent, steadfast, restoring the lost path').

Rāṣṭradā Rāṣṭramumuṣmai is thus interpreted as 'rashtra-giving, wishing for dazzling rashtra-resplendent'.

The metaphor evoked by the word mumuṣmai i in Rāṣṭramumuṣmai

is the dazzling nature of the

crucible-melted metal (as crucible steel).

It will be appropriate to interpret this invocation is to produce the

Rāṣṭra in a dazzling crucible for crucible-steel.

The refrain can thus be explained as 'wishing for a presented dazzling, surpassing light resplendent and restoring the steadfast path (for abhyudayam)'.

VS 10.4 provides the list of attributes in the Rāṣṭram starting with Āpah parivahiṇī stha:

Āpah parivahiṇī stha Rashtradā Rāṣṭram me datta svāhā

Āpah parivahiṇī stha Rāṣṭradā Rāṣṭramumuṣmai datta svāhā

Attributes of Vedic *Rāṣṭram*

The twin refrain lines are repeated twice invoking the following additional attributes:

Āpah parivahiṇī stha -- Place with (ocean) waves

apām patirasi – Place adjoining the ocean (*apām pati*)

apām garśnosi – Place moistened (endowed[28]) with water

sūryatvacas stha – Place covered by sunshine

māndā stha – Place with gladdening (potable) waters

vrajākṣita stha – Place with marked roads[29], cattle-sheds, enclosures or herdsmen stations

vāśā stha -- Place with plants (arable land)

śāviṣṭhā stha – Place with resolute, mightiest (craftsmen)(cf. RV 5.29.15[30])

śakvarī stha – Place with artificers

janа*śnṛta stha* – Place with agriculturists (*anṛta*)

viśvaśnṛta stha – Place with culture (cultivator tradition) of pitṛ-s.

vṛṣṇa ūrmirasi stha -- powerful wave (cutting like a sword)

vṛṣa senosi stha -- powerful battle-array[31] (cutting like a spear)

artheta stha -- place with work opportunities to create wealth[32]

ojasvatī stha -- place filled with water, vigour, lustre[33]

viśva bhṛtam -- place bearing, nourished by the dharma of pitr-s[34]

āpah svarāja stha -- place with self-luminous, resplendent rays of the sun[35] and water (springs)

मधुमतीर्मधुमतीभिँ पृच्यन्ताम्महि क्षत्रङ्क्षत्रियाय वन्वानाऽअनाधृष्टाँ

सीदत सहौजसो महि क्षत्रङ्क्षत्रियाय दधतीँ

Trans.

Pleasant great country with the earth bestowing bountifully,

endowed with water,

wealth, people valorous, resolute, unsubdued and with swabhimān (kṣatra),

dwelling on earth endowed with splendor and holding wealth (kṣatra).

Such is the Rāṣṭram bestowed by Devi. Rāṣṭradā, dadhatīm, Rāṣṭram the giver of wealth.

The prayer is a powerful invocation: Rāṣṭram is desired to be put together with these endowments of water, skilled artificers, arable land and wealth on earth on the rim of the ocean.[36].

The operative verb is *pṛcyanta*, 'to unite'; *pṛcyantām* 'put together'. (VS 10.4)

वाजस्येमम्प्रसवँ सुषुवेग्रे सोमँ राजानमोषधीष्वप्सु ।

ताऽअस्मभ्यम्मधुमतीर्भवन्तु वयँ राष्ट्रे जागृयाम पुरोहुताँ स्वाहा ।। (VS 9.23)

Trans.

Of old the furtherance of strength urged onwards this Rājā

Soma (Rājā) in the plants and waters.

For us may they be stored with honey. Stationed in front

Āhutam svāhā: Invoking you, Devi.

May we be awaken in the Rāṣṭram. Devi.

Chandogya Upanishad explains soma: *eṣa somo Rājā, tad devānām annam;*

tam devā

bhakshyanti). *Rājā* is the annam of *devā*. Annam is the form in which the

supreme *ātman* is

manifested, the coarsest envelope of the supreme *ātman*, *paramātman*.

Rāṣṭram in Śukla Yajurveda points to the unity and wealth achieved in waters (as in Indian Ocean?)

VS 9.23

वाजस्येमम्प्रसवँ सुषुवेग्रे सोमँ राजानमोषधीष्वप्सु ।ताऽअस्मभ्यम्मधुमतीर्भवन्तु वयँ राष्ट्रे जागृयाम पुरोहिताँ स्वाहा ।। Of old the furtherance of strength urged onwards this Raja

Soma in the plants and waters.

For us may they be stored with honey. Stationed in front

May we be watchful in the Rashtram. Svaahaa.

VS 10.2-4 (Rashtra as an anugraham)

वृष्णऽऊर्मिरसि राष्ट्रदा राष्ट्रम्मे देहि स्वाहा वृष्णऽऊर्मिरसि राष्ट्रदा राष्ट्रममुष्मै देहि

वृषसेनोसि राष्ट्रदा राष्ट्रममुष्मै देह्यर्थेत स्थ । 2 ।

अर्थेत स्थ राष्ट्रदा राष्ट्रम्मे दत्त स्वाहार्थेत स्थ राष्ट्रदा राष्ट्रमुष्मै दत्तोजस्वती स्थ राष्ट्रदा राष्ट्रम्मे दत्त स्वाहौजस्वती स्थ राष्ट्रदा राष्ट्रममुष्मै दत्ताप-:- परिवाहिणी स्थ राष्ट्रदा राष्ट्रम्मे दत्त स्वाहाप-:- परिवाहिणी स्थ राष्ट्रदा राष्ट्रममुष्मै दत्तापाम्पतिरसि

राष्ट्रदा राष्ट्रम्मे देहि स्वाहापाम्पतिरसि राष्ट्रदा राष्ट्रममुष्मै देह्यपाङ्गर्भोसि राष्ट्रदा राष्ट्रममुष्मै स्वाहापाङ्गर्भोसि राष्ट्रदा राष्ट्रममुष्मै देहि सूर्यत्वचस स्थ । 3 ।

सूर्यत्वचस स्थ राष्ट्रदा राष्ट्रम्मे दत्त स्वाहा सूर्यत्वचस स्थ राष्ट्रदा राष्ट्रममुष्मै दत्त स्वाहा सूर्यत्वचस स्थराष्ट्रदा राष्ट्रम्मे दत्त स्वाहा सूर्यत्वचस स्थ राष्ट्रदा राष्ट्रममुष्मै दत्त

मान्दा स्थ राष्ट्रदा राष्ट्रम्मे दत्त स्वाहा मान्दा स्थ राष्ट्रदा राष्ट्रममुष्मै दत्त

व्रजक्षित स्थ राष्ट्रदा राष्ट्रम्मे दत्त स्वाहा व्रजक्षित स्थ राष्ट्रदा राष्ट्रममुष्मैदत्त

वाशा स्थ राष्ट्रदा राष्ट्रम्मे दत्त स्वाहा वाशा स्थ राष्ट्रदा राष्ट्रममुष्मै दत्त

शविष्ठा स्थ राष्ट्रदा राष्ट्रम्मे दत्त शक्वरी स्थ राष्ट्रदा राष्ट्रममुष्मै दत्त स्वाहा

शक्वरी स्थ राष्ट्रदा राष्ट्रम्मे दत्त जनभृतं स्थ राष्ट्रदा राष्ट्रममुष्मैदत्त

स्वाहा जनभृतं स्थ राष्ट्रदा राष्ट्रम्मे दत्त विश्वभृतं स्थ राष्ट्रदा राष्ट्रममुष्मै दत्त स्वाहा विश्वभृतं स्थराष्ट्रदा राष्ट्रम्मे दत्ताप-:- स्वराज स्थ राष्ट्रदा राष्ट्रममुष्मै दत्त ।

मधुमतीर्मधुमतीभिँ पृच्यन्ताम्महि क्षत्रङ्क्षत्रियाय वन्वानाऽअनाधृष्टाँ

सीदत सहौजसो महि क्षत्रङ्क्षत्रियाय दधतीँ । 4 ।

This verse talks about many concepts which through light on the nation of the supporters of people (janabhṛta) and supporter of world (vishvabhRta) and about the concept of self rule (svarāja).

The Gods drew waters with their store of sweetness, succulent
and observant, king-creating,
Wherewith they sprinkled Varuna and Mitra, wherewith
they guided Indra past his foemen.

2 Wave of the male art thou, giver of kingship. Do thou—
All-hail!—bestow on me the kingdom.
Wave of the male art thou, giver of kingship. Do thou on
So-and-So bestow the kingdom.
Thou hast a host of males, giver of kingship. Do thou—
All-hail!—bestow on me the kingdom.
A host of males hast thou, giver of kingship. Do thou on
So-and-So bestow the kingdom.
3 Swift at your work are ye, givers of kingship. Do ye—

All-hail!—bestow on me the kingdom.
Swift at your work are ye, givers of kingship. Do ye on
So-and-So bestow the kingdom.
Endowed with strength are ye, givers of kingship, etc.
O'erflowing floods are ye, etc.
The Waters' Lord art thou, giver of kingship. Do thou, etc.
The Waters' Child art thou, etc.

4 With sun-bright skins are ye, givers, etc.
Brilliant as Suns are ye, etc.
Bringers of joy are ye, etc.
Dwellers in cloud are ye, etc
Desirable are ye, etc.
Most powerful are ye, etc.
Endowed with might are ye, etc.
Man-nourishing are ye, etc.
All-nourishing are ye, etc.
Self-ruling Waters are ye, giving kingship. On So-and-So
do ye bestow the kingdom.
Together with the sweet let sweet ones mingle, obtaining
for the Kshatriya mighty power.
Rest in your place inviolate and potent, bestowing on the
Kshatriya mighty power.

The binding feature of Rāṣṭram is emphasized in the following Rgvedic prayer:

yuvó rāṣṭarám bṛhád invati dyaúr
yaú setṛ́bhir arajjúbhiḥ sinīthá́ḥ
pári no héḷo váruṇasya vṛjyā
urúṃ na índraḥ kṛṇavad ulokám† (RV 7.84.2)

Trans.

Kings, Indra-Varuna, I would turn you hither to this sacrifice with gifts and homage. Held in both arms the ladle, dropping fatness, goes of itself to you whose forms are varied. Dyaus quickens and promotes your high dominion who bind with bonds not wrought of rope or cordage. Far from us still be Varuna's displeasure; may Indra give us spacious room to dwell in.

The upholding feature of the bonding provided by Rāṣṭram is elaborated in the Vājasneyisamhiatā (VS 20.8) prayer comparing Rāṣṭram to ribs :

पृष्टीर्मे राष्ट्रमुदरमँ सौ ग्रीवाश्च श्रोणी । ऊरूऽरत्नी जानुनी विशो मेङ्गानि सर्वत

– (Rashtra and me are one)-

My ribs be royal government, my belly, shoulders, neck, and hips, thighs, elbows, knees, the people, yea, my members universally!

This is the answer to the question: **When will the Rāṣṭram happen?**

When every citizen identifies himself or herself with the Rāṣṭram. When all the ribs and all the limbs of the body are at the service of the Rāṣṭram.

I take my stand on Rāṣṭram says VS 20.10:

प्रति क्षत्रे प्रतितिष्ठामि राष्टे प्रत्यश्वेषु प्रतितिष्ठामि गोषु ।

प्रत्यङ्गेषु प्रतितिष्ठाम्यात्मन्प्रति प्राणेषु प्रतितिष्ठामि पुष्टे प्रति द्यावापृथिव्योँ प्रतितिष्ठामि यज्ञे ।। (Whole)

10 I take my stand on princely power and Kingship, on cows am I dependent, and on horses. on vital breath On members I depend, and on the body, dependent and on welfare, on heaven and earth and sacrifice dependent.

Rāṣṭram is the framework for prosperity and defence of the realm in VS 22.22:

आ ब्रह्मन्ब्राह्मणो ब्रह्मवर्चसी जायतामा राष्ट्रे राजन्य-:-

शूरऽइषव्योतिव्याधी महारथो जायतान्दोग्घ्री धेनुर्वोढानड्वानाशुँ

सप्तिँ पुरन्धिर्योषा जिष्णू रथेष्ठाँ सभेयो युवास्य यजमानस्य वीरो

जायतान्निकामेनिकामे नँ पर्जन्यो वर्षतु फलवत्यो नऽओषधयँ पच्यन्ताँयोगक्षेमो न-:- कल्पताम् ।

22 O Brahman, let there be born in the kingdom the Brahman illustrious for religious knowledge; let there be born the Râjanya, heroic, skilled archer, piercing with shafts, mighty warrior; the cow giving abundant milk; the ox good at carrying; the swift courser; the industrious woman.

May Parjanya send rain according to our desire; may our fruit-bearing plants ripen; may acquisition and preservation of property be secured to us.

(Rajyam in AV 3.4.2 is an administering or governance aspect of rashtram. Ganrashtram is the nation of the people (gana).

This peoples' self-rule (*jānarājyam)* is reinforced by *Taittirīya Samhitā* (TS 1.8.10.3-5) which gives an insight into the Rāṣṭram of Bhāratam:

... *ya devaa devasuvah stha ta imamāmuṣyāyanamanamitrāya suvadhvammahate kshatrāya mahata ādhipatyāya mahate jānarājyāyaisha vo bharatā rājā somosmākam brāhmaṇānām rājā prati tyannāama rāyamadhāyi syām tanuvam..*

Trans.

O ye gods that instigate the gods, do ye instigate him, descendant of N.N., to freedom from foes, to great lordship, to great overlordship, to great rule over the people. This is your king, O Bharatas; Soma is the king of us Brahmanas. This rashtram hath verily been conferred... Note: 'jaanaraajyaayaisha' is a reference to 'the state of the people'.

In TS 3.4.6, there are references to rashtra and rashtrabhrta (rashtram, supporters of the rashtram):

Devaa vai yadyajne kurvata tadasuraa akurvata te devaa etaanabhyaataanaanapashyantaanabhyaatanyata yaddevaanaam karmaaseedaardhyata tadyasuraanaam na tadaarthyata yena karmanetsamtatra hotavyaa rghnotyeva tena karmana yaddhishve devaah samabharantasmaadabhyaataanaa vaishvadevaa yatprajaapatirjayaanpraayacchattasmaajjayaah praajaapatyaah yadrashtrabhrdbhii rashtramaadada ta tadraashtrabhrtaam rashtrabhrttvam te devaa abhyaataanairasuraanabhyaatanvata jayejayanrashtrabhrdbhii rashtramada datta yaddevaa abhyaataanairasuraanabhyaatanvata tadabhyaataanaanaamabhyaataanatvam yajjayairajayantajjayaanaam jayatvam yadrashtrabhrdbhii rashtramaadada ta tadraashtrabhrtaam rashtrabhrtvam tato devaa abhyavanparaasuraa yo bhaatruvaantsyaatsa etaanjuhuyadabhyaataanaireva bhaatrvyaanabhyaatanute jayerjayati rashtrabhrdbhii rashtramaadatte bhavatyaatmanaa paraasya bhraatruvyo bhavati

TS 3.4.6: What the gods did at the yajna, the Asuras did. The devas saw these overpowering (Homas), they performed them; the rite of the devas succeeded, that of the asura did not succeed. If he is desirous of prospering in a rite, then should he offer them, and in that rite he prospers. In that the All-divinities brought together (the materials), the Abhyatanas are connected with the All-divinities; in that Prajapati bestowed the victories (jayas), therefore the jayas are connected with Prajapati; in that they won the rashtram by the Rashtrabhrts, that is why the Rashtrabhrts (supporters of the rashtram) have their name. The devas overpowered the asura with the Abhyatanas, conquered them with the jayas, and won the

rashtram with the Rashtrabhrts; in that the devas overpowered (abhyatanvata) the Asuras with the Abhyatanas, that is why the Abhyatanas have their name; in that they conquered (ajayan) them with the jayas, that is why the jayas have their name; in that they won the rashtram with the Rashtrabhrts, that is why Rashtrabhrts have their name. Then the devas prospered, the Asura were defeated. He who has foes should offer these (offerings); verily by the Abhyatanas he overpowers his foes, by the jayas he conquers them, by the Rashtrabhrts he wins the rashtram; he prospers himself, his foe is defeated.
Abhyatana is the key dharma. Overpowering effort is the hallmark of the Rāṣṭram which overpowers evil and ensures victories for the Rāṣṭram.

TS 3.4.8 declares emphatically that the people united are the Rāṣṭram. This is a discussion the components of the Rāṣṭram and also refers to sangrām (struggle) for the well-being of the Rāṣṭram. In this prose, there is also a reference to plākṣa; it is noteworthy that the origin of Vedic River Sarasvati is surrounded by the plākṣa trees and is known as plakṣapraśravana. The six Vedic seasons are also indicated.

Rāṣṭrakaamaaya hetavyaa Rāṣṭram vai Rāṣṭrabhrto Rāṣṭrenevaas mai Rāṣṭramava rundve Rāṣṭrameva bhavatyaatmane hotavyaa Rāṣṭram vai Rāṣṭrabhrto Rāṣṭram prajaa Rāṣṭram pashavo Rāṣṭram yaccheshtho bhavati Rāṣṭrenaiva Rāṣṭramava rundve vasishthah samaanaanaambhavati graamakaamaaya hotavyaaRāṣṭram vai Rāṣṭrabhrto Rāṣṭram sajaataa rashtrenevaasmam Rāṣṭram sajaataanava rundve graamyeva bhavatyadhidevane juhotyadhidevana evasmai sajaataanava rundve tava enamavaruddha upa tishthante rathamukha ojakaamasya hotavyaa ojo vai Rāṣṭrabhrta ojo ratha ojasaivaasmaa ojova rundva ojasyeva bhavati yo Rāṣṭradpabhootah syaatasmai hotavyaa yavantosya sthaah syustaanbhooyaadyundhyamiti Rāṣṭramevaasmai yunaktyaahutayo vaa etasyaaklruptaa yasya Rāṣṭramanu kalpate svarathasya dakshinam chakrampravrhya naadiinabhi juhuyaadaahuteerevaasya kalpayati taa asya kalpamaanaa Rāṣṭramanu kalpate sangraame samyate hotavyaaRāṣṭram vai rashtrabhrto rashtre khalu vaa ete vyaahyacchante ye sangramam samyanti yasya poorvaasya juhvati sa eva bhavati jayati tam sangraamam maandhuka idhmo bhavatyangaaraa eva prativeshtamaanaa abhitraanaamasya senaamprati veshtayanti ya unmaadhyatyete hotavyaa evamunmaadayanti ya unmaadyatyete khalu vai gandharvaapsaraso yadrashtrabhrtasmai svaahaa taabhyah svaaheti juhoti tenaivainaacchamayati naiyagrodha audumbara aashwatthah plaaksha itidhmo bhavatyete vai gandharvapsarasaam gruhaah sva evainaanaanaayatane shamayatyabhicharataa pratilomam hotavyaah praanaanevaasya prateechah prati yaanti tam tato yena kena cha strunute svakruta harine juhoti pradare vaitadvaa asyai nirrtigrheetam evainam nirrtyaa graahayati yadvaachah krooram tena vashatkaroti vaaca evaina krooraana pra vrushcati taajagaartimaarchhati yasya kaamayetaannaadyamaa dadeeyeti tasya sabhaayaamuttaano nipadya bhuvanasya pata iti trunaani sam gruheeyaatprajaapativai bhuvanasya prajaapatinaivaasyaannaadyamaa datta idamahamamushyaayanasyaannaadyam haraameetyaahaannaadyamevaasya harati shadbhirharati shadyaa rtavah prajaapatinnaivaasyaannaadyamaadaayartavosmaa anu pra yacchanti yo jyeshthabandhurapabhootah syaatai sthalevasaayya brahmaudanam catuh sharaavampaktvaa tasmai hotavyaa varsh vai Rāṣṭrabhrto sthalama varshmanaivainam varshma samaanaanaam gamayati catuhsharaavo bhavati dikshyeva prati tishthati ksheere bhavati rucamevaasmindadhaatyuddharati shrutatvaaya sarpishvaanbhavati medhyatvaaya catvaarah aarsheeyaah praashnanti dishaameva jyotishi juhoti

They should be offered for one who desires the Rāṣṭram; the Rāṣṭrabhṛt are the Rāṣṭram; verily with the Rāṣṭram he wins the Rāṣṭram for him; he becomes the Rāṣṭram. They should be offered for oneself; the Rāṣṭrabhṛt are the Rāṣṭram, the people are the Rāṣṭram, cattle are the Rāṣṭram, in that he becomes the highest he is the Rāṣṭram; verily with the Rāṣṭram he wins the Rāṣṭram, he becomes the richest of his equals. They should be offered for one who desires a village; the Rāṣṭrabhṛt are the Rāṣṭram, his fellows are the Rāṣṭram; verily with the Rāṣṭram he wins for him his fellows and the Rāṣṭram; he becomes possessed of a village He offers on the dicing place; verily on the dicing-place he wins his fellows for him, and being won they wait upon him. They should be offered on the mouth of the chariot for him who desires force; the Rāṣṭrabhṛt are force, the chariot is force; verily by force he wins force for him; he becomes possessed of force. They should be offered for him who is expelled from his Rāṣṭram; to all his chariots he should say, 'Be yoked'; verily he yokes the Rāṣṭram for him. The oblations of him whose realm is not in order are disordered; he should take off the right wheel of his chariot and offer in the box; so he puts in order his oblation, and the Rāṣṭram comes into order in accord with their coming into order. They should be offered when battle is joined; the Rāṣṭrabhṛt are the Rāṣṭram, and for the Rāṣṭram do they strive who go to battle together; he for whom first they offer prospers, and wins this battle. The kindling-wood is from the Madhuka tree; the coals shrinking back make the host of his foe to shrink back. They should be offered for one who is mad; for it is the Gandharva and the Apsarases who madden him who is mad; the Rāṣṭrabhṛt are the Gandharva and the Apsarases. 'To him hail! To them hail!' (with these words) he offers, and thereby he appeases them. Of Nyagrodha, Udumbara, Açvattha, or Plaksa (wood) is the kindling-wood; these are the homes of the Gandharva and the Apsarases; verily he appeases them in their own abode . They should be offered in inverse order by one who is practising witchcraft; so he fastens on his breaths from in front, and then at pleasure lays him low. He offers in a natural cleft or hollow; that of this (earth) is seized by misfortune; verily on (a place) seized by misfortune he makes misfortune seize upon him. With what is harsh in speech he utters the Vasat call; verily with the harshness of speech he cuts him down; swiftly he is ruined. If he desire of a man, 'Let me take his eating of food', he should fall at length in his hall and (with the words), 'O lord of the world', gather blades of grass; the lord of the world is Prajapati; verily by Prajapati he takes his eating of food. 'Here do I take the eating of food of N. N., descendant of N. N.', he says;

verily he takes his eating of food. With six (verses) he takes, the seasons are six; verily the seasons having taken by Prajapati his eating of food bestow it on him. If the head of a family is expelled, they should be offered for him, placing him on a mound and cooking a Brahman's mess of four Çaravas in size; the Rāṣṭrabhṛt are pre-eminence, the mound is pre-eminence; verily by preeminence he makes him pre-eminent among his equals. (The offering) is of four Çaravas in size; verily he finds support in the quarters; it is made in milk; verily he bestows brilliance upon him; he takes it out, to make it cooked; it is full of butter, for purity; four descended from Rsis partake of it; verily he offers in the light of the quarters.

Bhadram icchanta rishayah swarvidah tapo deeksham upanishedush agre tato Rāṣṭram balam ojashca jaatam tadasmai devah uasannamantu

> The sages, aspiring for a higher and better standard, work with diligence and devotion; **they inspire people to do their duty with dedication.** This is the way how Rāṣṭram and communities grow strong. (Atharva Veda 19.41.1[37])

Atharvaveda underscores the action inspired by the divine to protect the Rāṣṭram:

brahmacharyena tapasā raja Rāṣṭram virakṣati
ācāryo brahmacaryena brahmacāriṇamicchati

> By brahmacharya and tapas, Rāṣṭram is protected. By brahmacharya acharya adores brahmachari. (Brahmacharya is

action inspired by the divine. Brahmacharyam is parameshtyam, evocation of parameśvara.) (Atharva Veda II-5-17)

That is the way for Rāṣṭram and communities grow strong.

Taking *rāṣṭram* as one nation, the features of a common bond which unite the community include many facets ranging from cultural to geopolitical.

In this context, for example, today's India can be viewed as a sub-set of an Indian Ocean 'Rāṣṭram' with a civilizational story of triumphs and travails including the foreign occupation into British India and later balkanisation with the formation of the states of Pakistan and Bangladesh. These administrative formations of states cannot negate the cultural community of Indian Ocean States governed by the common bond of dharma-dhamma continuum. (Dharma defined as a sustaining, upholding universal, eternal ethical order leading to personal emancipation -- *nihs'reyas* -- and community welfare -- *abhyudayam*).

Thus, Indian Ocean Community as *rāṣṭram*, One Nation can be seen as a pragmatic approach to get people together for a common cause, moving in union on the path of dharma-dhamma continuum. Based on this framework, a presentation will be made on the components of the common cause which can bind the people in the Indian Ocean Community together.

Many thinkers of yester-years have yearned for that One nation. In recent times, we can recall the phrase 'One nation' mentioned by Disraeli. The phrase comes from Disraeli's 1845 novel Sybil, in which he described the rich and poor as 'two nations between whom there is no intercourse and no sympathy; who are ignorant of each other's habits, thoughts and feelings, as if they were dwellers in different zones or inhabitants of different planets; who are formed by different breeding, are fed by different food, are ordered by different manners, and are not governed by the same laws'. BR Ambedkar echoed this in a more ephatic statement: "Every man who repeats the dogma of Mill that one country is not fit to rule another country must admit that one class is not fit to rule another class." Vivekananda predicted that modern science and education would break down the barriers between nations and prepare the ground for the fulfillment of the age-old dream of one united world.

Let us strive towards a vision larger than ourselves, the vision of a patriotic, loyal community of people dedicated to the common cause. The common cause 'courses through the veins of all and nobody feels left out.' It is a vision of the Indian Ocean Community coming together to overcome the shared challenges of the people in the Community.

Let us dedicate ourselves to achieve that common cause. We have a shared destiny and a common life we lead together.

Ōm Sam-gacchadhvam sam-vadadhvam, Sam vō
manāmsi jānatām;
Dēvā bhāgam yathā pūrvē Sam-jānānā upāsatē.
Samānō mantrah samitih samānī, samānam manah
saha-cittamēṣām; Samānah mantram abhi-
mantrayē vah, samānēna vō haviṣā juhōmi.
Samānīva ākūtih samānā hṛdayāni vah;
Samānamastu vō manō yathā vah su-sahāsati.

O Lord, may we move forward in harmony, in harmony shall we speak, in harmony shall our minds apprehend; so the shining ones of ancient times with united minds achieved their noble goals. We pray, that united be your deliberations, united be your assembly, united be your minds in harmonious understanding; united be your resolutions through friendly deliberations, make your offerings in perfect harmony, and united be your wills, united be your hearts, united be your thoughts, so that you may all be perfectly united for the well being of all and everything concerned for the progress in this planet.

According to tradition, the Dhammapada's verses were spoken by the Buddha on various occasions. Let us remember Gautama, the Buddha's exhortation remembering Dharma-Dhamma continuum:

Dhammapada Verse 5 Kalayakkhini Vatthu ***Yamaka-vaggo***

Na hi verena verani
sammantidha kudacanam
averena ca sammanti
esa dhammo sanantano.

(Trans.: Hatred is, indeed, never appeased by hatred in this world. It is appeased only by loving-kindness. This is an ancient law: esa dhammo sanantano, this is sanatana dharma.)

In the name of Dharma-Dhamma, let us resolve to work together for *abhyudayam*, welfare of the community.*Esha dhammo sanantano* to realize One nation, one Indian Ocean Community

Epistemological[38] underpinnings of *rāṣṭram* -- a connotation wider than a 'nation'

'Nation' itself was an idea to identify common and shared values of a group of people. Many definitions and scholarly formulation exist for the word, 'nation'.

Is a 'nation' a geographical identity? Is a 'nation' a group of people with shared values or common ideologies?

Is a 'nation' identified by the affinity of place of birth – some sort of territorial nation? Is it a modern construct for structural components of a society? Such identifications provide the basis for an ideology called 'nationalism'. Nationalists tend to define a community in ethnic, linguistic, cultural, historic, or religious terms calling such an identified community as a 'nation'.

'Nation' is a concept still unresolved as seen from the dissolution of the state of Union of Soviet Socialist Republic (USSR). But, Rāṣṭram is founded on ādhyatmika foundations from the Ṛgveda and is governed by the active terms, samgam, samgamanī –united movements of people towards *abhyudayam* (progress, welfare). Thus, Rāṣṭram is not a restricted construct related to a common language or territory but a common zeal to achieve welfare of people through united actions.

George Orwell's 1945 Notes on nationalism[39]: "By 'nationalism'… I mean the habit of identifying oneself with a single nation or other unit, placing it beyond good and evil and recognising no other duty than that of advancing its interests. *Nationalism is not to be confused with patriotism.* Both words are normally used in so vague a way that any definition is liable to be challenged, but one must draw a distinction between them, since two different and even opposing ideas are involved. By 'patriotism' I mean devotion to a particular place and a particular way of life, which one believes to be the best in the world but has no wish to force on other people. Patriotism is of its nature defensive, both militarily and culturally. Nationalism, on the other hand, is inseparable from the desire for power. The abiding purpose of every nationalist is to secure more power and more prestige, *not* for himself but for the nation or other unit in which he has chosen to sink his own individuality… There are, for example, Trotskyists who have become simply enemies of the U.S.S.R. without developing a corresponding loyalty to any other unit. When one grasps the implications of this, the nature of what I mean by nationalism becomes a good deal clearer. A nationalist is one who thinks solely, or mainly, in terms of competitive prestige. He may be a positive or a negative nationalist — that is, he may use his mental energy either in boosting or in denigrating — but at any rate his thoughts always turn on victories, defeats, triumphs and humiliations. He sees history, especially contemporary history, as the endless rise and decline of great power units, and every event that happens seems to him a demonstration that his own side is on the upgrade and some hated rival is on the downgrade. But finally, it is important not to confuse nationalism with mere worship of success. The nationalist does not go on the principle of simply ganging up with the strongest side. On the contrary, having picked his side, he persuades himself that it is the strongest, and is able to stick to his belief even when the facts are overwhelmingly against him."

In recent discourses by anthropologists in Europe, nationalism re-emerges as neo-nationalism under 'different global and transnational conditions'. "The end of the Cold War initiated these new global and European contexts, which are often summarized by the ambivalent term 'globalisatio'. They entail a wide range of transnational (economic, political and socio-cultural) dimensions to which neo-nationalists feel they have to adjust, and to react…Some of the most conspicuous reactions include the neo-nationalists' stance towards immigration, or on central EU decisions, as well as their populist appeals to the mass cultures of the present…" (Andre Gingrich & Marcus Banks, 2006, *Neo-nationalism in Europe and beyod – Perspectives from Social Anthropology*, Berghahn Boks, pp.2-3).

Indian Ocean Community as cultural identity

We have to remind all citizens of Indian Ocean Community about the heritage which our ancestors have bequeathed us, recollecting the memories of the cordial relations which had existed between Chola kings and the region of Kedaram (Malaysia) between the 10th and 12th centuries and the presence of hundreds of temples such as Angkor Wat, Borobudur, Prambanan (Brahma vana).

In fact, the largest Vishnu temple of the world is NOT in India, but in Angkor Wat, Cambodia. People of the region venerate the Buddha and traditions represented by the Hindu-Bauddha temples.[40] In Bali, Indonesia, the prayer position is namaste, as in India. And so goes the cultural metaphors in other parts of the IOC region who call themselves followers of dharma-dhamma. Now, it is time to provide economic content to this spiritual journey of millennia of a third of the world's population (about 2 billion people of the region).

Nobel Laureate, poet Tagore burst into song when he visited Jakarta referring to 'golden threads of friendship between India and Indonesia'. Biju Patnaik, father of Naveen Patnaik was the one who suggested the name of Meghawati to the daughter of President Soekarno. Soekarno named her Meghawati Soekarna putri.

Dharma-dhamma is the principal foundational value of the Indian Ocean Community. Dharma-dhamma continuum is inviolate, dharma-dhamma is divine, sacred. As one attains the full potential of his ātman, one attains divinity. The very performance of one's responsibility makes the action, the motion, divine. Sacredness inheres in the responsibility. That is why, dharma-dhamma is sacred.

In a comparative study of cultures, many states of Indian Ocean Community can be categorized as entities governed by the universal ethic, the perennial philosophia of dharma-dhamma.

In the intellectual evolution of the modern Indian Ocean Community, dhamma is a reification of dharma. The people of the Community turn Dharma-dhamma continuum for protection because dharma-dhamma postulate an ethical order independent of any path chosen for salvation. This is a universal postulation like the universal declaration of human rights. Rights inhere by the mere fact that one is a human being. Just as even a stateless person has human rights, a non-believer is also a part of the ethical order simply because he or she is a part of the order.[41]

Dhamma in Pali and Bauddha tradition refers to the "truth" or the ultimate reality of "the way that things really are" (Tib. Cho). Dharma sets forth an ideal to strive for, an ideal for all humanity; dharma is thus a universal ethic, which evolved over time as an eternal satyam (truth) which should govern every human endeavour which should result in the good of all living entities, bhūtahitam.

Dharma as a principle of motion, of tradition (parampara): jaina, bauddha continuum

Dharman, satya, ṛta

kim satyam? bhūtahitam. What is truth? That which leads to well-being of all living beings. This is the question and answer provided by śankara. The same applies to Dharma. Satya, 'the idea of morality' is 'verily planted in the heart', says Katha Up. 3.9.23. Śankara notes that while the idea of dharma may be in the breast of a human being, in reality it is activated only in relation to the specific social environment (nimitta-vis'es.a). Thus, the sense of right and wrong is a unique characteristic of a human being within sentient creation.[42]

A word often used in the Rgveda is satya (truth), defined as that on which the universe rests, almost an elucidation of ṛta, the law, principle, or order of things. (RV 10.85.1). Aghamarṣaṇa notes that ṛta is the eternal law and order of the universe (RV 10.190.1). The concepts of satya and r.ta are expanded in dharman, used in the R.gveda.

satyenottabhitā bhūmih sūryeṇāttabhitā dyāh

ṛtenādiyās tiṣṭhanti divi somo adhiśritah

RV 10.85.1 Earth is upheld by truth; heaven is upheld by the sun;
the ādityas are supported by sacrifice, Soma is supreme in heaven. [Truth: i.e., Brahman, the eternal soul].

Milestones of Bauddha Dhamma[43]

29 BCE: According to the Sinhalese chronicles, the Pali Canon is written down in the reign of KingVattagamini (29–17 BCE)[44]

247 King Asoka sends his son, Ven. Mahinda, on a mission to bring Bauddham to Sri Lanka. King Devanampiya Tissa of Sri Lanka is converted.

240 Ven. Mahinda establishes the Mahavihara (Great Monastery) of Anuradhapura, Sri Lanka. The Vibhajjavadin community living there becomes known as the Theravadins. Mahinda compiles the first of the Tipitaka commentaries, in the Sinhala language. Mahinda's sister, Ven. Sanghamitta, arrives in Sri Lanka with a cutting from the original Bo tree, and establishes the bhikkhuni-sangha in Sri Lanka.

100 Famine and schisms in Sri Lanka point out the need for a written record of the Tipitaka to preserve the Buddhist religion. King Vattagamani

convenes a Fourth Council, in which 500 reciters and scribes from the Mahavihara write down the Pali Tipitaka for the first time, on palm leaves.

100 Theravada Bauddham first appears in Burma and Central Thailand.

200 Buddhist monastic university at Nalanda, India flourishes; remains a world center of Buddhist study for over 1,000 years.

ca. 5th c. Ven. Buddhaghosa collates the various Sinhala commentaries on the Canon — drawing primarily on the Maha Atthakatha (Great Commentary) preserved at the Mahavihara — and translates them into Pali. This makes Sinhala Buddhist scholarship available for the first time to the entire Theravadin world and marks the beginning of what will become, in the centuries to follow, a vast body of post-canonical Pali literature. Buddhaghosa also composes his encyclopedic, though controversial, meditation manual *Visuddhimagga (The Path of Purification).* Vens. Buddhadatta and Dhammapala write additional commentaries and sub-commentaries.

ca. 600's Bauddham in India begins a long, slow decline from which it would never fully recover.

ca. 6th c.? 9th c.? Dhammapala composes commentaries on parts of the Canon missed by Buddhaghosa (such as the Udana, Itivuttaka, Theragatha, and Therigatha), along with extensive sub-commentaries on Buddhaghosa's work.

1050 The bhikkhu and bhikkhuni communities at Anuradhapura die out following invasions from South India.

1070 Bhikkhus from Pagan arrive in Polonnaruwa, Sri Lanka to reinstate the obliterated Theravada ordination line on the island.

1164 Polonnaruwa destroyed by foreign invasion. With the guidance of two monks from a forest branch of the Mahavihara sect — Vens. Mahakassapa and Sariputta — King Parakramabahu reunites all bhikkhus in Sri Lanka into the Mahavihara sect.

1236 Bhikkhus from Kañcipuram, India arrive in Sri Lanka to revive the Theravada ordination line.

1279 Last inscriptional evidence of a Theravada Bhikkhuni nunnery (in Burma).

1287 Pagan looted by Mongol invaders; its decline begins.

ca. 13th c. A forest-based Sri Lankan ordination line arrives in Burma and Thailand. Theravada spreads to Laos. Thai Theravada monasteries first appear in Cambodia shortly before the Thais win their independence from the Khmers.

ca. 1400's Another forest lineage is imported from Sri Lanka to Ayudhaya, the Thai capital. A new ordination line is also imported into Burma.

1753 King Kirti Sri Rajasinha obtains bhikkhus from the Thai court to reinstate the bhikkhu ordination line, which had died out in Sri Lanka. This is the origin of the Siyam Nikaya.

1768 Burmese destroy Ayudhaya (Thai capital).

1777 King Rama I, founder of the current dynasty in Thailand, obtains copies of the Tipitaka from Sri Lanka and sponsors a Council to standardize the Thai version of the Tipitaka, copies of which are then donated to temples throughout the country.

1803 Sri Lankans ordained in the Burmese city of Amarapura found the Amarapura Nikaya in Sri Lanka to supplement the Siyam Nikaya, which admitted only brahmans from the Up Country highlands around Kandy.

1828 Thailand's Prince Mongkut (later King Rama IV) founds the Dhammayut movement, which would later become the Dhammayut Sect.

ca. 1800's Sri Lankan Sangha deteriorates under pressure from two centuries of European colonial rule (Portuguese, Dutch, British).

1862 Forest monks headed by Ven. Paññananda go to Burma for reordination, returning to Sri Lanka the following year to found the Ramañña Nikaya. First translation of the Dhammapada into a Western language (German).

1868 Fifth Council is held at Mandalay, Burma; Pali Canon is inscribed on 729 marble slabs. {2}

1873 Ven. Mohottivatte Gunananda defeats Christian missionaries in a public debate, sparking a nationwide revival of Sri Lankan pride in its Buddhist traditions.

1879 Sir Edwin Arnold publishes his epic poem *Light of Asia,* which becomes a best-seller in England and the USA, stimulating popular Western interest in Bauddham.

1880 Helena Blavatsky and Henry Steel Olcott, founders of the Theosophical Society, arrive in Sri Lanka from the USA, embrace Bauddham, and begin a campaign to restore Bauddham on the island by encouraging the establishment of Buddhist schools.

1881 Pali Text Society is founded in England by T.W. Rhys Davids; most of the Tipitaka is published in roman script and, over the next 100 years, in English translation.

1891 Maha Bodhi Society founded in India by the Sri Lankan lay follower Anagarika Dharmapala. Mahabodhi temple in Bodh Gaya built in the late Gupta period, is a UNESCO World Heritage Centre, is controlled by the state government of Bihar, which established a temple management committee. The committee has nine members, a majority of whom, including the chairman, must by law be Hindus.

Anagarika Dhammapala was born as David Hewavitarana in 1864. In 1893 he attended the World Parliament of Religions in Chicago. In 1931 he became a samanera in Sarnath and in 1933 a bhikkhu. He died in December 1933 aged 69 with a stellar contribution of 40 years of his life to spreading Dhamma. Dhammapala is remembered for his contribution to the spread of Bauddham in India and in the world.

1899 First Western Theravada monk (Gordon Douglas) ordains, in Burma.

ca. 1900 Ven. Ajaan Mun and Ven. Ajaan Sao revive the forest meditation tradition in Thailand.

1902 King Rama V of Thailand institutes a Sangha Act that formally marks the beginnings of the Mahanikaya and Dhammayut sects. Sangha government, which up to that time had been in the hands of a lay official appointed by the king, is handed over to the bhikkhus themselves.

1949 Mahasi Sayadaw becomes head teacher at a government-sponsored meditation center in Rangoon, Burma.

1954 Burmese government sponsors a Sixth Council in Rangoon.

1956 Buddha Jayanti Year, commemorating 2,500 years of Bauddham.

1958 Ven. Nyanaponika Thera establishes the Buddhist Publication Society in Sri Lanka to publish English-language books on Theravada Bauddham. » Sarvodaya Shramadana Movement is founded in Sri Lanka to bring Buddhist ideals to bear in solving pressing social problems. Two Germans ordain at the Royal Thai Embassy in London, becoming the first to take full Theravada ordination in the West.

ca. 1960's 3 Washington (D.C.) Buddhist Vihara founded — first Theravada monastic community in the USA. and Bhavana Society Brochure}

ca. 1970's Refugees from war in Vietnam, Cambodia, and Laos settle in USA and Europe, establishing many tight-knit Buddhist communities in the West. Ven. Taungpulu Sayadaw and Dr. Rina Sircar, from Burma, establish the » Taungpulu Kaba-Aye Monastery in Northern California, USA. Ven. Ajaan Chah establishes » Wat Pah Nanachat, a forest monastery in Thailand for training Western monks. » Insight Meditation Society, a lay meditation center, is founded in Massachusetts, USA. Ven. Ajaan Chah travels to England to establish a small community of monks at the Hamsptead Vihara, which later moves to Sussex, England, to become Wat Pah Cittaviveka (Chithurst Forest Monastery).

ca. 1980's Lay meditation centers grow in popularity in USA and Europe. First Theravada forest monastery in the USA (» Bhavana Society) is established in West Virginia. » Amaravati Buddhist Monastery established in England by Ven. Ajaan Sumedho (student of Ven. Ajaan Chah).

ca. 1990's Continued western expansion of the Theravada Sangha: monasteries from the Thai forest traditions established in California, USA (» Metta Forest Monastery, founded by Ven. Ajaan Suwat; » Abhayagiri Monastery, founded by Ven. Ajaans Amaro and Pasanno). Bauddham meets cyberspace: online Buddhist information networks emerge; several editions of the Pali Tipitaka become available on-line.

In the Buddhist thought: anussava itiha-itiha-paramparā piṭaka-sampadā dhamma – a system of moral discipline which is based upon customs, usages, or traditions handed down from time immemorial. (Majjhima-nikāya, I.520). In broad terms, dhamma may have meant phenomena. Buddhist thought recognized the dhamma as applied to the upāsaka (layperson), pabbajita (wanderer), and the arhat (enlightened). Dhamm as an ideal already accepted by many people and as it applied to the upāsaka (layperson) was elaborated, about 250 BCE, in Aśoka's Rock

Edict Nos.1,3,7,9 and 11, 12, Pillar Edict, No. 2 and 3 1, In the 13th Edict, Aśoka also notes, in an address to his sons and grandsons that he himself found pleasure in conquests by the Dhamma and not in conquests by the sword. On monuments of the third century BCE, there is a reference to a donor described with the epithet, dhamma-kathika; the term is explained as, 'preacher of the system', dhamma signifying the philosophical and ethical doctrine as distinct from the Vinaya, the Rules of the Order.[45]

Bauddham in Sri Lanka

Eternal dhamma (esa dhammo sanantano); noble eightfold path (ariyo atthangiko maggo); true dhamma (saddhammo); pure dhamma (visuddhi-dhammo); dhamma leading to full liberation (vimutti-dhammo); noble dhamma (ariyo-dhammo); stainless dhamma (sukka dhammo); foremost dhamma (aggo dhammo); ancient dhamma (purano dhammo).[46]

History blends into the lives of every ordinary Indian positing . Sri Rāma and Sri Kṛṣṇa as role-models in polity to protect dharma. Valmiki who wrote the story of Rāma in Rāmāyaṇa calls Vyāsa who wrote the story of Kṛṣṇa in Mahābhārata depicts Krsna as the Gītācharya, teaching the world the basic tenets of Hindu dharma in action.

Sri Rāma and Sri Kṛṣṇa are engaged in the struggles of the Rāṣṭram, harsh tests of life and time, to establish and sustain dharma. Rāmāyaṇa and Mahābhārata are itihāsa. Yāska (11:25) notes that Aitihāsika explains Vedic thought while commenting upon pāramparika kathā (traditional narratives). Thus, itihāsa teaches philosophy of life supported by historical evidence.

Sri Rāma and his vānara sena led by the architects Nala and Nīla accomplish the historic feat of constructing Setubandha to provide a bridge across Setusamudram between India and Sri Lanka to rescue Sita devi held captive by Rāvaṇa in a blatant act of adharma. Sita's rescue from captivity is a dharmic action, par excellence, narrated in the Itihāsa, *Rāmāyaṇa*. Rāma is maryāda puruṣottama, the perfect among men, leading a life of self-control and virtue governed by the global ethic, dharma.

Varaha Mahakuta, Deccan 7th C.

In the Jaina thought, dharma and adharma are defined as the principle of motion and principle of rest. The two phenomena are said to pervade the whole of *loka-ākāśa*; they are subtle; movement is associated with either a *jīva* or pudgala (being sakriya dravyas); the movement is dependent upon the presence of dharma.

Dharma dravya makes movement possible; an analogy is provided by fish swimming, while swimming is impossible without the presence of water.

Adharma dravya enables a moving object, living or non-living to come to rest. The analogy is of a bird coming to a stop by ceasing to beat its wings; this is contingent upon the bird ceasing to fly perching on a tree branch or on the ground. The two principles, dharma and adharma account for the definite structure of the world. So, too, *kāla* is a *dravya*. [cf. S.K. Chatterji et al. (eds.), 1937, The Cultural Heritage of India, Vol. I, Calcutta, Ramakrishna Mission, p. 425].

In the Buddhist thought: anussava itiha-itiha-parampara_-pit.aka-sampada_ dhamma – a system of moral discipline which is based upon customs, usages, or traditions handed down from time immemorial. (Majjhima-nikāya, I.520).

Deviations from dharma have to be rectified.

• Premise: Movement is needed to realize human potential, nihśreyas (samanya dharma, 'ethic'), social capital, abhyudaya

• Harmonise the quest for inner peace (inner space) and abhyudaya – general welfare, loka hitam -- of social order (outer space)

Re-establish the primacy of Human responsibility and duties (juxtaposed to Human rights) : Rights flow from performance (vratam, vratā 'law')

Re-establish the freedom to enquire (different pantha-s, realizing that cosmic order is knowable) Dharma is celebration of freedom, freedom to move from Being to Becoming.[47]

Just as philosophia gives moral meaning to a world view, dharma-dhamma continuum gives a secular meaning to the imperative of modernity. In such a construct, 'religion' and 'politics' are merely two 'modes of negotiating modernity'[48] and dharma-dhamma are not in opposition to modernity.

During Middle Ages, the term was used to distinguish clergy who belonged to 'religious' orders from those who only served local parishes and hence termed 'secular'. Later ages saw the term getting used to isolate public institutions from being fettered by influences of associations promoting particular moral creeds.The term 'secular' is often presented as the only means of promoting 'modernity'. The term is derived from Latin—*saeculum,* of an age—and the French word *siecle*, meaning century or age. By this etymological definition, Dharma-dhamma continuum is of the 'current' age and is consistent with negotiating modernity. The evolutionary history of the term 'secular' is instructive.

This is an echo from the statement of Brihadaranyaka Upanishad:

> *sa naiva vyabhavat* |
> *tac chreyo rūpam atyasṛjata dharmam* |
> *tad etat kṣatrasya kṣatraṃ yad dharmaḥ* |
> *tasmād dharmāt paraṃ nāsti* |
> *atho abalīyān balīyāṃsam āśaṃsate dharmeṇa* |
> *yathā rājñaivam* |
> *yo vai sa dharmaḥ satyaṃ vai tat* |
> *tasmāt satyaṃ vadantam āhur dharmaṃ vadatīti* |
> *dharmaṃ vā vadantaṃ satyaṃ vadatīti* |
> *etad dhy evaitad ubhayaṃ bhavati* || BrhUp_1,4.14 ||

" Verily, that which is Dharma is truth.

Therefore they say of a man who speaks truth, 'He speaks the Dharma,'

Or of a man who speaks the Dharma, 'He speaks the Truth.'

Verily, both these things are the same."

(Brh. Upanishad, 1.4.14)

Let us bring states of the Indian Ocean Community to the eminent position held before the colonial era.

A metaphor for Dharma-Dhamma as the upholding, ordering principle is provided by Varāha upholding Mother Earth: Mahakuta, Deccan, 7th cent.

Dharma-Dhamma is universal and applies to all cosmic phenomena and personal responsibilities. Prithivīm dharmaṇā dhṛtam (Atharva Veda) Trans. Globe is upheld by DharmaSanatana Dharma is eternal ordering principle which is elucidated in many social or personal facets:

Svadharma (Dharmacarth = dharma carati = inherent nature (Thai) ; svadharma = responsibility, according to one's nature), Yuga Dharma (responsibility in the age or period in history), Mānava Dharma (human responsibility).

Sāmānya Dharma (common), Viśeṣa Dharma (special) Varṇāśrama Dharma or Kula dharma (kula and social order), Rāja Dharma (ruler's responsibility) Pravṛtti Dharma (responsibility to realize outer -- worldly life), Nivritti Dharma (responsibility to realize inner -- spiritual life).

Social facet is denoted by abhyudayam as dharma: *Ramo vigrahavan dharmah* (R. Bala. 1.21.10)
Personal facet relates to nihśreyas, self-realization:

Padma Purāṇa notes that Dharma proceeds from ten facets: continence, truthfulness, austerity, charity, self-control, forbearance, purity, non-violence, serenity and non-thieving. These facets are related to human responsibility.

Pravṛtti-Nivṛtti: Social action, Personal knowledge

In Patanjali Yoga Sūtra 3.13 three aspects of change are identified:

> transformation of a thing (dharmi) into a property (dharma),
>
> transformation of a property into a mark (lakṣaṇa), and
>
> the transformation of a mark into a condition (avasthā).

This is then the basis of the "unreasonable effectiveness" of mathematics in the description of the world.

Change applies both to physical substance (bhūta) and to the senses (indriya),i.e.,to sensations.

Pravṛtti relates to social action (trivarga: dharma, artha ka_ma == righteousness, prosperity. desire) **Nivṛtti** i relates to inward contemplation.

Addressing his father, Suka said: The declaration of the Vedas are twofold. They once lay down the command, "Do all acts." They also indicate the reverse saying, "Give up acts." Where do persons go by the aid of Knowledge and where by the aid of Acts? Indeed, these declarations about knowledge and acts are dissimilar and even contradictory. I desire to hear this. Do tell me this.

Vyasa said: I shall expound to thee the two paths, viz., the destructible and the indestructible, depending respectively upon acts and knowledge. Listen with concentrated attention, O child, to me, as I tell thee the place that is reached by one with the aid of knowledge, and that other place which is reached with the aid of acts. The difference between these two places, is as great as the limitless sky. These are the two paths upon which the Vedas are established; the duties indicated by **Pravṛtti**, and those based on **Nivṛtti**.[49]

Gita propounds: "In this world there is a two fold path; the path of knowledge of the Sankhyas and the path of action of the Yogis." --"The Vedic dharma (religion) is verily two-fold, characterised by **Pravṛtti** (social action) and **Nivṛtti** (inward contemplation), designed to promote order in the world; this twofold dharma has in view the true social welfare and spiritual emancipation of all beings."[50]

The history of dharma and dhamma as regulatory principles of life and maintenance of order in the cosmis is exemplified by the following expositions, many of which are echoed in the ancient texts of Bauddham:

Kanada of Vaiśesṣika declares:

Athā to dharma vyā khyā syā mah Yatobhyudaya nihśreyasa siddhih sa dharmah (Vaiśeṣika Sutra 1.11.2)

Dharma is that which exalts and bestows the Supreme Good or Absolute Bliss (cessation of pain). "That which leads to the attainment of Abhyudaya (prosperity in this world) and Nihśreyasa (total cessation of pain and attainment of eternal bliss hereafter) is Dharma".

Note: *Kauśītakī Brāhmaṇa Upaniṣad* uses the term nihśreyas in the context of ātman: II-13. Now, with reference to the Self II-14. Now, next, the assumption of superior excellence. Ni*hs*reyasâdâna (the accepting of the pre-eminence of prâ*n*a (breath or life) by the other divinities). cf. Â*s*valâyana G*ri*hya-sûtras I, 13, 7.

Rāṣṭram is the ātman. Country is the body. State is the protective robe.

A person with faith in dharma-dhamma realizes the fact that every living being and phenomenon on the globe is a divine manifestation. No dogma or doctrine governs the dharma-dhamma way of life. The only emphasis is on responsibility, duty: protection of dharma-dhamma since dharma-dhamma protects us. The accent is on collective responsibility, not on individual, atomised rights.

Bauddham exhorts: Buddham, dhamma, sangham śaraṇam gacchāmi.

The mantra of Viśvāmitra (RV 3.53.12 *viśvāmitrasya rakṣati bráhmedám bhāratam jánam*) (trans. This mantra of Viśvāmitra protects the people of *bhāratam*).

A ' Rāṣṭram of ten generations ' {Daśapurusāmrājya) is mentioned in the Śathapathabrāhmaṇa, xii. 9. 3. 3. Cf. v. 4. 2. 8. sāmrājya is dharmeṇa pālanam, righteous governance. Sāmrājyam is sārvabhaumam padam, position of a purveyor of every aspect of governance. Sāmrājya, bhaujya, svarājya, vairājya are variants of the padam of sārvabhauma.

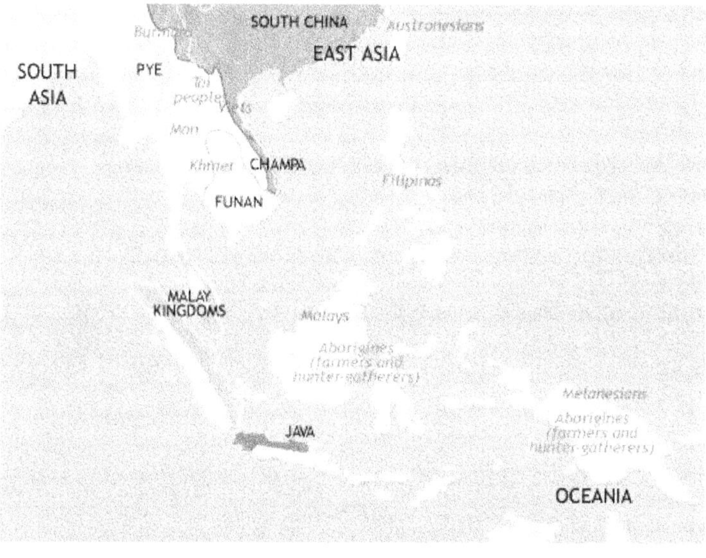

Mahā nārayaṇopaniṣad (Section 79.7) declares thus:

dharmo viśvasya jagatah pratiṣṭhā

loke dharmiṣṭha prajā upasarpanti

dharmeṇa pāpamapanudati

dharme sarvam pratiṣṭhitam

tasmāddharmam paramam vadanti (Mahā nārayaṇopaniṣad Section 79.7)

Dharma constitutes the foundation of all affairs in the world. People respect those who adhere to Dharma. Dharma insulates (man) against sinful thoughts. Everything in this world is founded on Dharma. Dharma, therefore, is considered supreme.

This foundational value of dharma-dhamma continuum provides a set of shared cultural values for the Indian Ocean Community.

Greater Indian Ocean Region: cultural and historical vignettes

At this stage in its history the region's strong trading and cultural links with India are at their height. Buddhism has gained a firm foothold in Burma, and Hinduism is a major cultural force throughout much of the rest of South East Asia. With these faiths has come Indian influences in art, architecture and political organization.

In present-day Vietrnam, an area formerly full of "wild tribes" has been moulded into a kingdom by leaders of Chinese origin. Like Funan, to the south, it is organized along Indian lines, as are the numeous small kingdoms on the Malayan peninsula, eastern Sumatra and eastern Java.

In nortehrn South East Asia, Mon tribes are expanding in modern-day southern Burma and northern Thailand. This movement may be linked to the drift of Tai (Thai) tribes southwards into Laos and northern Thailand.

"Hinduism in Southeast Asia gave birth to the former Champa civilization in southern parts of Central Vietnam, Funan in Cambodia, the Khmer Empire in Indochina, Langkasuka Kingdom, Gangga Negara and Old Kedah in the Malay Peninsula, the Srivijayan kingdom on Sumatra, the

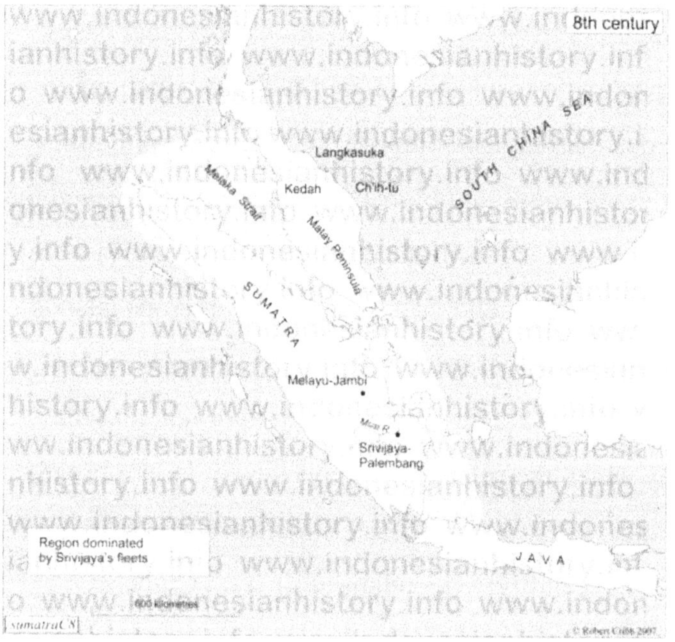

Singhasari kingdom and the Majapahit Empire based in Java, Bali and parts of the Philippine archipelago. The civilization of India influenced the languages, scripts, calendars, and artistic aspects of these peoples and nations…Southeast Asia was frequented by traders from eastern India, particularly Magadha, as well as from the kingdoms of South India."[51]

South East Asia

979 CE

"The Sri Vijayan empire continues to dominate many of the coasts and islands of South East Asia. However, the kingdoms of Java have won their independence. Here, one of the most remarkable structures in the entire region has been constructed, the massive Buddhist temple complex at Borobodur."[52]

Likely extent of Srivijaya's maritime empire
Maps are after *Indoanesian History Atlas* of Robert Cribb (2007); an excerpt on the writeup:

[quote]The power of the ruler of Srivijaya rested on three distinct bases: the courtiers of the capital, who managed the port facilities which made Srivijaya an attractive destination, the chiefs of the interior communities, who supplied produce, trade goods and probably labour to the city, and the orang laut, or people of the sea, semi-piratical people whose homes were aboard small, fast vessels which sheltered amongst the numerous islands and inlets of the Sumatra coast. These seafarers played a crucial role in forcing ships to call at Srivijaya whether they wished to or not, and they were also the means by which the ruler of Srivijaya kept at least a broad suzerainty over potential rivals along the coast. Successive rulers of Srivijaya also appear to have cultivated a relationship with China by sending regular tribute missions and making other gestures of respect for Chinese emperors. This relationship may have assisted the activities of Srivijaya traders in the ports of China. Wealth from trade was used to support a sophisticated civilization, one in which Chinese monks came to study Buddhism and whose scholars were known for their mathematical expertise.

In the 11th century, Srivijaya went into abrupt decline, particularly as a result of destructive raids from Java in 992 and from the Chola rulers of southern India in 1025. Shortly thereafter the empire's capital appears to have moved from Palembang to Jambi (Melayu), though the reasons for this move are not clear. From about this time, however, Srivijaya appears to have ceased to be the dominant power in the region.

Although Jambi inherited some of the authority of Srivijaya, the balance of power in Sumatra and the peninsula shifted dramatically in the 12th and 13th centuries. On the northern coast of Sumatra, several small trading states, Aru, Tamiang, Perlak, Pasai, Samudra and Lamuri now came to prominence. These states were the first in Indonesia to convert to Islam, Perlak probably being the earliest in about 1290. In central Sumatra, the

Buddhist kingdom of the Minangkabau, sometimes called Pagarruyung after its capital, emerged in about 1250 and extended its hegemony down into the coastal regions facing the strait. Palembang and Jambi, however, declined in importance, though they remained significant regional ports. Late in the 13th century, both became the target of Javanese expansionism, when king Kertanegara of Singhasari launched what was called the pamalayu expedition.[unquote][53]

The Indians nowhere engaged in military conquest and annexation in the name

of a state or mother country. And the Indian states that were set up in Farther India during the first centuries of the Christian Era had only ties of tradition with the dynasties reigning in India proper ; there was no political dependence. . .

Meanwhile within India there developed an elaborate and finely honed economic system (which might be described in contemporary terms as Economic Nationalism) which made India an economic hub of the ancient world. Hence too, the development of the Rashtra Kuta, democratic assemblies of Rashtram.The Kuta being the economic spoke in the wheel and after which we have the name for the Rashtrakuta empire. This and as well the development of varṇa and jāti and the growth of srenis and sreni dharma, the economic cell of Indian's prosperity (similar but not identical with the European guild of medieval times).

A scene from the Reamker; a battle between Rama and Ravana performed in the courtyard of the Silver Pagoda, c. 1900s~1920s by Royal Ballet of Cambodia.

A Borobudur ship carved on Borobudur, c. 800 CE.

Indonesian outrigger boats may have made trade voyages to the east coast of Africa as early as the 1st century CE

Borobudur, a UNESCO World Heritage Site, Borobudur, or Barabudur, is a 9th-century Mahayana Buddhist monument in Magelang, Central Java, Indonesia.The monument consists of six square platforms topped by three circular platforms, and is decorated with 2,672 relief panels and 504 Buddha statues.

Candi

Prambanan or Candi Rara

Jonggrang is a 9th-century Hindu temple compound in Central Java, Indonesia, dedicated to the Trimurti, the expression of God as the Creator (Brahma), the Sustainer (Vishnu) and the Destroyer (Shiva). The temple compound is located approximately 18 kilometres (11 mi) east of the city of Yogyakarta on the

boundary between Central Java and Yogyakarta provinces.

An architectural model of the Prambanan temple complex; originally there were 240 temples in this temple compound

The statue of Durga Mahisasuramardini in northern cella of Shiva temple.

Ravana kidnapping Sita while
the Jatayuon the left tried to help her.
Prambanan bas-relief
Indonesian Rupiah with Ganesh inscription

Statue of Bhima, Bali

Official mascot of Military Intelligence in Indonesia is Hanuman who in Ramayana traced Sita Devi

A dancer dressed as Hanuman, a monkey god in Hindu mythology, waits for his turn to perform during a celebration that marks the end of the holy fasting month of Ramadan in Bantul, Indonesia.

Krishna-Arjuna statue at Jakarta main square

Ghatotakach statue near the Ngurah Rai International Airport (also known as Denpasar Airport, Bali)

SHANTI SHANTI SHANTI

Brand logo of Bali “*The tagline ‘Shanti, Shanti, Shanti’ represents peace upon Bhuwana alit dan agung (yourself and the world)…” says a* Indonesian Ministry of tourism publication. “The triangle (shape of logo) is a symbol of stability and balance. It is formed out of three straight lines in which both ends meet, taking the symbols of a blazing fire (Brahma – the creator), lingga. The triangle also represents the three Gods of the universe (Trimurti – Brahma, Wisnu, and Siwa), three stages of nature (Bhur, Bwah and Swah Loka), and three stages of Life

(Born, Live, and Die). The tagline 'Shanti, Shanti, Shanti' represents peace upon Bhuwana alit dan agung (yourself and the world) that will deliver a sacred and holy vibe that awakens a deep aura that balance and make peace to all living creatures."

Kaalachakra ('wheel of time') exhibition in Singapore celebrates the early

Indian influences in Southeast asia. "Aligning with the National Library Board (NLB)'s mission to promote a knowledgeable and engaged society, this exhibition aims at acknowledging the historical past of the Indians with a Singaporean identity rooted in our multicultural heritage."[54]

Model of Khmer Chariot[55] "Chola – Khmer Alliance: Some historians have interpreted that the gift of the Khmer chariot from Suryavarman I to Rajendrachola is the Khmer response to a threat and military pressure from Srivijaya. The date of the gift would correspond to the strongest period of Srivijaya's control over the Straits trade route."[56]

" The Anaimangalam Copper Plates[57] Period: Early 11th Century CE

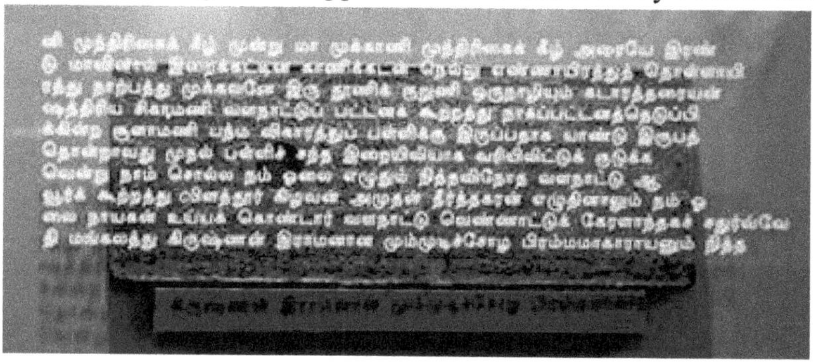

Script: Tamil-Grantha

Language: Tamil Found in: Anaimangalam, India Material: Copper Present Location library of Leiden University, Netherlands. This is the second side of the sixthth plate of Anaimangalam Copper Plates. The content is in Tamil referring to Rajaraja Chola's gift to Chulamanivarma Vihara"Another long-established South East Asian state, the Pye kingdom in Burma, is coming under increasing pressure from Burman tribes, from the north. Meanwhile, the Mon people have established powerful kingdoms in southern Burma and northern and central Thailand.

Ganesha murti from Banon Temple, Magelang, Central Java. 8th cent. is kept in National Museum, Jakarta.

Ganesha on logo of Bandung Institute of Technology.

Ganesha is called Ts'ogsbdag

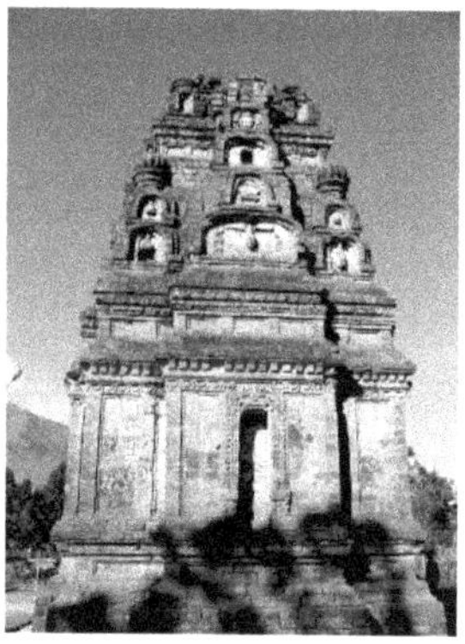

(Tibetan), Maha-Pienne (Burmese), Totkharour Khagan (Mongolian), Prah Kenes (Cambodian), Vinayaksha or Sho-ten (Japanese). Bara temple

in Tuliskaiyo village of East Java (1239 CE) has a 3 metre-high statue of Ganesha. Buddha shrine in Kelaniya, on the banks of Kelaniya Ganga River near Colombo, Sri Lanka, has Ganesha friezes. Fourteen Ganesha temples are in Jaffna, Alaveddy, Batticaloa, Kandy and Katargma. In Kashmir, Ganesha idols are also found in 1) Ganeshbal, on the banks of Lidar River, 2) Ganesha as Bhimasvamin at the foot of the Hariparbat Hill near Srinagar and 3) in Ganeshghati, on a cliff along the Kishenganga River. Candi Sukuh and Candi Ceto are the last Hindu temples built towards the end of the Magapahit period of Javanese history. Candi Loro Jongrang-Prambanan built by the Sanjaya Hindu kings in the 7th-8th centuries has shrines of Shiva Mahaguru, Ganesha and Durga Mahishasuramardini. Other Prambanan temples are at Kalasan, Sari and Sewu.

In Malay and Bhasa Indonesia, bhasha (language), swami (husband), guru (teacher), mahaguru (senior teacher), siswa (student), maha siswa (senior student), building names such as Citra graham (Art gallery), Swargi (Heaven) PlazaChhaya Surya, Wisma Putra, Arya Duta, Wisma Duta, Parambanan (Brahma vana), Yogyakarta, Madura, Sumatra, Bali, Surabaya, are echoes from Sanskrit and Hindu traditions. Cities bear names like Ayodhya, Lavapuri, Kanchanapuri, Chandrapuri, Vishnulok, Singapore (simhapura, the city of lions), Jayakarta, the city of victory (Capitol of Indonesia), Bandar Sri Bhagwan (capitol of Brunei). In the region, all rivers are reverently addressed as Mae which is Maa or Mother. Thus the river flowing through Bangkok, the capital of Thailand is Mae Chaophraya. The river that flows from the Himalayas through Burma, China, Laos, Thailand and Cambodia is called Maa Ganga pronounced as Mae Kong (Mekong river).

Mr Gus Dur Abdul Rehman Wahid, the former President of Indonesia, who was requested to attend the consecration of an ancient mosque in Surabaya City in the island of Java asked the organizers to arrange for a Hindu pundit from India to perform the Vigneswara Pooja before the Quran could be recited by the Islamic priest. A Hindu Tantrik priest was flown in from Kerala exclusively for the purpose. Late Swami Ranganathanandaji, in his book "Eternal Values For a Changing Society", has mentioned about a discussion he had with Sukarno, the late Indonesian president, during his visit to Indonesia in 1964. "Though the President agreed to meet me for just 20 minutes, our discussion went on for more than an hour. Sukarno told me that every night he reads at least two pages from the collected volumes of Swami Vivekananda before going to bed." Sukarno, was named after Karna, the legendary hero of Mahabharata. Sukarno's father used to read Koran on Fridays and Ramayana and Mahabharat on other 6 days. Karna was his favourite character in Mahabharat. He wanted his son to be as brave and philanthropic as Karna. He also wanted his son to be on the right side of Dharma and Righteousness which made him name his son as "SuKarno" meaning a good Karna. The name of his daughter, "Sukarnoputri Meghawati", literally, "full of clouds". Sukarnoputri is yet another Sanskrit word meaning Sukarno's daughter. The name of the present President of

Indonesia Susilo Yudhoyono literally means, 'Warrior of good character'. A prominent politicians in Indonesia is named Karthikeya Mohammed.

Formation of Rastram, a federating comity of nations

The legacy of Hinduised states celebrating Hindu culture lives on the Farther Orient. In Durban, South Africa, Swamiji Sharadananda of Sivananda Divine Life Society runs more than 40 schools for the African people. In recognition of the heritage left by the activities of this Society, South African Government there has names an airport in Natal province after Swami Sivananda. Governments in Singapore, Malaysia, Sri Lanka, Kenya, Mauritius, Trinidad, Guyana and Fiji celebrate the annual Deepavali festival (Festival of lights). Half a million Hindu, Chinese and Western devotees congregate every year in Malaysia, at Batu Caves Lord Subramanya temple on the occasion of Thai Pusam. Half a million devotees turn up at the Ganga sagar in Mauritius on the occasion of Shiv Ratri. About 1,00,000 Thai and Chinese devotees partake in the Vijaya Dashami Ratha Yatra celebrations of the Maha Mariamman (Mata Parvati) Temple on Silom Road, Bangkok. Thai Bharat Cultural Lodge, Bangkok runs several schools in Thailand. Satya Sai Foundation in Thailand runs a residential school for Thai children. Hindu Samaj, Gita Ashram, Sindhi Samaj and Indo-Thai Chamber of Commerce in Bangkok give scholarships to deserving Thai students. The teachings of Swami Vivekananda have been an inspiration to freedom fighters like Soekarno who fought for freeing Indonesia from the Dutch colonial rule.

After Vietnam fought successfully against the American army, Vietnam's Defence Minister Madame Binh visited India in 1977., She expressed to India's Defence minister Jagjivan Ram her keen desire to garland the statue of Chhatrapati Shivaji Maharaj in memory of his successful guerilla warfare against the Mughals. The heroic saga of Shivaji was an inspiration to Vietcong soldiers, leading them ultimately to victory in their guerilla war between 1955 to 1975.

The present UN Secretary General, Ban Ki-moon, spoke of United States of Asia when he took office. IOC will make this vision a reality with the formation of a federation of 59 states along the Indian Ocan Rim, as a milestone.

Time is now for states of the Indian Ocean Rim to raise above the

constraints and preoccupation with issues such as corruption, social inequality, ethnic demography, poverty, infiltration, hostile neighbours, terrorism, maritime security and set a goal which fulfils their destiny in the lands spanned by Himalayas and Indian Ocean.

This is an opportunity for federating a comity of nations to create Indian Ocean Community (IOC) as a 6 trillion dollar combined Gross Domestic Product, as a counterpoise to the European Community.

The IOC will be a tribute to George Coedes who identified Hinduised states of the Farther Orient, and also to Arnold Joseph Toynbee (1889–1975) who said, “It is already becoming clearer that a chapter which has a western beginning will have to have an Indian ending if it is not to end in the self-destruction of the human race... At this supremely dangerous moment in history the only way of salvation for mankind is the Indian Way. Here we have the attitude and spirit that can make it possible for the human race to grow together in to a single family”.
Prayer with namaskar at Bali.

Terracotta toys show yogic asanas including namaskar posture: 1-4, from Harappa; 5-6, from Mohenjo-daro.

Candi Prambanan Candi Mendut

Prambanan)Candi Pawon (Prambanan)Candi Kalasan

Candi Sari

Candi Sewu

Other Java Hindu temples are: Candi Badut (7th cent.), near Malang, Java; Gunung Gangsir (10th cent.); Candi Kidal (13th cent.); Candi Jago (14th cent.); Candi Jawi (14th cent.)Candi Bhima (8th cent.)(1 km. from Candi

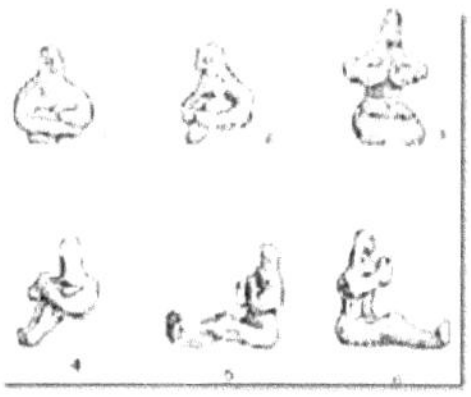

Gatotkaca), Java. Other temples of Dieng temple group are: 3.Candi Abiyasa 4.Candi Arjuna 5.Candi Dwarawati 6.Candi Darawati 7.Candi Pandu

8.Candi Parikesit 9.Candi Puntadewa 10.Candi Magersari 11.Candi Nakula 12.Candi Sadewa 13.Candi Sembadra 14.Candi Senjaka 15.Candi Semar 16.Candi Srikandi

The two Great Epics, Ramayana and Mahabharata together with the teachings of Tathagata the Buddha, encapsulate the dharma-dhamma value system of the Indian Ocean Rastram. In Indonesia, Ramayana and Mahabharata are taught in schools and universities at all levels true to the proud statement: 'Islam is a religion but Ramayana and Mahabharata are our culture'.

In Indian historical tradition, recorded actions and thoughts of two persons have become part of the collective cultural consciousness or *citta*. Trials and tribulations, tests of virtue and righteous, ethical behaviour of these two persons have defined dharma in the reality of Rāṣṭram.

They are Sri Rama and Sri Krsna who are avataras (divine manifestations) in the dashavatāra tradition. Viṣṇu Purāṇa recounts Sri Rama as Viṣṇu's seventh avatāra and Kṛṣṇa as the eighth avatāra. The life-activities of these two avatāra puruṣas are an integral part of the Hindu tradition of received memories of ancient History of India. They are inalienable parts of the living Hindu tradition. They are revered and are divinities. Sri Rāma navami and Sri Kṛṣṇa janmāṣṭami are celebrated every year in their memory which can never be erased from the Hindu understanding of citta,

ritam, satyam and dharma. Recollecting the memories of their lives, esha dhammo sanantano shines resplendent as every Hindu household lights up a dīpam in an eternal flickering flame moving people from darkness to light, tamaso mā jyotirgamaya ('lead meone from darkness to light').

Rama Setu in sculptures (9th and 10th centuries CE)[58]

Stone steles from the Ramayana wall carvings at Prambanan Temple, Java, Indonesia (built during the ninth and tenth centuries Common Era). Classical Javanese dance performances of the Ramayana are held seasonally at Prambanan temple. A 2006 earthquake in Central Java, however, caused considerable damage to the World Heritage Site.

- Devi Sita talking to Sri Hanuman

- Vaanara Sena carrying stones, in their arms and on their heads, to build Rama Setu, followed by Sri Rama, carrying a sword.

- Fish and other sea creatures handling stones from Rama's bridge to Lanka, during the construction of Nala Setu (Rama Setu).

Setubandha narrative is so compelling that the truth is recounted in many forms, many disciplines, as in the Rājā Ravi Verma's painting of Rāma's encounter with Samudraraja, the king of the Indian Ocean. Vālmiki *Rāmāyaṇa*, Sarga 21, Yuddhakāṇḍam Describes Rāma's victory over the ocean; he releases the arrow which makes a volcano erupt, resulting in a tsunami. This episode is validated by the heatflow and geotectonic maps of Bhāratam in the Rāma Setu region.

Sri Kṛṣṇa and his associates Pandavas involve the entire nation of Bhāratam in the Great War fought to restore fairness and justice in the polity. Pandavas were denied a fair share of the land by Kauravas and the war ensues. Sri Kṛṣṇa is the strategist who defeats the adharmic Kauravas in battle and presents the imperative of dharmakshetra in kurukshetra. Dharmakshetra is the punyabhumi Bhārat, the mahābhārat, which has many tīrthasthānas (sacred pilgrimage places) for adherents of dharma-dhamma to travel on pilgrimage yatras offering prayers to pitṛ-s, ancestors who have given them their identity.

Both Itihāsa are remembered with fondness in the Indian Ocean Region.

Mahatma Gandhi said of the Ramayana: 'Ramanama is for the pure in heart and for those who want to attain purity and remain pure.' Describing Rama, Valmiki notes: *Ramo vigrahavān dharmah*, 'Rama is the embodiment of dharma'. Ramayana is a timeless story which narrates the triumph of dharma over adharma, the triumph of good over evil.

Ramayana is found in many versions in many languages and communities of the world. In Khmer, it is *Reamker*; in Thailand it is *Ramakien*, in Myanmar (Burma), it is *Yama Watthu*, in Laos it is *Palak Palang*. The capital of early Thailand was names Ayutthaya, in memory of Ayodhya, Rama's capital. The royalty of Thailand take the title, 'Bhumipal Athulyatj, Rama'. Murals in Bangkok's Wat Phra Kaew (temple of Emerald Buddha) celebrate the episodes of Ramayana. A Mon language stone inscription proclaims that King Kyanzittha (1084-1113 CE) of Bagan dynasty in Myanmar was a ruler in the lineage of Rama of Ayodhya. The capital of Brunei is Bandar Sri Bhagwan, literally, 'Port of the Lord (Rama divine)'. Large statues of Sugriva and other heroes of the epic decorate the courtyard of the Thai Royal Palace with episodes from the Ramayana painted as murals on walls and ceilings. *Ramakien* of King Rama I is a masterpiece of Thai literature and taught in Thailand schools.

Malaysian ministers take their oath of office in the name of Rama's Paduka, 'Urusan Seri Paduka Beginda' (literally, 'by the orders of Sri Rama's Paduka) or; the President (elected from amont the 9 sultans) takes his oath of office in the name of the dust of Rama's Paduka, 'Urusan Seri Paduka Dhuli', and takes 'Ganga snan' before ascending to the throne called 'simhasana'. Government orders in Malaysia (gazette notifications) are issued in the name of 'Urusan Seri Paduka'. Paduka is an extraordinary evocation of the episode of Ramayana when Bharata enthrones the Paduka (sandals) of Sri Rama in Ayodhya to continue to recognise Sri Rama in vanavas (exile into the forest) as the King of Ayodhya. The President is titled Raja Parameswara, Royal Queen is Raja Parameswari, second son of the sultan is Laxmana. The name plate at a mosque in Penang translated into English reads "This mosque has been built by the orders of Seri Paduka in 1974."

In weddings, yellow rice is sprinkled as blessings on bride and bridegroom. The association of wives of Malaysian leaders is 'vanitha pushpavalli'. The coronation of the King of Cambodia is complete only with the handing over of murti-s of Shiva and Vishnu by Rajaguru to the King. This is a Southeast Asian tradition continuum of the worship of Shiva, Vishnu, Brahma and the Buddha evidenced by hundreds of Hindu-Bauddham temples with the pinnacle represented by Angkor Wat which has the largest Vishnu temple of the world with a 2.7 km. long circumambulatory passage, decorated along the temple walls with bas relief from Hindu-Bauddha heritage.

In most states of the Indian Ocean Rim, puppet shows (*wayang kulit* in Malaysia), artistic presentations, stage shows, temple festivals celebrate the events of Ramayana and Mahabharata. Southeast Asian Games of 1997 has Hanuman of Ramayana as the mascot. Hanuman is called by various names in the region: Hanoman in Balinese, Anoman and Senggna in Javanese, Haliman in Karbi, Anjat or Anujit in Khmer, Hanmone(e), Hulahman, Hunahman, Hounahman, Hourahman in Lao, Haduman, Hanuman Kera Putih, Kera Kechil Imam Tergangga, Pahlawan Udara, Shah Numan in Malay, Laksamana (distinguished from Mangawarna the brother of Rama) in Maranao, Hanumant in Sinhalese, Anchat or Wanon in Thai and Hanumandha or Hanumanta in Tibetan.

Banteasy Srei temple (10th cent.), Angkor Wat (12th cent.), Parambanan temple complex of Central Java (9th cent.), Panataran temple in East Java (14th cent.) celebrate in bas-reliefs the epics Ramayana and Mahabharata. Vishnu temple of Bagan, known as Nat Hlaung Kyaung in Burma has murti-s of Rama and Parasurama. Terracotta panels on Petlcik Pagoda in

Bagan depicts the story of Rama. Sculptures depict Rama, Krishna and other avatars of Vishnu on the panels of Siva temple, a UNESCO World Heritage Monument, at Wat Phu Champasak (southern Laos). Thousands of Hindu temples are places of worship in Bali. Besakih Mother Temple in Bali (8th cent) with Padmasana Tiga or seats of the trinity of divinities: Brahma, Wisnu and Siwa.

Besakih Mother Temple, Bali

Panataran temple (12th cent.), East Java.

Three-or-four-day performance series or Ramayana ballet are held on Denspasarnese stage through the Wayang Wong classical dance drama

tradition, to the accompaniment of Gamelan gong orchestra, depicting the events from Ramayana. Ramayana Grand Ballet performances are held in Yogyakarta, Central Java in the Parambanan temple complex. *Kakawin Ramayana* is a 9th century rendering in Javanese of Kawi. Other versions are: Janakiharan of Sri Lanka (7th cent.), of Bali, *Maradia Lawana* and *Darangen* of the Philippines, *Reamker* of Cambodia, *Serat Rama* of Indonesia (used in leather puppet theatre shows, wherein the puppeteer (*dalang*) makes the shadows of the leather puppets dance across a white screen). Cambodian *nang sbek thom* and Thai *nang yai* are dance spectacles to the accompaniment of gongs, drums and wind instruments, many dancers animate large leather-cut-

out figures across a huge screen. *Ramakien* of Thailand has Sita as the daughter of Ravana and Mandodari (T'os'akanth = Dasakanth; and Mont'o). Vibhishana (P'ip'ek) is the astrologer brother of Ravana. Ravana throws Sita into the waters from where Janaka (Janok) picks her up. *Phra Lak Phra Lam* is Lao Ramayana, with the title including the names of Lakshmana and Rama and their story told as the previous life of the Buddha. *Hikayat Seri Rama* is Malaysian rendering, showing Dasaratha as the great-grandson of the Prophet Adam and Ravana receiving boons from Allah, replacing the Dewata Mulia Raya (the Hindu Divinity). Another version is *Cherita Maharaja Wana* (16th or 17th cent.) U Thein Han of Burma identifies nine Myanmar versions: three in prose (i) *Rama Watthu* (17th century), (ii) *Maha Rama* (late 18th or early 19th century), (iii) *Rama Thonmyo* (1904); three in verse (iv) *Rama Thagyin* (1775), (v) *Rama Yagan* (1784), (vi) Alaung Rama Thagyin (1905), and three in drama (vii) *Thiri Rama* (late 18th or early 19th century), (viii) *Pontaw Rama*, Pt.I (1880) and (ix) *Pontaw Rama and Lakkhhana*, Pt.I (1910). *Maharadia Lawana* of the Maranao seafaring people of the Philippines and *Rajah Mangandiri* of Southern Philippines are dance-drama versions of Ramayana episodes. *Dastan-e-Ram O Sita, Razmnama* are versions in Persian (Iran, 16th century), *Pothi Ramayan* is a version in Urdu (Pakistan). *Ramayan-e-Masih* was composed by Sheikh Sadullah Masih Panipati during the reign of Shahjahan and Jehangir.

Garuda Wisnu Kenchana, Bali

Krishna-Arjuna statue at Jakarta main square in front of Bank Indonesia. Garuda is Indonesia's national insignia and the national carrier is Garuda Airlines.

Frits Staal notes how the scripts in use in many regions of Asia find their roots in

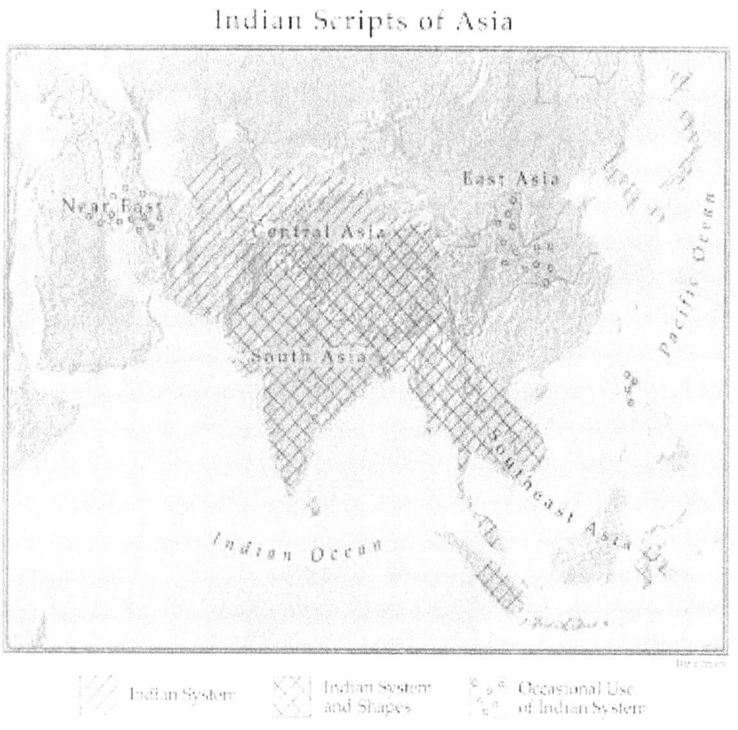

Hindustan. "I derive five conclusions from our brief discussion. The first is that the sound pattern of Sanskrit was adopted and adapted by many writing systems of Asia. The exporters were Indian brahmans and Buddhist monks. The second is that the pattern that underlies the system was not always understood. The third is that those Asian writing systems are applications of a theory of language, just as airplanes are applications of the laws of aerodynamics. The fourth, closely connected, is that a writing system is only as good as the theory upon which it is based. (Since the accuracy of theories is measured in degrees, absence of any theory points to probability zero.) My fifth and final conclusion is hypothetical in character. If the sound pattern of Sanskrit had also reached the Near East and Europe, there would not be so many clumsy alphabets around and the modern world would have the benefit of rational and practical Indic syllabaries in addition to rational and practical Indic numerals…" [59]

Lord Shiva, Guimet Museum, Paris, France

Lord Buddha,Wat Pra Men,Thailan

Vanaspati- Buddha on the Vehicles of Shiva, Vishnu, and Brahma[60]

Gracing the southwestern corner of the Monas(Freedom Square), at the downtown central business district in Jakarta, the capital city of Indonesia, this statue depicts Arjuna Wijaya, the charismatic archer from the Indian legend Mahabharata, with a bow and arrow, riding an eagle-faced chariot of eight galloping horses - a scene supposedly taken from Bharata Yuddha War when Arjuna defeated Karna. The monument holds great significance for the Indonesians, with some believing that the very figure opens a door to the spiritual world...

Golden threads of friendship that existed between India and Indian Ocean Region

"Ramayana and Mahabharata are most popular in Indonesia. They were probably translated in the 11th century during the reign of King Airlangga in the ancient Kawi language. King Airlangga was himself a great scholar and ascetic who spent many years in the jungle in meditation. Ramayana and Mahabharata are the basis of innumerable dances, plays, sculptures, paintings and music themes."

President Susilo Bambang Yodhoyono was the chief guest of the celebrations of India's Republic Day on 26 January 2011.

“In August 1927 when Rabindranath Tagore, the Nobel prize winner arrived at Tanjung Priok harbor, he burst into a verse in the memory of the golden threads of kinship that have existed between India and Indonesia.”

“In 1947, Biju Patnaik flew a private plane full of medicines to Indonesia and also rescued Mohammad Hatta and P.M. Sutan Sjahrir from the Dutch and brought them to India. In 1951 when Nehru visited Bali he said, "this is the morning of the world."

“The earliest historical record is in Ujung Kulon National Park, West Java. An early Hindu archeological relic of a Ganesha statue from the 1st Century CE has been found on the summit of Mount Raksa in Panaitan Island. The next historical record is in the area of Kutai on the Mahakam River in east Kalimantan. Three rough plinths dating from the beginning of the fourth century are recorded in the Pallavi script of India. The inscription reads: "A gift to the Brahmin priests."

"The famous Batu Tulis (stone writing) near Bogor in Western Java is on a huge black boulder in, around 450 A.D king Purnawarna inscribed his name and made an imprint of his footprints, as well as his elephant's footprints. The accompanying inscription reads, 'Here are the footprints of King Purnawarna, the heroic conqueror of the world'. This inscription is in Sanskrit and is still clear after 1500 years. This is the oldest archeological monument in Java. (Candi) Badut near Malang in East Java was built in A.D 760. Candi is the name of the Hindu Goddess of Time and Death. This area is literally strewn with ancient Hindu temples and even today temples are being dug out from the ground".

“The famous Batu Tulis (stone writing) near Bogor in Western Java is on a huge black boulder in, around 450 A.D king Purnawarna inscribed his name and made an imprint of his footprints, as well as his elephant's footprints. The accompanying inscription reads, 'Here are the footprints of King Purnawarna, the heroic conqueror of the world'. This inscription is in Sanskrit and is still clear after 1500 years. This is the oldest archeological monument in Java. (Candi) Badut near Malang in East Java was built in A.D 760. Candi is the name of the Hindu Goddess of Time and Death. This area is literally strewn with ancient Hindu temples and even today temples are being dug out from the ground”.

“During the 8th and 9th century, the world's largest Buddhist complex Borobudur and Prambanan the largest Hindu temple complex in Indonesia were built near Yogyakarta in Central Java. In the 10th Century, students were sent to Nalanda Buddhist University in N.E.India”.

“The national emblem of the Republic of Indonesia"Garuda Pancasila" is adorned with the Garuda in the Indonesian history holds a place of honor. It is a symbol of national emblem with Wishnu riding it. Garuda sculpture is shown in countless temples. Garuda stands for complete devotion to Lord Vishnu and subsequent freedom from evil. Garuda also stands for the freedom of the people of Indonesia from foreign rule”.

“The (Candi) Badut near Malang in East Java built in A.D 760. Candi is the name of the Hindu Goddess of Time and Death. This area is literally strewn with ancient Hindu temples and even today temples are being dug out from the ground."

"In Sumatra in the 12/13th Century arose the great Kingdom of Sriwijaya. However, it was during the reign of King Hayam Wuruk of the Majapahit Kingdom that the Prime Minister Gajah Mada united the entire Indonesia into a single state. It was the golden era of Indonesia."

"The national emblem of the Republic of Indonesia – "Garuda Pancasila" is adorned with the with the words Bhineka Tunggal Ika- which means Unity in Diversity. The concept of Bhineka Tunggal Ika was started during the 8th–9th centuries in Central Java to create an understanding between Hinduism and Buddhism. Classic example is Candi Shiwa - Buddha. Afterwards King Airlangga made use of it in the 11th century. However it was Mpu Tantular the court poet of the Majapahit kingdom who during the reign of King Hayam Wuruk propagated this idea of a Unity in Diversity, in his poem".

Mention must be made here of Panca Sila, the 5 basic principles of the Republic of Indonesia. They are: Faith in one God, Nationalism, Democracy, Humanity and Just Society. All over Indonesia, at Govt. places you see Garuda, the vehicle of the Hindu God Vishnu alongside with a Panca Sila plaque. Indonesians are extremely proud of their historical cultural past. Indonesia like India is secular and even one of their currency notes carries a picture of Lord Ganesha".

"Although there are hundreds of dialects throughout Indonesia, yet Bahasa Indonesia in roman script is understood everywhere and this is what unites them all in their outlook. Indeed “Bhineka Tunggal Ika” ‘Unity in Diversity’ stands proved through Bahasa Indonesia, which shares many common words with Sanskrit like Guru, istri, suami, putri, putra, warna, Akasha and niscaya. Bahasa Indonesia is a very artistic language. Matahari means eye of the day which means Sun.”[61]

Mehru Jaffer wrote, in 2001, recollecting the memory of Tagore’s arrival in Java: “Tagore's visit to Java and Bali were part of a series of lecture tours he organized for himself to share with the rest of Asia his romantic and idealized concept of a single eastern civilization. Most of Asia at that time was a slave of colonial masters and Tagore felt that Asia must find her voice if humanity was to be saved. The greed of western countries caused him great concern…

Over the years, the Indian poet's initial concept of a spiritual East standing aloof from a materialistic West flowered into a world ideal that he hoped would one day unify all humankind. His religion, he explained to Albert Einstein during their 1930 conversation at Einstein's home near Berlin, was in the reconciliation of the super personal man, the universal human spirit in his own individual being.

Tagore advocated a worldwide commerce of heart and mind so that the individual's sense of purpose in life is enhanced. He took the initiative to contact leading thinkers in other parts of Asia. In Java one of his closest allies was Ki Hajar Dewantoro, founder of the Taman Siswa schools, and the country's first minister of education. Dewantoro was inspired by Tagore's talk of nationalism without closing the door to modernism.

A literal translation of kindergarten or the garden of children, the Taman Siswa schools remain the oldest national education institutions here, started in 1932. Dewantoro was impressed with Tagore's school at Santiniketan and Viswa Bharati, the world university founded by Tagore in 1918 with all the money he received as Nobel laureate. Dewantoro, painter Affandi and Dr. Ida Bagus Mantra of Bali visited the university of universal learning which Tagore saw as a center of Indian culture and also the thread linking India to the world.

The idea was to revive the traditional Indian way of teaching, in the open, under a tree, in close contact with nature. Both Tagore and Dewantoro believed that all the elements in one's own culture have to be strengthened, not to resist western culture but to accept and assimilate it, to get mastery over it and not to live at its outskirts.

Tagore died in 1941 but his ideas continue to live through the works of all those who look upon all civilizations in different continents as being complementary to each other. It is in the same spirit that Abhyudaya, an Indonesia-India cultural assembly came into being half a decade ago. Since then every May is dedicated to the memory of Tagore whose birth anniversary falls this month.

Chitrangada, an episode about a warrior princess from the Mahabharata which Tagore wrote as a dance-drama, was performed in the past by Indian dancer Nilanjana Ghosh along with Balinese dancers, and also Tridhara, yet another offering of Indian dance, music and song to Indonesian audiences.

"As we live, work and bring up children in foreign countries it becomes our personal responsibility to keep them connected with our culture and values," says Aparesh Mukerjee, production manager and one of the founders of Abhyudaya."

The highlight of the evening with Tagore was an excerpt from a film on Tagore made by Satyajit Ray, perhaps the greatest film maker of India and an alumnus of Santiniketan. The Performance took place at Little Theater, the Jakarta International School, Cilandak Campus.

This event is a landmark pointing to the bonds based on dharma-dhamma continuum which continue to tie the states of Indian Ocean Rim in friendship.[62]

A remarkable heritage of Indian Ocean Community is recorded in temples of Tamil Nadu built in the 12th century. The temple at Gangaikondacholapuram has a Shivalingam larger than the one at Brihadishwara Temple of Thanjavur. Dimensions: 13.5 ft. tall, 60 feet. diameter. This image is a representation of the King Rajendra Chola being crowned by Shiva and Parvati. Shiva takes the snake from his neck and rolls it over the crown of the king. Brihadeeshwarar Temple,

Gangaikondacholapuram. Rajendra Chola-I (1012-1044 A.D) son of the Great Rajaraja-I, established this temple after his great victorious march to river Ganges on Northern India. The Sailendra dynasty had been in good relations with the Chola Empire during the period of Rajaraja Chola I. Rajaraja encouraged Mara Vijayatungavarman to build the Chudamani Vihara at Nagapattinam. Rajendra confirmed this grant in the Anaimangalam grants showing that the relationship with Srivijaya was still continued be friendly. The Cholas had an active trade relationship with the eastern island. Moreover the Srivijaya kingdom and the South Indian empires were the intermediaries in the trade between China. China is a Culture of China, an ancient civilization, and, depending on perspective, a national or multinational entity extending over a large area in East Asia and the countries of the Western world. Both the Srivijaya and Cholas had active dialog with the Chinese and sent diplomatic missions to China. Tanjavur inscriptions also state that the king of Kambhoja (Kampuchea) requesting Rajendra's help in defeating enemies of his Angkor. Angkor is a name conventionally applied to the region of Cambodia serving as the seat of the Khmer empire that flourished from approximately the ninth century to the fifteenth century CE kingdom.[63]

A statue of Visnu found at Óc Eo (6–7th century CE). The Mekong Delta was likely inhabited long since prehistory; the empire of Funan and later Chenlamaintained a presence in the Mekong Delta for centuries. Archaeological discoveries at Oc Eo and other Funan sites show that the area was an important part of the Funan Kingdom., bustling with trading ports and canals as early as in the first century CE and extensive human settlement in the region may have gone back as far as the 4th century BCE. The region was known as Khmer Krom (lower Khmer, or lower Cambodia) to the Khmer Empire, which likely maintained settlements there centuries before its rise in the 11th and 12th centuries. The kingdom of Champa, though mainly based along the coast of the South China Sea, is known to have expanded west into the Mekong Delta, seizing control of Prey Nokor (the precursor to modern-day Ho Chi Minh City) by the end of the 13th century. Author Nghia M. Vo suggests that a Cham presence may indeed have existed in the area prior to Khmer occupation. Beginning in the 1620s, Khmer king Chey Chettha II (1618–1628) allowed the Vietnamese to settle in the area, and to set up a custom house at Prey Nokor, which they colloquially referred to as *Sài Gòn*."[64]

The delta is home to Prasat Angkor Wat. "Angkor Wat (Khmer: អង្គរវត្ត) is the largest Hindu temple complex in the world. The temple was built by King Suryavarman in the early 12th century in Yasodharapura (Khmer: យសោធរបុរៈ, present-day Angkor), the capital of the Khmer Empire, as his state temple... Breaking from the Shaivism tradition of previous kings, Angkor Wat was instead dedicated to Vishnu.

As the best-preserved temple at the site, it is the only one to have remained a significant religious centre since its foundation – first Hindu, dedicated to the god Vishnu, then Buddhist."[65]

Angkor empire flourished from the 9th to 13th centuries (including rule by Jayavarman VII of 12th century) and absorbed Mon kingdom of Dvaravati in Thailand in the west and Champa in the east. The great temple of Angkor Wat (Nagara Vatika) was built in the 12th century. Between 6th and 14th centuries, Maritime empires flourished in Hinduised Malay kingdom of Srivijaya (capital at Palembang in southern Sumatra) and the Indonesian islands of Sumatra and Java, influenced by the Kingdom of

Kalinga (southeastern coast of India). Indians in Indonesia are known as 'Klings' (a word derived from Kalinga). The Malay kingdom of Srivijaya commanded the sea-route from India to China between Sumatra and the Malay peninsula (now known as Straits of Malacca). Srivijaya, Hindu in culture and administration, venerating Bauddham, succeeded Funan in the 6th-7th centuries and was the leading state in Malay peninsula, western

Java and Sumatra. Eastern Java saw the rise of Sailendra rule exemplified by temple-building in Borobudur, eastern Java from 7th century.

Sailendra rule also spread to southern Sumatra. After the union of Srivijaya and the Sailendras much of Southeas Asia was Hinduised for about 500 years, between 9th to 13th centuries. In the 13th century, the great Hindu-Javanese kingdom, Majapahit was established with control spreading to part of Borneo, southern Celebes and the Moluccas. The remarkable nature of the links with India was that diplomatic and trade contacts between this region and India was maintained, while the peoples of the region remained politically independent of the Indian kingdoms. The only exception was the temporary accession of Kidaram (Kedah) by Chola kingdom of the 11th century, a region later brought under the control of Sailendra kings of Srivijaya. This is evidenced by the archaeological sites of Lembah Bujang kingdom (Bujang valley) of Kedah which forged an alliance with the Cholas. Kedah (Bujang valley) was known by the Tamils as Kedaram, Kidaram, Kalagam and Kataha, and Kalah or Kalaha by the Persians... In the early 11th century, Tamil Chola King Rajendra Chola I sent an expedition to invade Kadaram (Sri Vijaya) on behalf of one of its rulers who sought his assistance to gain the throne. Chola dominance was brief, but effectively crippled the power of Srivijaya.
In Kedah an inscription in Sanskrit dated 1086 A.D. has been found. This was left by Kulothunka Cholan I (of the Chola empire, Tamil country). This too shows the commercial contacts the Chola Empire had with Malaya.[66]

In geology, Greater India signifies "the Indian sub-continent plus a postulated northern extension" in plate tectonicmodels of the India-Asia. This 'Greater India' is called 'Hinduised states of south-east Asia' by George Coedes[67]. George Coedes concluded, after a study of fourteen centuries of history of Southeast Asia: " the importance of studying the Indianized countries of Southeast Asia– which, let us repeat, were never political dependencies of India, but rather cultural colonies – lies above all in the observation of the impact of Indian civilization on the primitive civilizations... We can measure the power of penetration of this culture by the importance of that which remains of it in these countries even though all of them except Siam passed sooner or later under European domination and a great part of the area was converted to Islam…we may ask ourselves if the particular aspect assumed by Islam in Java was not due rather to the influence that Indian religions exercised over the character of the inhabitant of the island for more than ten centuries…The literary heritage from ancient India is even more apparent that the religious heritage. Throughout the entire Indian period, the Ramayana and the Mahabharata, the Harivamsa, and the Puranas were the principal, if not the only, sources of inspiration for local literature, to which was added the Buddhist folklore of the Jatakas, still makes up the substance of the classical theatre, of the dances, and of the shadow-plays and puppet theatre."

The term "Greater India," now largely out of favor consists of "all the Asian lands including Burma, Java, Cambodia, Bali and the former Champa and Funan polities of present-day Vietnam in which pre-Islamic Indian culture left an "imprint in the form of monuments, inscriptions and other traces of the historic 'Indianising or hinduising' process." In some accounts, many Pacific societies and "most of the Buddhist world including Ceylon, Tibet, Central Asia and even Japan were held to fall within this web of Indianising 'culture colonies'" [68] Southeast Asia as "a single cultural process in which Southeast Asia was the matrix and South Asia the mediatrix."[69] Kertanegara was ruler (1268 to 1292 CE) of the Singhasari kingdom, reigning between 1268 and 1292 in the eastern part of Java. He described himself as *Sivabuddha*, a simultaneous incarnation of the Hindu Maheshwara and the Buddha.

The *'etats hindouises'* identified by George Coedes is essentially a Hindu-Buddhist dharma-dhamma cultural community evidenced by thousands of Hindu-Bauddha temples in Malaysia, Indonesia, Thailand, Cambodia, Vietnam, Laos, Burma and other states and historical presence of Hindu kings in the region for over one millennium. The arts, literature and statecraft are substantial replicas of the Indian civilization tradition. Tathagata, Gautama the Buddha called it esha dhammo sanantano (this sanatana dharma, this universal eternal ethic). The opportunities for carrying the cultural bonds into socio-economic spheres of cooperation are immense and have to be seized by USA and other developed nations supporting the emergence of an economic federation among the Indian Ocean Rim states.

Climate shift linked to rise of Himalayas, Tibetan Plateau[70]: "The picture that is emerging, drawn with the help of newly analyzed geologic records and a sophisticated computer-driven climate model, portrays the rise of the towering Himalayas and the adjacent Tibetan Plateau, the world's largest, as the primary driver of the onset of Asian monsoons about 8 million years ago, and hints that the rise of the world's tallest mountains and plateau may also have helped set the stage for the Ice Ages that began about 2.5 million years ago…The modern name, Angkor Wat, means "Temple City" or "City of Temples" in Khmer; *Angkor*, meaning "city" or "capital city", is a vernacular form of the word*no kor* (នគរ), which comes from the Samskrtam word *nagar* (नगर). *Wat* is the Khmerword for "temple grounds", derived from the Pali word "vatta" (वत्त). Prior to this time the temple was known as *Preah Pisnulok* (Vara Vishnuloka in Sanskrit), after the posthumous title of its founder."[71]

Angkor Wat temple shows a bas relief of the Churning of the Sea of Milk shows Vishnu in the centre, his turtle Avatar Kurma below, asuras and devas to left and right, and apsaras and Indra above. The northern gallery shows Krishna's victory over Bana. The north-west and south-west corner pavilions both feature scenes from the Ramayana or the life of Krishna.

Samudra manthanam image in Suvarnaphom (suvarnabhumi) airport of Bangkok. Vishnu in the centre, his turtle avatar Kurma below, asuras and devas to left and right. This metaphor from Bhagavatam is a memory-marker for cooperative endeavor of all peoples to harness sustainably the riches of the ocean and the earth for the benefit of present and future generations.

In some ports of northern Sumatra Indian merchants from Gujarat converted some people to Islam in the 13th century and from here, Islam spread to the Malay peninsula, Java and the Philippines. The settlement of

Malacca on the west coast of Malaya was founded ca 15th century by a Sumatran prince, Parameswara who later converted to Islam. Malacca was a strategic trading port of the East, situated on the trade routes which linked India, Southeast Asia and China. Majapahit empire splintered into Moslem states and the island of Bali alone maintained the Hindu religious identity. However, Islam made little impact on the mainland of Southeast Asia which continued overwhelmingly to venerate Bauddham. Thai people founded the kingdom of Sukothai in west central Thailand in 1238 CE with the King Ramkamhaeng adopting the Khmer alphabet and introducing Bauddham in his kingdom. After the founding of a Thai kingdom in 1350 by Prince Ramatibodi with capital at Ayuthhia, the regime survived for 400 years. In 1353, a Bauddham Thai settlement was founded at Luang Prabhang in northern Laos. Heralding colonialism, 15th century saw the arrival of Portuguese, Spaniards and the Dutch into the region seeking trade routes to India and the Spice islands (the Moluccas). Between 1595 and 1620 CE, the Dutch formed the Dutch East India Company in 1601 with a main settlement at Batavia (now Jakarta) in Java. In 1824, the British East India Company acquired Malacca from the Dutch and Britain controlled from 1826, the 'Straits Settlements' of Penang, Singapore and Malacca. Labour for the rubber plantations in Malay peninsula came from southern India. The colonial rule was focused on trade; the cultural foundations of the region continued to be governed by the spiritual foundations of Hindu dharma and Bauddha dhamma.

Sri Lanka is the oldest continuously Bauddha nation.

Theravāda (Sthaviravāda 'way of elders') Bauddham being the major religion in the island since its official introduction in the 2nd century BCE by Venerable Mahinda, the son of the Emperor Ashoka of India during the reign of King Devanampiya- Tissa. Later, the nun Sanghamitta, the daughter of Asoka, was said to have brought the southern branch of the original Bodhi tree; this was planted at Anuradhapura.

'Way of the elders' is evocative of the enormous respect held for the pitr-s, the ancestors who have the people of all regions their identity and shared values. The pitr-rinam became a governing principle in all walks of life; living itself was considered a discharge of the debt owed to the ancestors as role models for ethical, dharmic behavior.

The Pali *Tipitaka* ("Three Baskets")—the *Sutta Pitaka* ("Basket of Discourse"), which contains the Buddha's sermons; the*Vinaya Pitaka* ("Basket of Discipline"), which contains the rule governing the monastic order; and the *Abhidhamma Pitaka*("Basket of Special [Further] Doctrine"), which contains doctrinal systematizations and summaries have been the abiding basis for a rich tradition of commentaries by Theravada followers.

It was in Sri Lanka, in the 1st century Common Era during the reign of King Vatta Gamini that the Bauddha monks assembled in Aloka-Vihara and wrote down the Tripitaka, the three basket of the Teachings, known as the Pali scriptures. It was Sri Lankan nuns who introduced the Sangha of nuns into China in 433 CE. In the 16th century Sri Lanka withstood the onslaughts of the Portuguese and the Dutch colonialists. It is a tribute to the Bauddha monks that Bauddham was sustained in Sri Lanka despite colonial regimes.[72]

Indian Ocean Community as a geographical identity

"About twenty years ago Cleuziou and Tosi (1989: 15) referred to the prehistoric Arabian peninsula as a "conveyor belt between the two continents, channelling an early dispersal of domestic plants and animals." The question of how precisely African crops reached India beginning around 2000 BCE has now attracted the attention of archaeologists and botanists for decades...First, there was an earlier circum-Arabia or Arabian Sea phase of the Middle Bronze Age (from 2000 BCE), in which domesticates were transferred between the northern African savannahs and the savannah zones of India (Figure 1). Then there was a later mid-Indian Ocean phase that may be regarded as generally Iron Age (late centuries BCE to early centuries CE), which began to draw South India, South-east Asia and East Africa into the wider remit of trade/contact, setting the stage for a genuinely Indian Ocean world. In addition, we would like to draw attention to the significance of transfers of commensal animals and weeds, a largely unstudied but potentially revealing body of evidence for early human contacts across the Arabian Sea and the Indian Ocean." **Figure 1. A schematic representation of some key Arabian Sea-Savannah zone biotic transfers of prehistory (the "Bronze Age horizon").** [73]

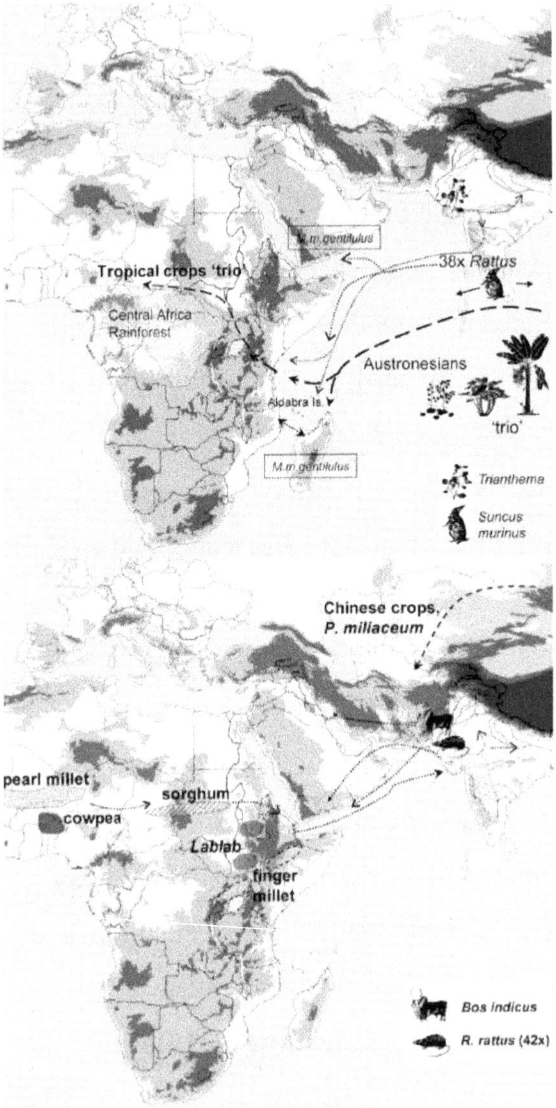

In the extraordinary journey of humanity of several millennia, genetic studies show y-chromosome, mtDNA identity of bharatam janam, starting 50000 years ago. Human movements begin along the Indian Ocean Rim which is now home to people of 59 present-day countries, from South Africa to Tasmania.

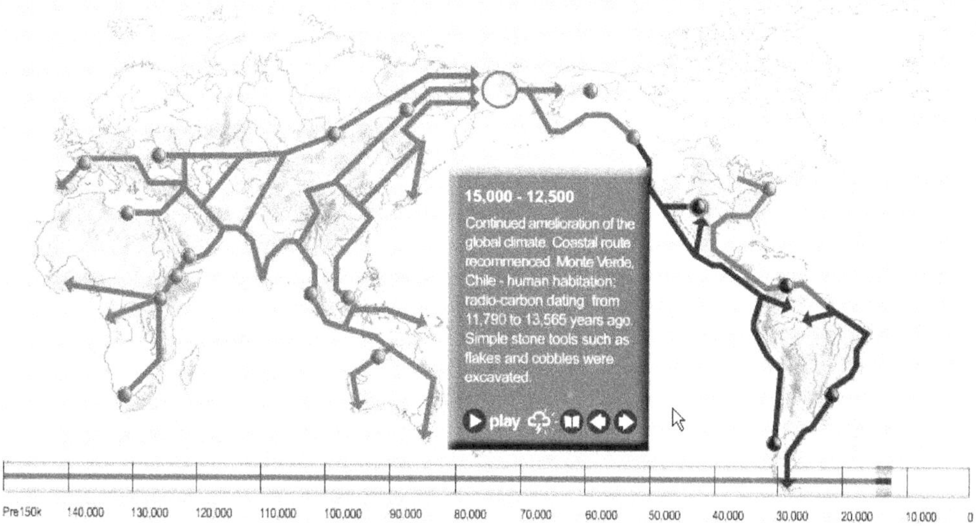

Map depicting the human journey along the coastal route of Indian Ocean or peopling of the world.[74]

The rim of the Indian Ocean unites countries of the Indian Ocean into one geographical entity. The bond provided by cosmic forces of planetary movements and the Indian Ocean is exemplified by two gigantic factors: 1. Ongoing formation of the dynamic Himalayas structurally governed by the glacial cycles formed by the axial tilt of the earth as it rotates around the Sun; and 2. Monsoon cycles and continuing rise of the Himalayas controlled by geo-tectonics of the northward movement and thrust of Indo-Australian continental plate into Eurasian plate, recurring tectonic events caused by geo-tectonics, resulting in recurrent tsunamis along the Indian Ocean rim and spread of volcanic ash across continents, when volcanic eruptions such as the supra-eruptions of Krakatoa occur. Equitable harnessing of the water-resources provided the Himalayas as the Greatest Water Reservoir of the world and united action to protect the coastal people against natural hazards such as tsunamis and earthquakes are the *raison d'etre* for the Indian Ocean Community.

The Himalayas are among the youngest mountain ranges on the planet and consist mostly of uplifted sedimentary and metamorphic rock. They are the result of a collision between two continental tectonic plates. The highest rate of uplift is nearly 10 mm/year at Nanga Parbat which is the ninth highest mountain in the world and the western anchor of the Himalayas, with a summit elevation of 8,126 metres (26,660 ft). Karakoram mountain rage has the highest concentration of peaks over 8000m. in height to be found anywhere on earth including K2, the second highest peak of the world (8,611 m/28,251 ft). K2 is just 237 m (778 ft) lower than the 8,848 m (29,029 ft) tall Mount Everest.

Baltoro glacier in the central Karakoram with 8000ers Gasherbrum I & II.

Milanković[75] shows that variations in eccentricity, axial tilt, and precession of the Earth's orbit determined climatic patterns on Earth through orbital forcing. The angle between Earth's rotational axis and the normal to the plane of its orbit (obliquity) oscillates between 22.1 and 24.5 degrees on a 41,000-year cycle. It is currently 23.44 degrees and decreasing.

The angle of the Earth's axial tilt (obliquity of the ecliptic) varies with respect to the plane of the Earth's orbit. These slow 2.4° obliquity variations are roughly periodic, taking approximately 41,000 years to shift between a tilt of 22.1° and 24.5° and back again. When the obliquity increases, the amplitude of the seasonal cycle in insolation increases, with summers in both hemispheres receiving more radiative flux from the Sun, and winters less. Conversely, when the obliquity decreases, summers receive less insolation and winters more.

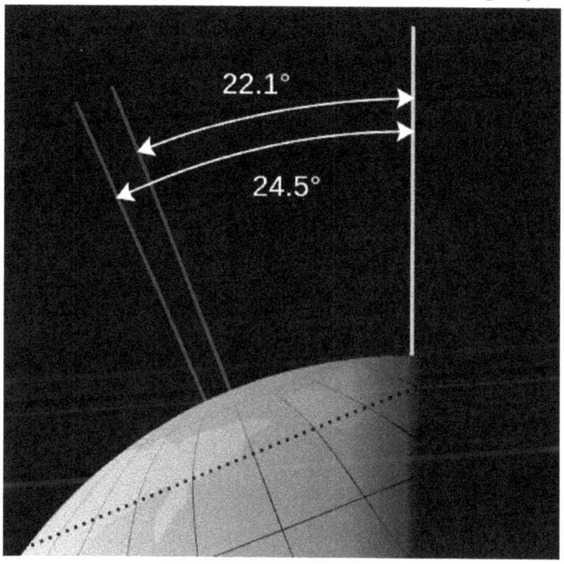

22.1–24.5° range of Earth's obliquity.

"""Today's axial tilt is about 23.5 degrees... One hypothesis for Earth's reaction to a smaller degree of axial tilt is that it would promote the growth of ice sheets. This response would be due to a warmer winter, in which warmer air would be able to hold more moisture, and subsequently produce a greater amount of snowfall. In addition, summer temperatures would be cooler, resulting in less melting of the winter's accumulation. At present, axial tilt is in the middle of its range…The episodic nature of the Earth's glacial and interglacial periods within the present Ice Age (the last couple of million years) have been caused primarily by cyclical changes in the Earth's circumnavigation of the Sun. Variations in the Earth's eccentricity, axial tilt, and precession comprise the three dominant cycles, collectively known as the Milankovitch Cycles… These times of increased or decreased solar radiation directly influence the Earth's climate system, thus impacting the advance and retreat of Earth's glaciers."[76]

AXIAL TILT

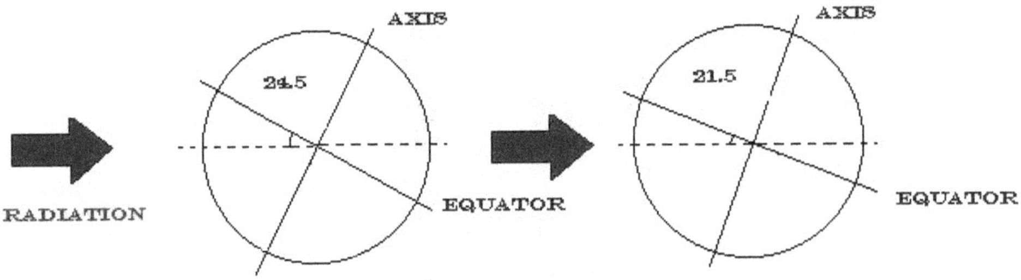

PERIODICITY:

41,000 YEARS

Axial tilt, the second of the three Milankovitch Cycles, is the inclination of the Earth's axis in relation to its plane of orbit around the Sun. Oscillations in the degree of Earth's axial tilt occur on a periodicity of 41,000 years from 21.5 to 24.5 degrees.

2004 Indian Ocean earthquake resulted in a great tsunami on December 26, 2004 event

The 9.1-9.3 moment magnitude 2004 Indian Ocean earthquake was caused by the release of stresses built up along the subduction zone where the Indian Plate is sliding under the Burma Plate in the eastern Indian Ocean, at a rate of 6 cm/yr (2.5 in/yr).

[quote]416 CE event

The Javanese *Book of Kings* (*Pustaka Raja*) records that in the year 338 Saka (416 AD):

"A thundering sound was heard from the mountain Batuwara [now called Pulosari, an extinct volcano in Bantam, the nearest to the Sunda Strait] which was answered by a similar noise from Kapi, lying westward of the modern Bantam [Bantam is the westernmost province in Java, so this seems to indicate that Krakatoa is meant]. A great glowing fire, which reached the sky, came out of the last-named mountain; the whole world was greatly shaken and violent thundering, accompanied by heavy rain and storms took place, but not only did not this heavy rain extinguish the eruption of the fire of the mountain Kapi, but augmented the fire; the noise was fearful, at last the mountain Kapi with a tremendous roar burst into pieces and sank into the deepest of the earth. The water of the sea rose and inundated the land, the country to the east of the mountain Batuwara, to the mountain Rajabasa [the most southerly volcano in Sumatra], was inundated by the sea; the inhabitants of the northern part of the Sunda country to the mountain Rajabasa were drowned and swept away with all property[13] ... The water subsided but the land on which Kapi stood became sea, and Java and Sumatra were divided into two parts."

"The eruption of Krakatoa in the Sunda Strait, in 1883, produced not only large immediate loss of life due to severe local tremors, pyroclastic clouds, lava flows, tsunamis and ash fall, but also more widespread damage due to ash destroying crops, and weather disruption globally. The large scale eruption of Krakatoa in 535 CE has been implicated in much greater damage, on a global scale, resulting in large scale crop and pasture

failures, in turn resulting in large scale population displacements... A major volcanic eruption in the near region has enormous potential for damage effects, both locally, and given population density, elsewhere in the region. The tsunami of 2004 with its

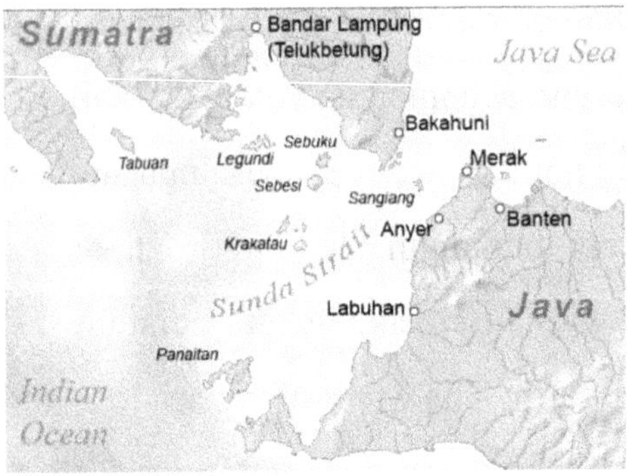

epicentre near Aceh in northern Sumatra resulted in massive loss of life, mostly in Indonesia and Thailand."[77]

Apra Harbor, Guam (U.S. Navy). Apra is home port to Submarine Squadron 15, comprising a tender and three Los Angeles class attack submarines (U.S. Navy).

There is no geological evidence of a Krakatoa eruption of this size around that time; it may describe loss of land which previously joined Java to Sumatra across what is now the narrow east end of the Sunda Strait; or it may be a mistaken date, referring to a later eruption in 535 AD, for which there is some corroborating historical evidence.[14]

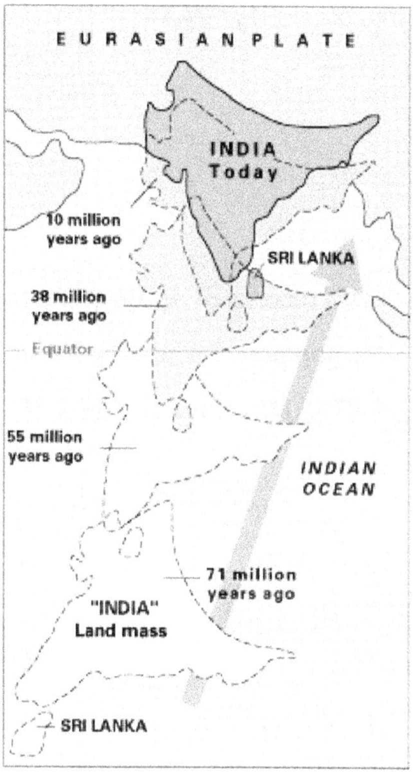

535 CE event

David Keys, Ken Wohletz, and others have postulated that a violent volcanic eruption, possibly of Krakatoa, in 535 may have been responsible for the global climate changes of 535–536.[14] Keys explores what he believes to be the radical and far-ranging global effects of just such a putative 6th-century eruption in his book *Catastrophe: An Investigation into the Origins of the Modern World*. Additionally, in recent times, it has been argued that it was this eruption which created the islands of Verlaten, Lang, and the beginnings of Rakata—all indicators of early Krakatoa's caldera's size. To date, however, little datable charcoal from that eruption has been found.

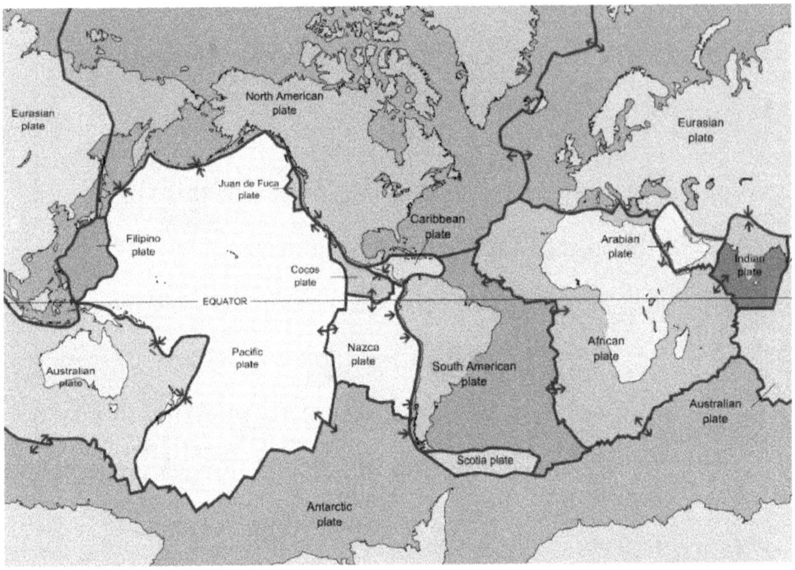

Thornton mentions that Krakatoa was known as "The Fire Mountain" during Java's Sailendra dynasty, with records of seven eruptive events between the 9th and 16th centuries.[15]Template:47 These have been tentatively dated as 850 AD, 950 AD, 1050 AD, 1150 AD, 1320 AD, and 1530 AD.[unquote][78]

Krakatoa

Sumatra strait map.

An 1888 lithograph of the 1883 eruption of Krakatoa.

Indonesia has over 130 active volcanoes which make up the axis of the Indonesian island arc system, which was produced by northeastward subduction of the Indo-Australian Plate. Krakatoa is directly above the subduction zone of the Eurasian Plate and the Indo-Australian Plate where the plate boundaries make a sharp change of direction, possibly resulting in an unusually weak crust in the region.

Recent studies, and seismic events such as the 2012 Indian Ocean earthquake, suggest that the Indo-Australian Plate may be in the process of breaking up into two separate plates due primarily to stresses induced by the collision of the Indo-Australian Plate with Eurasia along the Himalayas.[79]

The Indian plate shown in bold

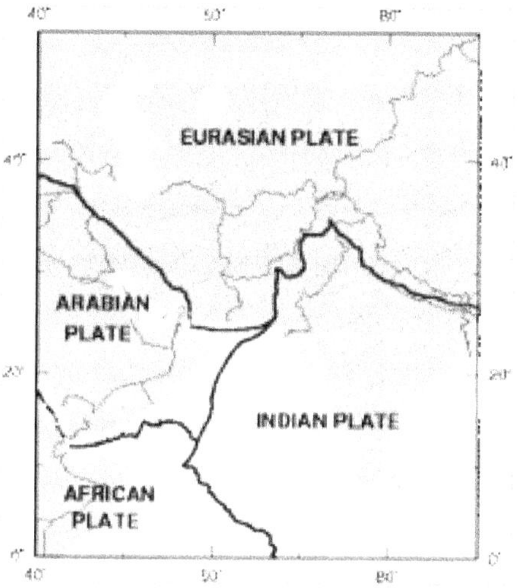

The India Plate or Indian Plate is a tectonic plate that was originally a part of the ancient continent of Gondwana from which it split off, eventually becoming a major plate. About 55 to 50 million years ago (contested), it fused with the adjacent Australian Plate. It is today part of the major Indo-Australian Plate, and includes most of South Asia and a portion of the basin under the Indian Ocean, including parts of South China and Eastern Indonesia, and extending up to but not including Ladakh, Kohistan and Balochistan.

Due to plate tectonics, the India Plate split from Madagascar and collided (c. 55 Ma) with the Eurasian Plate, resulting in the formation of the Himalayas.

140 million years ago the Indian Plate formed part of the supercontinent Gondwana together with modern Africa, Australia, Antarctica, and South America. Gondwana broke up as these continents drifted apart with

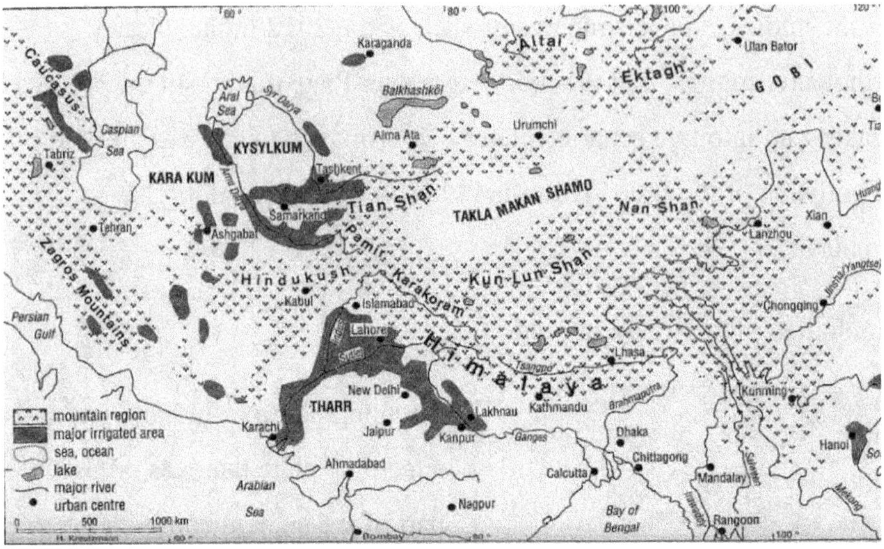

different velocities, a process which led to the opening of the Indian Ocean.[80]

The "hard collision" between India and Asia occurred at ~25 Ma together with subduction of the resulting ocean basin that formed between the Greater Himalayan fragment and India.

The Indian Plate is currently moving north-east at 5 centimetres (2.0 in) per year, while the Eurasian Plate is moving north at only 2 centimetres (0.79 in) per year.

Closeup of the boundary with the Eurasian, African and Arabian plates; the 2005 Kashmir earthquake occurred at the northern tip of the Indian plate.

The Himalayan range encompasses about 15,000 glaciers, which store about 12,000 km^3(3000 cubic miles) of fresh water.

Himalaya is the source of major rivers for 2.5 billion people; Manasarovar in Tibet yields Sindhu, Sutlej, Sarasvati, Mahakali-Karnali-Sharada and Tsangpo-Lohitya-Brahmaputra rivers; other rivers flowing from eastern Himalaya are: Irawaddy, Salween, Mekong, Yangtse and Huanghe. Precipitation levels increase along the Himalaya from Karakorm (250 cm. per annum) to Cherrapunjee, Assam (1410 cm p.a.) registering the highest rainfall regions of the world. Since 1959, Chinese government estimates that they have removed over $54 billion worth of timber.

Indian Ocean Community can contribute to a collective pan-Asian effort to share the waters of the Himalayan rivers with all the people of the Community. The major river systems of Ganga, Brahmaputra, Indus, Irawaddy, Salween, Mekong can meet the water requirements (for irrigation water and drinking water) of IOC working towards the creation of a series of national water grids harnessing and sharing the water resources of the Great Fresh Water Reservoir of the World, the Himalayas.

Indian Ocean Community is home to about 2 billion of the globe.

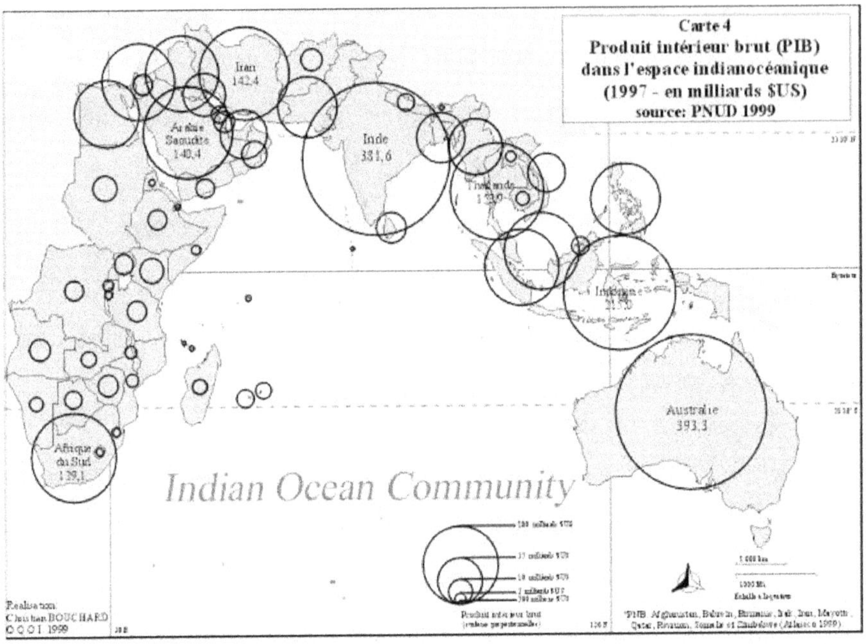

Decades after many countries of Indian Ocean Community attained freedom from colonial rule, sporadic efforts have been made to formalize this *IOC* and many of these efforts have not resulted in any significant advance towards the constitution of *IOC*. The contribution made by these diverse steps should not be underestimated. The small steps together provide the firm ground on which the geographic reality can be transformed into One nation.

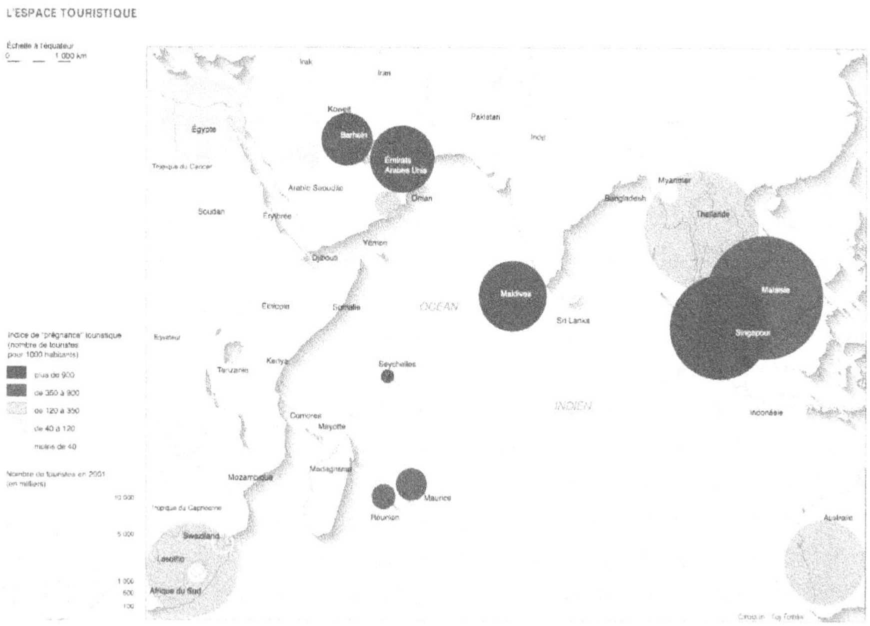

There are many facets of any community of people. *Indian Ocean Community* is a geographical entity comparable to European Community as a geographical entity.

In a 1995 speech in New Delhi, Senator Gareth Evans,who was then Foreign Minister of Australia observed:

> "… the region is so diffuse … it contains sovereign states ranging in size from India with over 900 million people, to Seychelles with less than 80,000 people. Economies range in size from over $250 billion for our two countries [India and Australia], to less than $400 million for the Maldives and Comoros."

Just as European Coal and Steel Community preceded the formation of European Community, Indian Ocean Community can be seen to have started with *Indian Ocean Tuna Commission (IOTC)* was established in

1993. IOTC members were Indian ocean island or littoral states or countries whose ships fish in the Indian Ocean.Thus IOTC has now 28 members including extra-regional countries. The Indian Ocean Tuna Commission (IOTC)[81] is an intergovernmental organization mandated to manage tuna and tuna-like species in the Indian Ocean and adjacent seas. Its objective is to promote cooperation among its Members with a view to ensuring, through appropriate management, the conservation and optimum utilisation of stocks and encouraging sustainable development of fisheries based on such stocks.

Indian Ocean Naval Symposium (IONS) set up in 2008 has participants from across the region and beyond.

Indian Ocean Centre for Peace Studies (IOCPS) was set up in the 1990s by the late Professor Kenneth McPherson. IOCPS was renamed *Indian Ocean Centre (IOC)* after McPherson moved to Curtin University of Technology. *IOCPS* and *IOC* played think-tank or advisory roles. Another policy-oriented dialogue was *Indian Ocearn Research Group (IORG)* initiated in India partnership, among governments, industries, NGOs and communities. *IORG* brings *out Journal of the Indian Ocean Region*, (Routledge Taylor & Francis Group)

*Indian Ocean Rim-Association for Regional Cooperation (IOR-ARC)*which started in 1990 as an inter-governmental meeting forum. Initially known as the Indian Ocean Rim Initiative, *IOR-ARC* is an international organization with 18 member states. It was first established in Mauritiuson March 1995 and formally launched on 6–7 March 1997.

The time has come to institutionalise this regional cooperation by setting up a federal framework for the Indian Ocean Community, the way the European Community was an evolution from the European Coal and Steel Community (ECSC) formed in the 1950's as a six-nationinternational organisation serving to unify Western Europe during the Cold War.[82]

In 1971, Sri Lanka brought forth in the United Nations, a proposal for *Indian Ocean Zone of Peace (IOZOP).* Same year, Malaysia proposed Zone of Peace, Freedom and Neutrality (ZOPFAN). Both proposals remained as mere proposals with no consensus achieved in the UN deliberations.

In 1985, UNESCO initiated *Organisation for Indian Ocean Marine Affairs Cooperation (IOMAC)*[83] which did not get any significant backing. Fields of co-operation[84] in marine affairs in the Indian Ocean envisaged were:

(a) marine science, ocean services and marine technology;

(b) living resources;

(c) non-living resources;

(d) ocean law, policy and management;

(e) marine transport and communications;

(f)

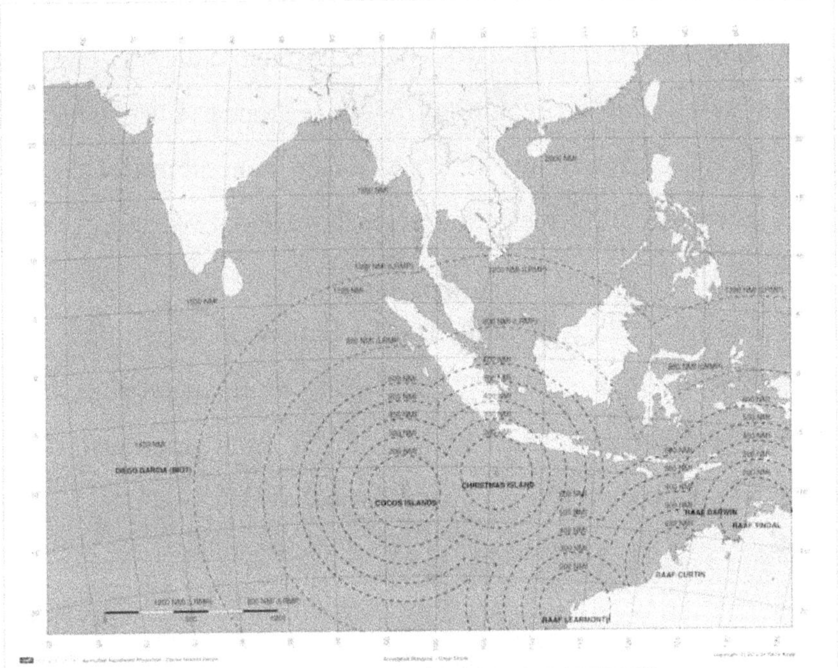

INDIAN OCEAN STRATEGIC AIR DEFENCE AND MARITIME PATROL ENVIRONMENT

marine environment; and

(g) other fields relevant to co-operation in marine affairs.

In a scintillating and brilliantly illustrated monograph (February 2012), Dr. Carlo Kopp, discusses basing infrastructure considerations in the defence of Australia's Indian Ocean [85]Approaches. The insights provided by Carlo Kopp should extend to the defence of the entire Indian Ocean Region with involvement of all countries of the Indian Ocean Region to guard the fragile environment in this geographical region, martime activities and strategic sealanes of traffic of fossil fuels from the Straits of Hormuz through the Straits of Malacca reaching the westcoast of United States of America. "Stragetic importance of the Indian Ocean Sea Lanes of Communication: "The industrialisation of Asia began with Japan during the 1920s, and has been an accelerating process as South Korea, Taiwan, and most recently mainland China have pursued industrialisation, with India following. These Asian nations collectively now account for much of global manufacturing activity, in areas ranging from heavy industries such metal processing and shipbuilding, down to the operation of high density microelectronic foundries. A key characteristic of industrial economies is that they are insatiable consumers of energy and raw materials. This reality was observed first during the industrialisation of Europe, then during the industrialisation of North America, and most recently, during the industrialisation of Asia. The consequence of this is high *per capita* energy consumption in most if not all industrialised nations, spread across transportation, industrial manufacturing, and consumer markets. Other consequences of industrialisation are a strong drive to individual ownership of housing and automobiles. In turn this yields higher energy consumption and thus increased demand over time as a result. It is often not well understood that one of the major motivations underpinning the Great War was intensive competition over colonial raw materials and energy, between the established colonial powers, and latecomers on the European continent. "

Other areas of concern relate to sea-lane security to promote maritime trade across the Indian Ocean. One aspect relates to sea piracy which calls for regional level cooperation among the coast guards of the Indian Ocean Community countries. Discussing the strategic basing options, Carlo Kopp notes: "An additional dimension to consider is that of the strategic needs of our principal ally, the United States.The United States had an excellent basing network across the Pacific during the Cold War, including multiple bases in Japan, South Korea, the Philippines, the Marianas and Hawaii, with leased access to Britain's Diego Garcia in the Indian Ocean. Two decades after the Cold War the North Asian bases are demonstrably indefensible against Chinese air assets, cruise missiles and ballistic missiles. The large Subic Bay and Clark bases in the Philippines were closed down at the end of the Cold War. While Diego Garcia and Guam have become central basing "hubs", the remaining bases are of limited utility due to their exposed locations. A crisis in South East Asia or the eastern Indian Ocean would present major challenges, especially for tactical air and tanker aircraft basing. This would be true of a conflict, as much as a major natural disaster."

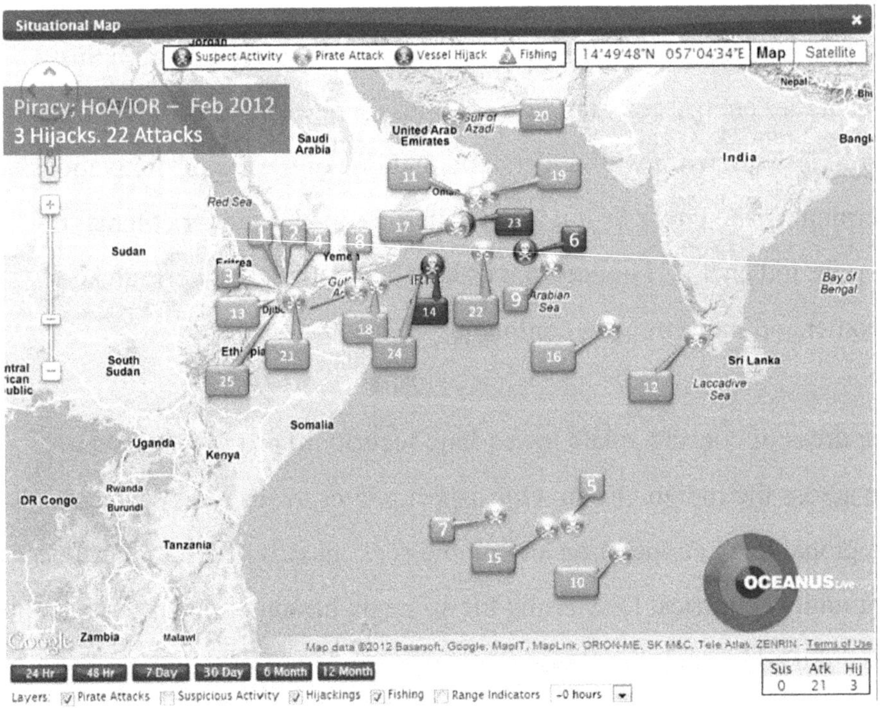

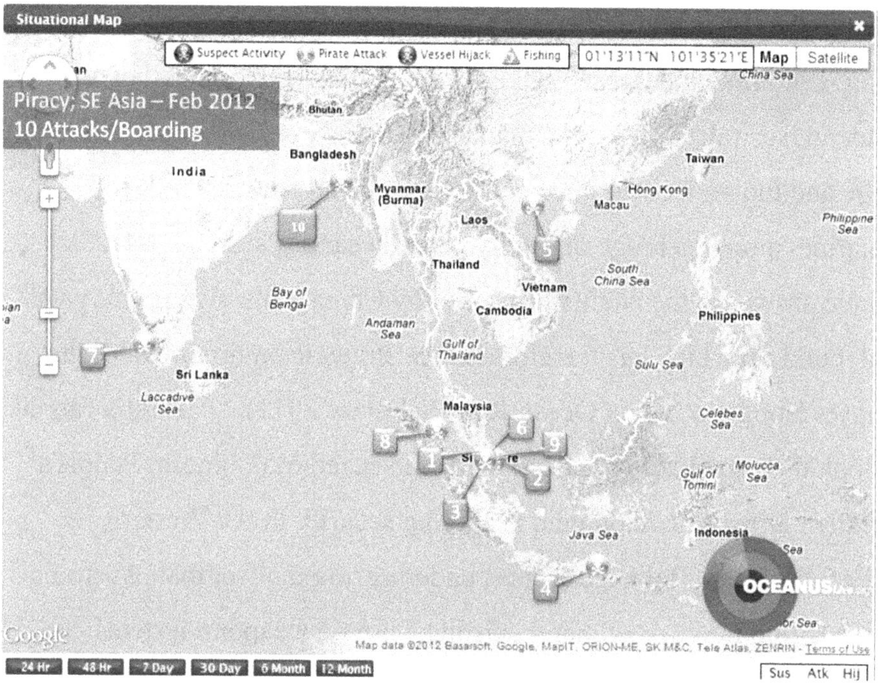
Situational Map
Suspect Activity
Pirate Attack
Vessel Hijack
Fishing
01°13'11"N 101°35'21"E
Map
Satellite
Piracy; SE Asia – Feb 2012
10 Attacks/Boarding
Bhutan
Bangladesh
India
Myanmar (Burma)
Laos
Taiwan
Hong Kong
Macau
Philippine Sea
Thailand
Vietnam
South China Sea
Bay of Bengal
Cambodia
Philippines
Andaman Sea
Gulf of Thailand
Sulu Sea
Sri Lanka
Laccadive Sea
Malaysia
Celebes Sea
Molucca Sea
Gulf of Tomini
Java Sea
Indonesia
OCEANUS
Google
Map data ©2012 Basarsoft, Google, MapIT, ORION-ME, SK M&C, Tele Atlas, ZENRIN - Terms of Use
24 Hr
48 Hr
7 Day
30 Day
6 Month
12 Month
Sus Atk Hij

Indian Ocean is a pirate-infested region of the world, as may be seen from the map depicting number of pirate attacks in 2005-

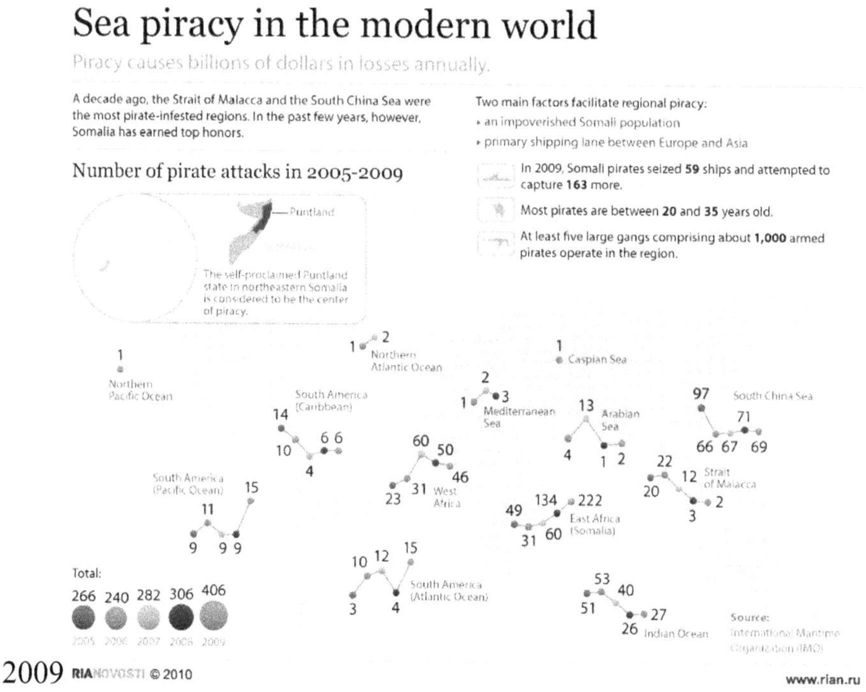
Sea piracy in the modern world
Piracy causes billions of dollars in losses annually.
A decade ago, the Strait of Malacca and the South China Sea were the most pirate-infested regions. In the past few years, however, Somalia has earned top honors.
Two main factors facilitate regional piracy:
• an impoverished Somali population
• primary shipping lane between Europe and Asia
Number of pirate attacks in 2005-2009
In 2009, Somali pirates seized 59 ships and attempted to capture 163 more.
Most pirates are between 20 and 35 years old.
At least five large gangs comprising about 1,000 armed pirates operate in the region.
Puntland
The self-proclaimed Puntland state in northeastern Somalia is considered to be the center of piracy.
1 Northern Pacific Ocean
1 2 Northern Atlantic Ocean
1 Caspian Sea
South America (Caribbean) 14 10 4 6 6
2 1 3 Mediterranean Sea
13 4 1 2 Arabian Sea
97 66 67 71 69 South China Sea
60 23 31 50 46 West Africa
22 20 12 3 2 Strait of Malacca
South America (Pacific Ocean) 11 9 9 9 15
49 31 60 134 222 East Africa (Somalia)
10 12 3 4 15 South America (Atlantic Ocean)
53 51 40 26 27 Indian Ocean
Total:
266 240 282 306 406
2005 2006 2007 2008 2009
Source: International Maritime Organization (IMO)
2009 RIANOVOSTI © 2010
www.rian.ru

Added to the concerns of sea piracy is the strategic military environment leading a prominent defense thinker of Australia, Professor Babbage to commend Australian Navy to enhance Australia's presence straddling the Pacific and Indian Oceans and acquire 12 nuclear-powered attack submarines among a range of highly potent weapons systems, as a strategic answer to the challenges posed by China's massive military and naval build-up which has transformed the strategic environment of the countries along the Indian Ocean Rim (February 2011). "Australia cannot overlook the way that the scale, pattern and speed of (Chinese) People's Liberation Army's development is altering security in the Western Pacific," Professor Babbage argues, underscoring the fact that .Australia itself is within the rnge of many existing Chinese weapons systems. http://www.kokodafoundation.org/Resources/Documents/KP15StrategicEdge.pdf

It would appear that the lack-lustre results of the sporadic efforts at forming a pan-regional organization were due to the absence of substantial 'socio-economic content' or 'trade and investment' of the type the European Coal and Steel Community provided to give a definitive push to the formation of European Community.

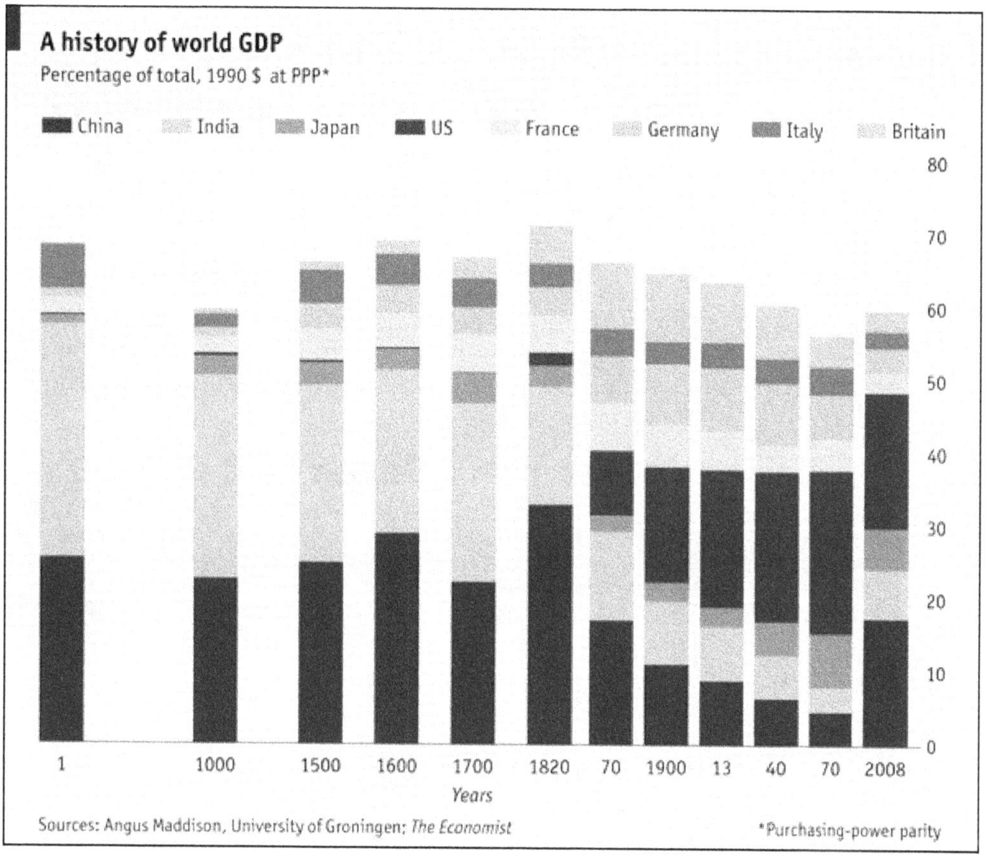

Economic history of two millennia

59 countries along the Indian Ocean Rim now realize that the devastation caused by colonial domination and colonial loot has to be undone and a new era of socio-economic development has to be realised.

The formation of an Indian Ocean Community will provide a multiplier effect for providing for increase in employment among the 2 billion (1/3rd of the world population) people of the IOC region, while providing an unprecedented opportunity for the developed world led by USA to get involved in investing in large projects in the region: Trans-Asian Highway and Trans-Asian Railway from Bangkok to Vladivostok and extending the terrotorial waters of the Indian Ocean Rim states to 200 nautical miles under the amended Law of the Sea (which has the effect of a marked increased increase, lebensraum, for expanding economic opportunities to harness the riches of the ocean).

The rationale for a supra-nation of European Community was initially premised on a Coal and Steel Community but got expanded to full-fledged economic cooperation with Euro as a Common currency and a European

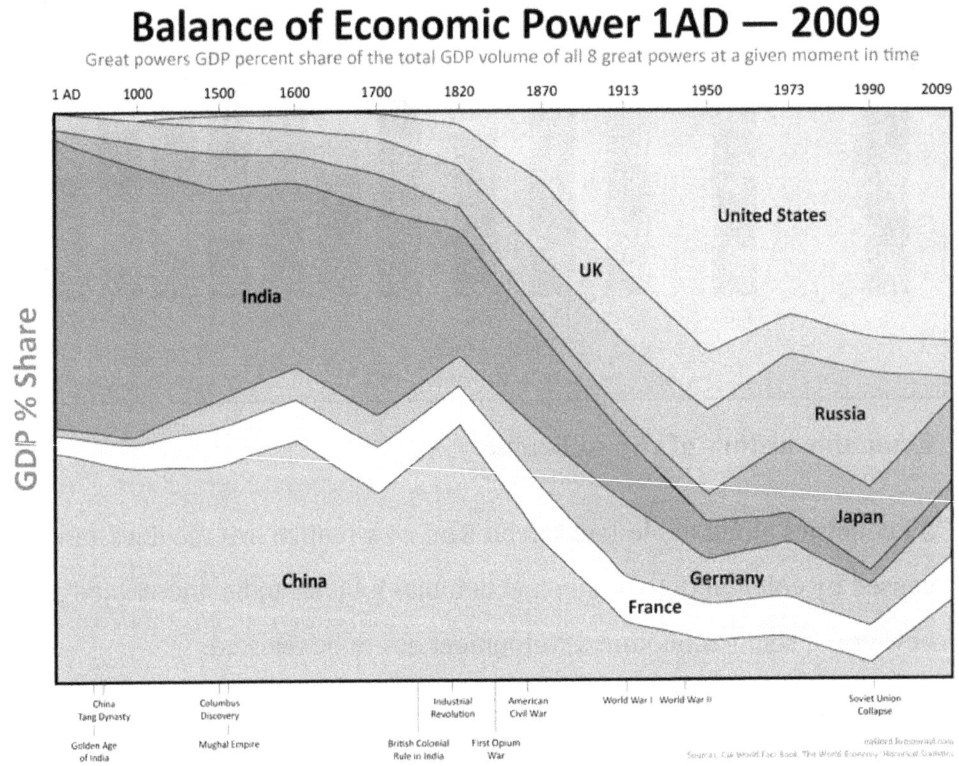

Central Bank. This happened as an economic imperative despite the two world wars fought among the European nations. Similarly, Indian Ocean Community (IOC) can be initiated as a Free Trade Zone, to start with and later to provide for a Common Currency (Mudra) to provide for free

movement of goods and services among the 59 states of the Indian Ocean Rim stretching from South Africa to Tasmania along the 63,000 long Indian Ocean Rim.

Economic history of China and other major powers
Share of world GDP

Source: "Statistics on World Population, GDP and Per Capita GDP, 1-2008 AD", Angus Maddison, University of Groningen

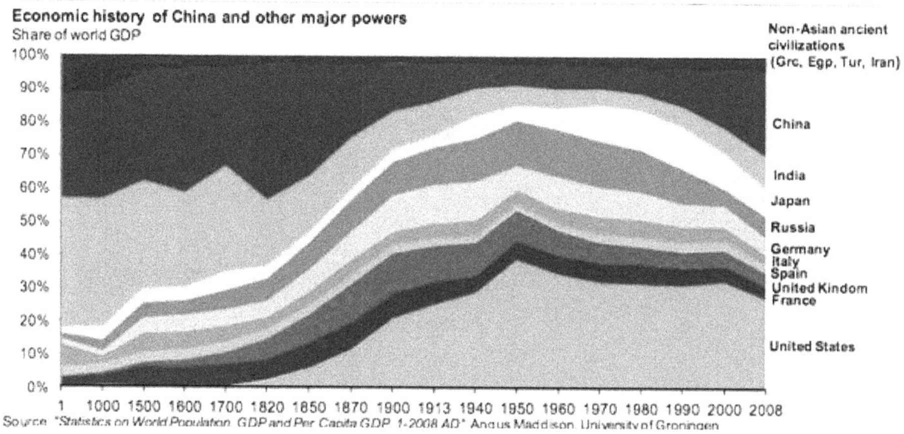

Making common cause to gain multiplier effects with specific developmental projects

IOC will be a socio-economic powerhouse contributing to creation of wealth and new lives for about 2 billion people of the ocean rim states.

Areas of economic strengths of the Community:

- skilled labor forcecompetence in IT and space, ocean development technologies (including tsunami warning and protection systems against future tsunami-s, desalination of seawater)
- Higher education in basic sciences and agriculture technologies (e.g. Intl. Rice Research Institute, Philippines)

- agricultural services sector, -- in particular: dairy development, aquatic resources and rice cultivation technologies
- water-management systems and national/regional water grids (Mekong-Ganga cooperation initiative)
- exploration and sustainable development of mines and minerals

safeguarding sea-lanes

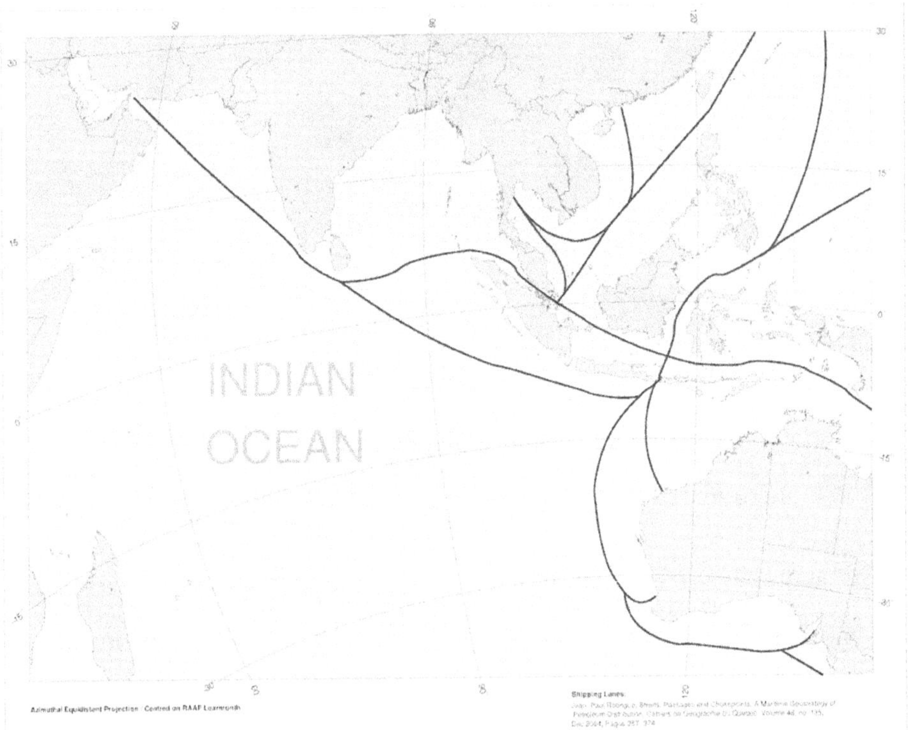

INDIAN OCEAN SEA LINES OF COMMUNICATION

- preservation of cultural artefacts and sites such as Angkor Wat, Prambanan

establishment of Indian Ocean Free Trade Agreement for a multi-trillion-dollar economic community

- scholar-exchanges for better understanding of dharma-dhamma continuum governing a common shared set of socio-cultural values

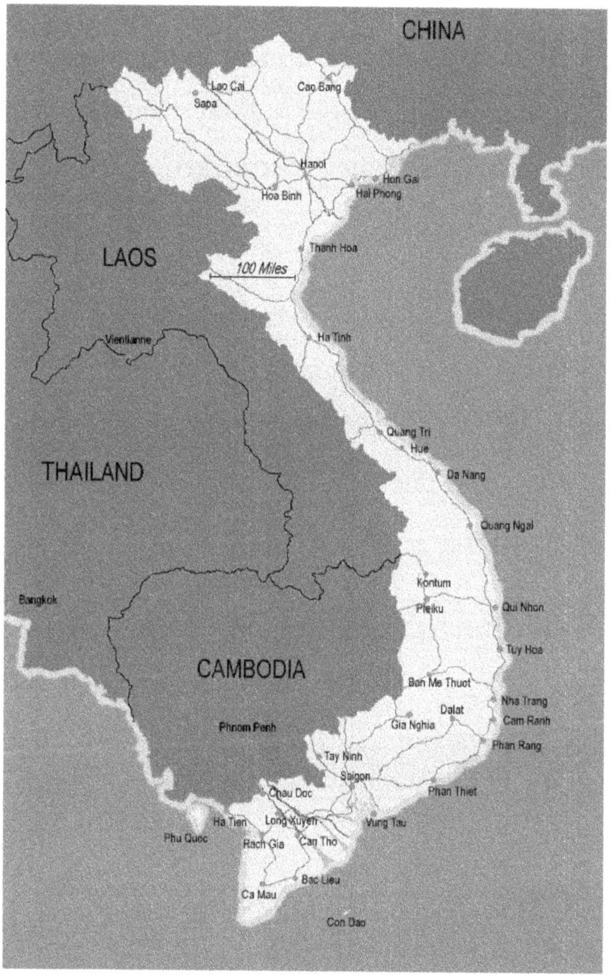

strengthening economies of Mekong countries comprising Cambodia, Lao People's Democratic Republic (PDR), Myanmar, Thailand and Vietnam with economic linkages in transport, energy and telecommunication. Mekong delta The Mekong-Ganga Cooperation (MGC) established in 2000 with six member-countries namely, Thailand, Myanmar, Cambodia, Lao PDR, Vietnam and India. should expand areas of cooperation in tourism, culture, education and transportation, promoting trade and investment. which RITES Ltd, a government of India undertaking has completed a preliminary study in 2006 to set-up a railway line from Delhi to Hanoi. India has proposed to extend BIMSTEC highway (India–Myanmar–Thailand trilateral highway) to Lao PDR and Cambodia. Opening of the second 'Friendship Bridge' connecting the town of Savannakhet in Lao PDR with Mukdahan in Thailand has made it possible to travel by road from anywhere in India right up to Danang in Vietnam through Mekong's East-West Economic Corridor to set up.special economic zones at borders—India-Myanmar and Myanmar—Thailand.

> India offers 10 scholarships every year to MGC member countries in culture-related subjects, such as ancient history of MGC countries and Buddhism, Sanskrit, Pali, dance, preservation of manuscripts, archaeology, handicrafts and museology.
>
> India continues its support for the MGC initiative. With the help of India's Entrepreneurship Development Institute (EDI), the India–Cambodia and India–Vietnam Entrepreneurship Development Centres became operational recently. The India–Lao Centre has been operational since November 2004.
>
> India always attaches special attention to the Cambodia–Lao PDR–Myanmar–Vietnam (CLMV) countries among the ten Asean countries, and is committed to assisting them to bridge the gap with the other six.[86]

A suggestion can be mooted for forming a Task Force of intellectuals and economists to study the modalities for forming an Indian Ocean Community, taking the cue from the formation of European Community.

How to create a multiplier effect to accelerate the pace of development of the Indian Ocean Community?Asia accounted for 75.1% of world GDP at the turn of the Common Era. It declined to 36.0% in 1870 and to 29.5 in 1998. Africa's share for the turn of the Common Era, 1870 and 1998 were: 6.8%, 3.6% and 3.1%. Most of the Indian Ocean Countries are in these Asia and Africa regions and all of them were impoverished, registerin steep declines in their share of the world GDP.

Shares of World GDP, select countries, regional totals

	0	1000	1500	1700	1870	1998
W. Europe	10.8	8.7	17.9	22.5	33.6	20.6
E. Europe	1.9	2.2	2.5	2.9	4.1	2.0
Japan	1.2	2.7	3.1	4.1	2.3	7.7
China	28.2	22.7	25.0	22.3	8.9	11.5
India	32.9	28.9	24.5	24.4	7.6	5.0
Other Asia	16.1	16.0	12.7	10.9	5.4	13.0
Total Asia (excldg. Japan)	75.1	67.6	62.1	57.6	21.9	29.5
Africa	6.8	11.8	7.4	6.6	2.7	3.1
WORLD	100	100	100	100	100	100
	0	1000	1500	1700	1870	1998

This was counterbalanced by the increase in the wealth of Western offshoots from a share of 0.5 at the turn of the Common Era to 30.6% in 1950 and 25.1% in 1998

The principal objective of establishing Indian Ocean Community is to restore Asia and Africa to the share the continents had at the turn of the common era (0 CE): to 83.1% of World GDP (from the 19998 level of 40.3%).

Source: Table B-20, Maddison; Contours of the World Economy 1-2030 CE by Angus Maddison (2007)[87]

Table 2: Basic Economic Indicators by Region and Subregion

	Share of World Population (%) 2010	Share of World GDP (%, PPP) 2011	Real GDP Growth (%)[1] Average 2000–2007	Real GDP Growth (%)[1] Average 2008-2011	Per Capita GDP (PPP) $ 2011	Per Capita GDP (PPP) Average Growth (%) 2000–2007
Asia	56.2	36.6	6.2	5.8	7,376	7.0
East Asia	22.5	23.5	6.3	5.9	11,896	7.7
Central Asia	1.2	0.7	10.3	5.9	6,396	9.8
Southeast Asia	8.7	4.2	5.5	4.5	5,476	6.0
South Asia	23.3	6.9	6.8	7.0	3,325	7.4
The Pacific and Oceania	0.5	1.3	3.4	2.0	29,623	3.5
European Union	7.2	20.1	2.6	0.0	31,607	3.6
North America	6.6	23.0	2.6	0.4	39,450	3.1
World[2]	100.0	100.0	4.2	2.8	10,821	4.7

GDP = gross domestic product, PPP = purchasing power parity.

Notes: The list of countries in each subregion is shown in Table 3. European Union (EU) refers to the aggregate of the 27 EU members. North America includes Canada, Mexico, and the United States.

[1]Weighted by nominal GDP in PPP.

[2]Per capita GDP as of end-2010.

Source: ADB calculations using data from *Asian Development Outlook 2012*, Asian Development Bank; *World Economic Outlook Database April 2012*, International Monetary Fund; and *World Development Indicators*, World Bank.

Table 5: Trade-to-GDP Ratio by Region and Subregion (%)

	1990	2000	2010	2011
Asia	**30.1**	**40.4**	**54.1**	**57.3**
East Asia	26.7	34.1	51.1	52.8
People's Republic of China	29.9	39.6	50.2	49.9
Southeast Asia	89.4	130.8	107.2	116.1
ASEAN-4	62.9	103.7	78.1	86.0
BCLMV	75.3	84.4	110.1	130.8
Singapore	293.1	289.3	292.3	299.4
Central Asia	–	62.8	52.4	59.7
South Asia	16.0	23.0	36.7	44.0
India	12.9	19.5	35.9	44.2
The Pacific and Oceania	28.3	37.3	36.3	37.8
European Union	–	**57.6**	**62.5**	**67.2**
North America	**18.4**	**25.6**	**27.4**	**29.9**
World	**31.1**	**40.2**	**48.0**	**51.9**

ASEAN-4 = Indonesia, Malaysia, the Philippines, and Thailand; BCLMV = Brunei Darussalam, Cambodia, the Lao People's Democratic Republic, Myanmar, and Viet Nam; GDP = gross domestic product; North America = Canada, Mexico, and the United States; – = unavailable.

Notes: Figures refer to the ratio of total trade to gross domestic product (GDP) for the specified years. Values were derived by dividing total trade (exports plus imports) by nominal GDP (both in $).

Source: ADB calculations using data from *Direction of Trade Statistics* and *World Economic Outlook Database April 2012*, International Monetary Fund; and CEIC for Taipei,China.

Basic economic indicators of 'Developing Asia' such as population data, GDP, Trade-to-GDP ratio, are provided in a July 2012 publication (Titled as Tables 2 and 5).There are indications of increasing trade within the region itself as Asia's share of world exports rose from 23.4% in 1990 to 34.3% in 2011. By 2050, the region could exceed 50% of global trade. The following table (also taken from the same publication)[88] shows GDP growth (year-on-year) in 'Developing Asia' (which includes many countries of the Indian Ocean Community compared with the GDP growth in major industrialized economies. Though the growth rates between 2009 and 2012 range between 1.4 to 9.2% in most Indian Ocean Community nations, the rates are a slow process of catch-up to attain the situation which existed before the colonial era.

Table 1: Regional GDP Growth[1] (y-o-y, %)

				ADB Forecast	
	2009	**2010**	**2011**	**2012**	**2013**
Developing Asia	6.0	9.1	7.2	6.6	7.1
Central Asia[2]	3.2	6.6	6.2	5.8	6.2
East Asia[3]	6.8	9.8	8.0	7.1	7.5
PRC	9.2	10.4	9.2	8.2	8.5
South Asia[4]	7.5	7.7	6.2	6.2	6.9
India	8.4	8.4	6.5	6.5	7.3
Southeast Asia[5]	1.4	7.9	4.6	5.2	5.6
The Pacific[6]	4.3	5.5	7.0	6.0	4.2
Major industrialized economies					
United States	-3.5	3.0	1.7	1.9	2.2
eurozone	-4.4	2.0	1.5	-0.7	0.8
Japan	-5.5	4.4	-0.7	2.2	1.5

PRC = People's Republic of China, GDP = gross domestic product, eurozone = Austria, Belgium, Cyprus, Estonia, Finland, France, Germany, Greece, Ireland, Italy, Luxembourg, Malta, the Netherlands, Portugal, Slovakia, Slovenia, and Spain.
[1]Aggregates are weighted according to gross national income levels (Atlas method, current $) from *World Development Indicators*, World Bank.
[2]Includes Armenia, Azerbaijan, Georgia, Kazakhstan, the Kyrgyz Republic, Tajikistan, Turkmenistan, and Uzbekistan.
[3]Includes the People's Republic of China; Hong Kong, China; the Republic of Korea; Mongolia; and Taipei,China.
[4]Includes Afghanistan, Bangladesh, Bhutan, India, Republic of the Maldives, Nepal, Pakistan, and Sri Lanka. Data for Bangladesh, India, and Pakistan are recorded on a fiscal-year basis. For India, the fiscal year spans the current year's April through the next year's March. For Bangladesh and Pakistan, the fiscal year spans the previous year's July through the current year's June.
[5]Includes Brunei Darussalam, Cambodia, Indonesia, the Lao People's Democratic Republic, Malaysia, the Philippines, Singapore, Thailand, and Viet Nam. Excludes Myanmar as weights unavailable.
[6]Includes the Cook Islands, Fiji, Kiribati, the Marshall Islands, the Federated States of Micronesia, Nauru, Palau, Papua New Guinea, Samoa, Solomon Islands, Timor-Leste, Tonga, Tuvalu, and Vanuatu.

The pace of growth has to be quickened and the multiplier effect can be provided by the formation of Indian Ocean Community.

In an impressive presentation on ASEAN Economics – Characteristics and Management, Lee Yoong Yoong of Institute of Policy Studies asks a rhetorical question which is shown on a slide:

ASEAN Economic Community (AEC)

Trading Bloc or Blocked?

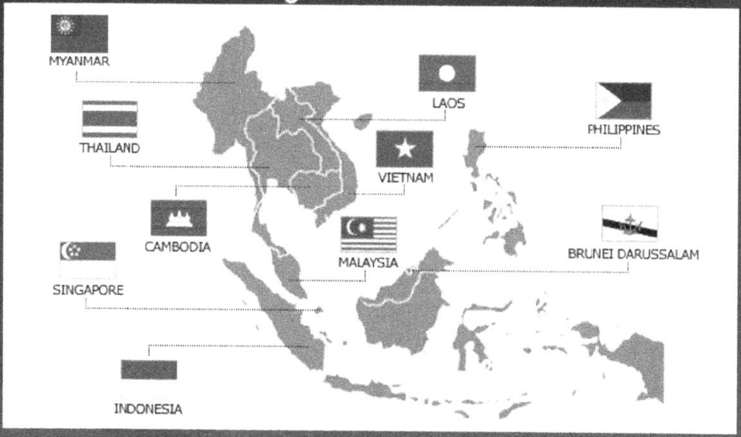

Path towards an AEC

- The ASEAN Charter - signed on 20 Nov 2007.
- Also issued a Declaration on the ASEAN Economic Community (AEC); Adopted the AEC Blueprint for the implementation of the AEC by 2015.
- The Declaration says that "…the AEC Blueprint will transform ASEAN into a single market and production base, a highly competitive economic region, a region of equitable economic development, and a region fully integrated into the global economy."

Economic Architecture of Regional and Trans-regional Forum

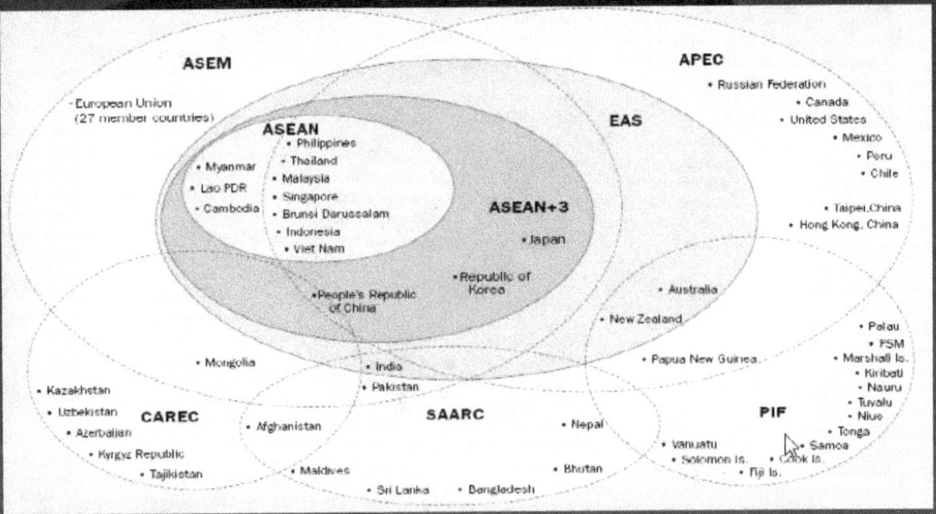

Source: Emerging Asian Regionalism, A Partnership for Shared Prosperity

Single Market?

- To most people, a single market is synonymous with a ***custom union*** which also includes not just free movement of goods but also of labour, services and capital.
- The most famous single market: European Union (EU)
  - Began life as the European Coal and Steel Community in 1951 (Treaty of Paris (1951)
  - Become the European Economic Community (EEC) in 1957 (Treaty of Rome (1957)
  - The abolition of internal tariff barriers was achieved in 1968.
  - The Single European Act was signed in 1986 to establish a Single European Market by 1992, by removing the barriers to free movement of capital, labour, goods and services.

ASEAN EC will have free movement of goods, services, ***skilled*** labour and ***freer*** movement of capital but is unlikely to be a custom union.

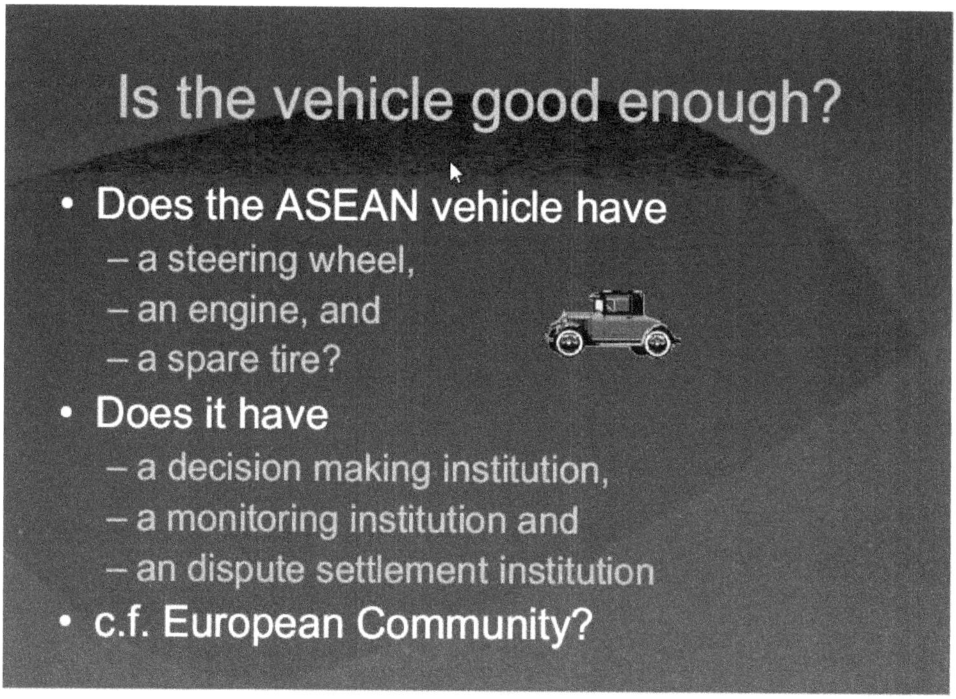
Is the vehicle good enough?
• Does the ASEAN vehicle have
– a steering wheel,
– an engine, and
– a spare tire?
• Does it have
– a decision making institution,
– a monitoring institution and
– an dispute settlement institution
• c.f. European Community?

Lee Yoong Yoong finds the traditional approach of tariff and non-tariff barriers insufficient and recommends a strategy to upgrade competitiveness of ASEAN – a region where 44% live below US$2 per day (source: Asian Development Bank, 2009). We suggest that the strategy should break out of the ASEAN vision and declaration and move towards the formation of an Indian Ocean Community on the lines of the European Community leading towards full integration of the economies of 59 countries of the Community in a series of measured steps: financial, fiscal, free-trade, embark on new pan-regional development initiatives and common currency steps.

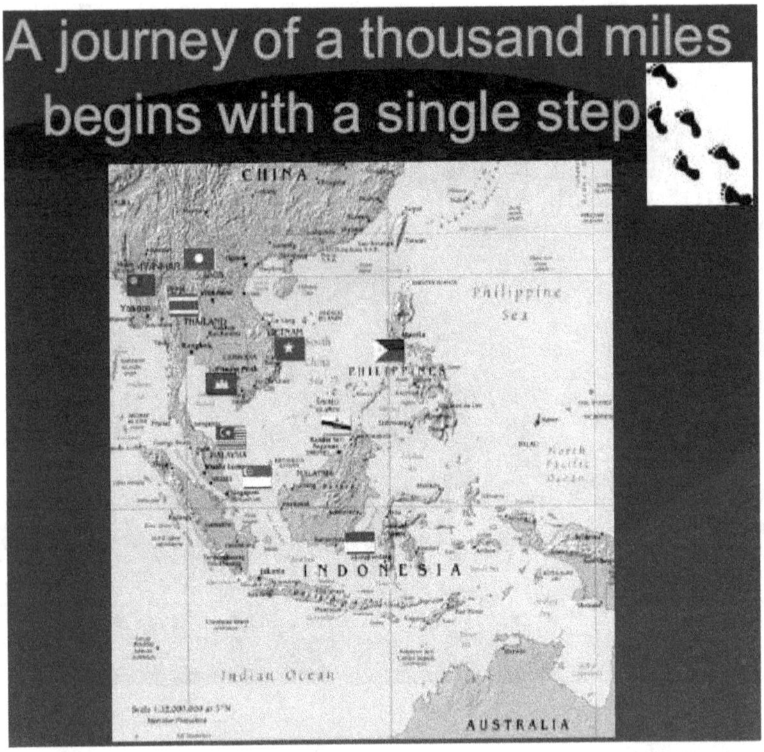

The land that The Buddha walked is a roadmap for opening up the path of the Community with more rapid steps to reach the destination:

We are, however, impacted by our neighbors:

- ASEAN is only as strong as the weakest member. It is thus compelling to help the newer ASEAN economies - CLMV;
- On a wider Asian and world stage, geopolitical dynamics are shifting dramatically. How should ASEAN react?
- Important factors impacting on ASEAN include:

  (a) generational change-youths who do not know how hard the struggle was for survival;

  (b) identity change: now a stronger national identity, which implies a more nationalistic reactions to pressures from neighbors;

  (c) leadership changes in most ASEAN Member States, who are largely technocrats/non-charismatic: can they mobilise the people?

abhyudayam, welfare of about 2 billion people. With the framework of Dharma-Dhamma, institutional frameworks can be established to make the pilgrimage a tryst with destiny – dhamma and sangha, protected by the Buddha dhamma and Sanatana Dharma.

ASEAN+6 set to launch world's biggest free-trade market[89]

Monday, Oct 22, 2012

ASEAN and six Asian leaders will this November announce the official establishment of the Regional Comprehensive Economic Partnership (RCEP), which will make it the biggest free-trade market on the globe.

"The leaders should come up with a formal statement to form the RCEP. The negotiations are expected to start early next year in order to wrap up the pact by 2015, just in time for the full implementation of the ASEAN Economic Community," Somkiat Triratpan, deputy director-general of the Trade Negotiations Department, said

... ASEAN groups 10 countries in Southeast Asia. The six partner countries are China, Japan, South Korea, India, Australia and New Zealand.

The provocative question can be answered. Indian Ocean Community formation will unblock the trade and investment opportunities in the 59 countries of the Community and open up a new era of quickened pace of socio-economic development of the Community.

Indian Ocean Community can help avoid a global financial meltdown

I recall with fondness the brilliant monograph titled *Economic Consequences of the Peace* by John Maynard Keynes (1919). This became the voice of a genius to shape the financial system of the world for almost a century thereafter. Now, we need a person of the stature of Keynes to take the world financial system out of the recessionary mess resulting from a chaotic order of puts and calls, fiscal irresponsibility, and bogus instruments like credit swaps and participatory notes.

A historic opportunity exists to reshape the world economic order to create a win-win situation for both the developed world and the IOC with the potential for a multi-trillion dollar GDP growing at over 10 percent per annum for the next century. Hindu economic thought governed by dharma-dhamma provides a solution to the present mess and we have to actively promote this solution.

The financial crisis faced by the developed world requires firm, decisive action to get out of the recession worse than the 1929 depression. When the world had to reckon with the cost of financing the Second World War, PM Winston Churchill turned to John Maynard Keynes for an economic framework to prosecute the war. Keynes came up with a brilliant document titled: *'How to Pay for the War (1940)'*. This landmark document suggested an economic policy for compulsory saving (essentially wage-earners loaning money to the government), rather than deficit spending, in order to avoid inflation. This measure predicated a substantial increase in the national product, to be effected by a net increase in employment, a longer working day, and a livelier tempo of labor. A solution analogous to this can be found to overcome the present recessionary market place in the developed world.

IOC has a millennium of socio-cultural interaction and bonds which existed among the present-day states of the Indian Ocean Rim. This is exemplified by the statement of the late French epigraphist George Coedes (who wrote about the largest vishnu temple of the world in Angkor Wat, Cambodia and other Hindu temples of the Farther Orient) who called the region: Hinduised States of the Farther Orient. The title of his work is: Histoire ancienne des États hindouisés d'Extrême-Orient, 1944; translated into English by Hawaii University Press as Indianised States of Southeast Asia). The 'etats hindouises' is essentially a dharma-dhamma continuum evidenced by thousands of Hindu-Bauddha temples in Malaysia, Indonesia, Thailand, Cambodia, Vietnam, Laos, Burma and other states and historical presence of Hindu kings in the region for over one millennium.

The arts, literature and statecraft are substantial replicas of the Indian civilization tradition. Tathagata, Gautama the Buddha called it esha dhammo sanantano (this sanatana dharma, this universal eternal ethic). When Tagore visited Java, he sang about the golden threads of friendship between India and Indonesia. The Republi Day of 26 Jan. 2011 was graced by the presence of President Susilo Yodhoyono of Indonesia. The opportunities for carrying the cultural bonds into socio-economic spheres of cooperation are immense and have to be seized by India looking east and by USA and other western leaders supporting the emergence of an economic federation among the Indian Ocean Rim states. The earlier experiences of ASEAN and Asea Pacific Cooperation have to be formalised in an institutional set up as a counterpoise to the European Community.

The IOC will be a six trillion dollar powerhouse which can provide for new opportunities for expanded creation of national wealth in the region by providing employment opportunities and integrating the region's finances into the global economic order. A beginning can be made by expanding the Free Trade Agreements of the type just signed (July 2011) between India and Malaysia to all states of the IOC and by promoting Buddha tourism to India's Buddhist pilgrimate centres. The archaeological monuments of the region need to be restored and the priests of the states trained in the performance of traditional festivities and prayers in the Hindu-Bauddha temples of the region. Cultural exchanges in the fields of higher technical education, use of satellite and IT technologies, exchanges among oceanographers will go a long way in strengthening cooperation among the states of IOC.

IOR-ARC has to be given economic content through Free Trade agreements and MOUs for bilateral, multi-lateral cooperation in project such as the development of the Mekong River delta, Irrawady River delta which are economic infrastructure projects related to Himalayan rivers.

This need not be seen as a competition between India and China for presence in the region. India and China, together with USA and other developed countries can participate in a common enterprise of promoting economic development in the region which is struggling to wriggle out of the slow pace of post-colonial economic development initiatives. A region which accounted for about 80% of the world GDP (pace Angus Maddison) just three centuries ago can find its rightful place in the comity of nations.

Many opportunities exist to provide an economic push to many of the poorest countries among the Indian Ocean Rim States (Indian Ocean Community). While India and Australia account for almost 40% of the total GDP of this Community, by increased regional cooperation, it should be possible to raise the income levels of the least developed countries (mainly islands) of the Community.

Infrastructure projects which are ready to take-off and can provide the economic push include: Trans-Asian Railway, Trans-Asian Highway, Indian Ocean Tuna initiative, Indian Ocean Hydrographic initiatives (including tsunami warning[90] and tsunami protection systems, control and management of climatic systems and projects to control erosion of the coastlines and desiccation of coral reefs). Member states India, Australia and China can provide the space imaging technologies and techniques for managing marine bioreserve resources in starting an initiative for Indian Ocean Aquatic and Mineral Resources Management initiative.

The devastating tsunami of Dec. 26, 2004 which took 260,000 lives is a stark reminder that the Indian Ocean is one integral entity which cuts across a vast Ocean Rim of over 63,000 miles stretching from Mauritius off the African coast to Tasmania (Australia).

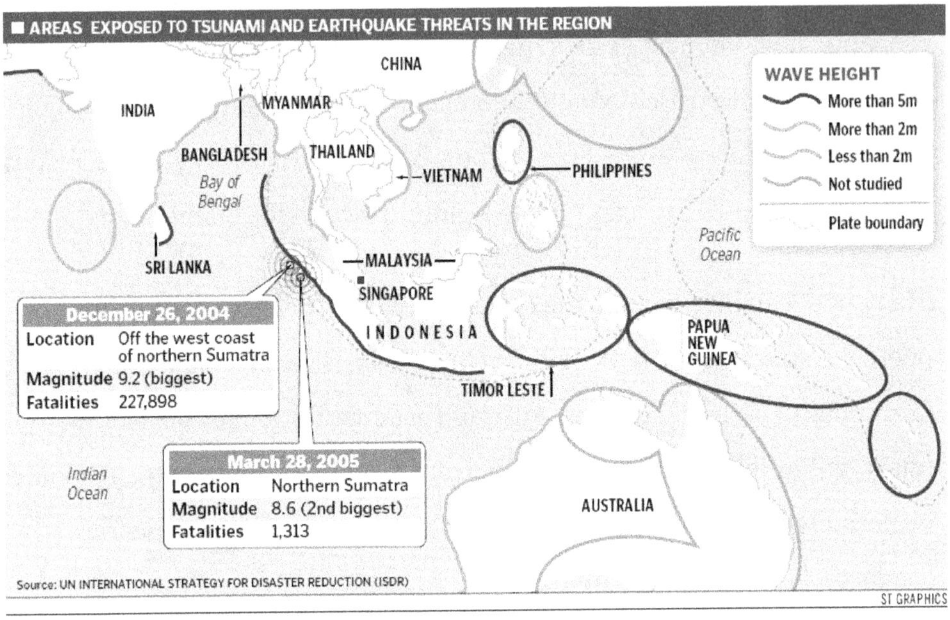

Tsunami effect: 2,60,000 lives lost

Destruction of Aceh island, damage in beaches north of Chennai and Nagapattinam

Sea-bed has risen by about 200 m. in some regions

2/3 of the aquatic life and corals devastated in the Biosphere Reserve/Marine National Parks

Religious and cultural sites, 8th-12th centuries[91]

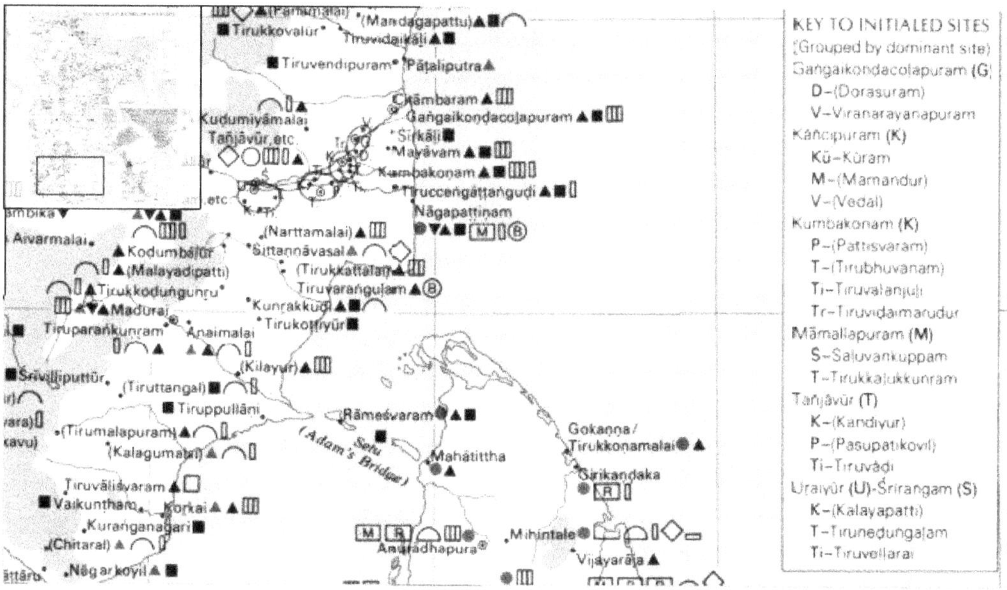

Islamic expansion and changing Western views of South Asia, 7th-12th centuries (Al-Biruni's record)

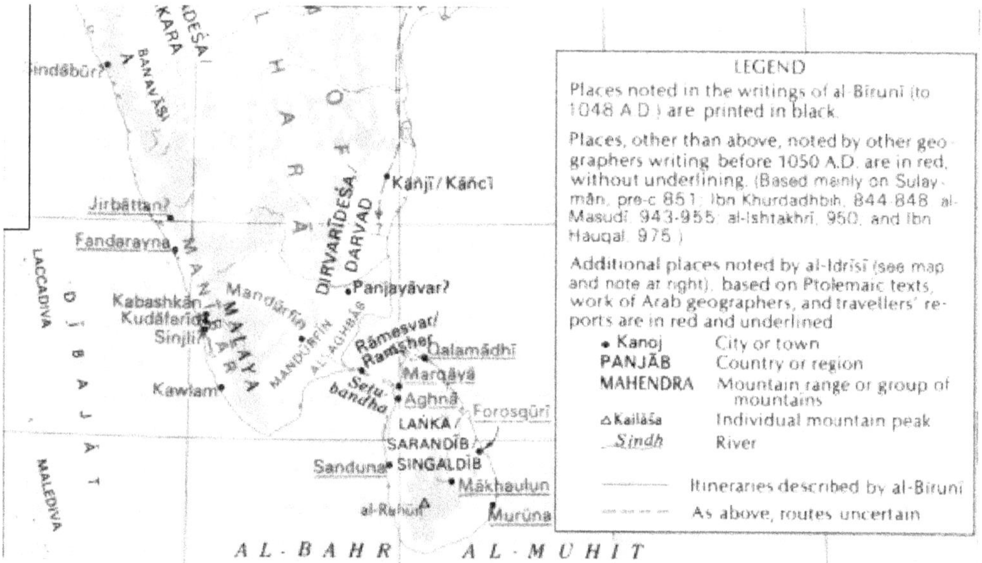

\

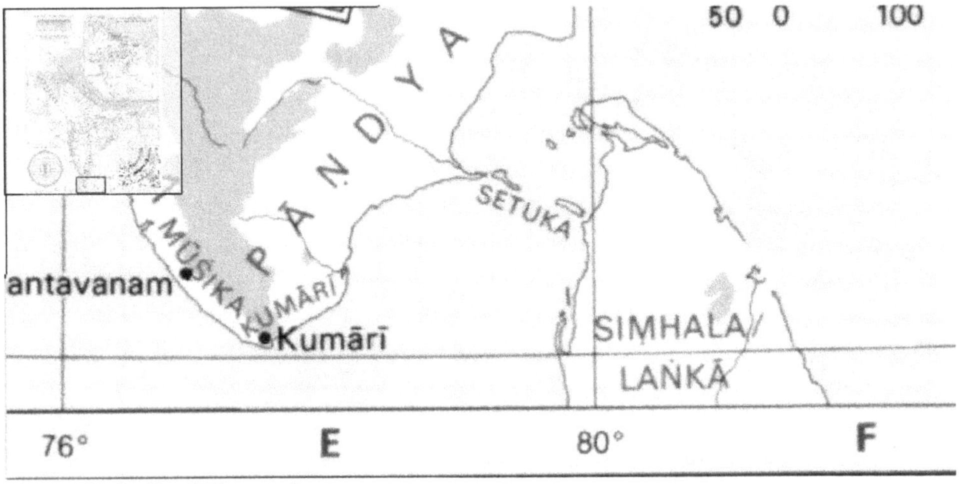

Puranic India (Bharata)

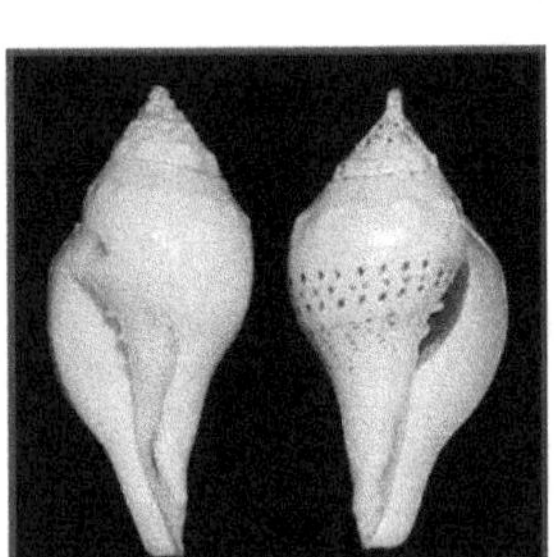

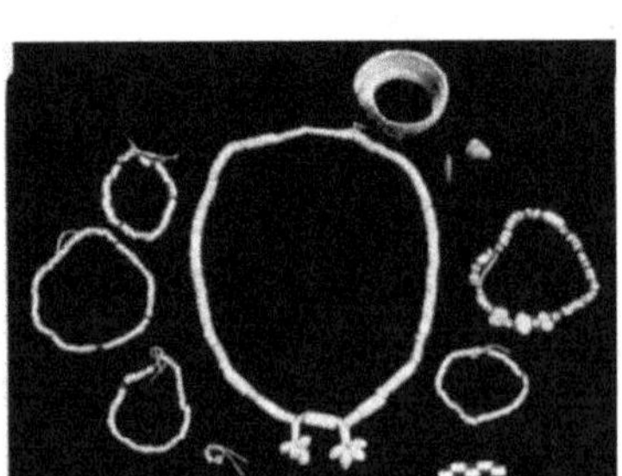

Mannar as trademark for aquatic species, śankha, green turtle in the marine bioreserve of Setusamudram

Kilakkarai and other places produce s'ankha, a cultural symbol venerated in Bharatiya traditions (West Bengal Dev. Corpn. In Kilakarai has an annual turnover of Rs. 100 crores to procure s'ankha from Rama Setu coastal zone)

Śankha is unique to Bharatam coastline, not found anywhere else in the world

Date of the woman's burial with ornaments 6500 Years

Before Common Era.

Save marine wealth:
Vegetarian sea-cow, green turtle

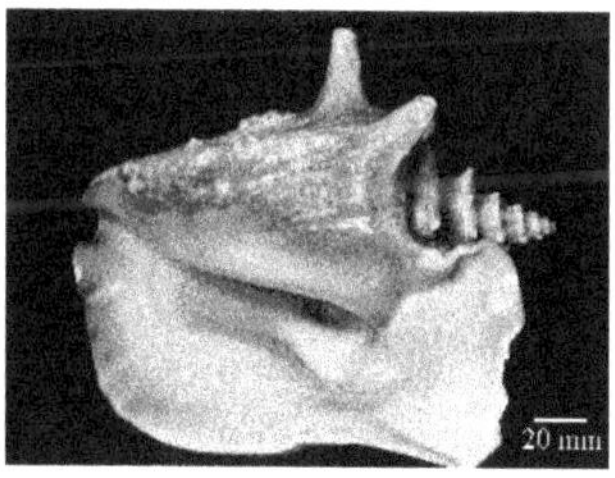

The only place in the world where dugong lives.

Dugong is a sea-cow which eats only sea-grass.

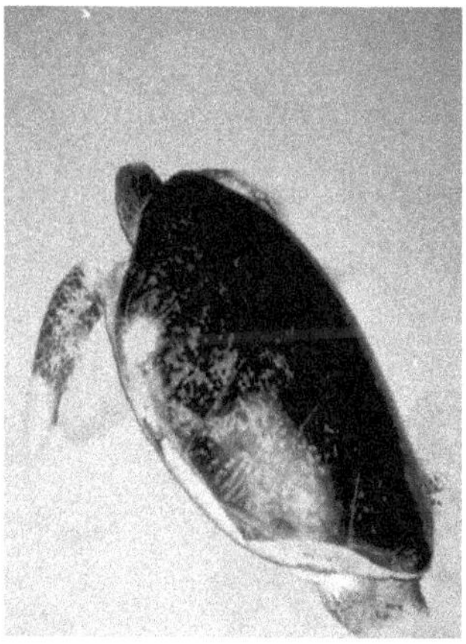

Green Sea Turtle Chelonia mydas nesting on Barrow Island off the Pilbara coast. Several thousand of this endangered species live in the Cocos

(Keeling) Islands area. Sea turtles are at risk due to hunting in developing

nations, loss of nesting habitats, disease, and collisions with boats (© 1979 - 2012 Carlo Kopp)

The critically endangered Hawksbill Turtle Eretmochelys imbricata (Bruno Navez, Creative Commons Licence).

The abundant and endemic Christmas Island terrestrial Red Crab Gecarcoidea natalis has suffered a claimed 30% population loss due to

invasive pest species, primarily the Yellow Crazy Ant Anoplolepis gracilipes. The Red Crab is a critical component of the local rainforest ecosystem and its loss presents as an "ecological cascade failure", where loss of a species produces cascading

damage effects across the habitat (Jarich / Rebecca Dominguez, Creative Commons Licence).

Christmas Island is claimed to host the world's largest single population of the terrestrial Coconut crab Birgus latro, which can grow to a weight in excess of 4 kg, and has a claimed lifespan in excess of sixty years. While the species is widespread across the Indo-Pacific islands, including the Cocos (Keeling) Islands, it is hunted by humans and uncommon in populated areas. On Christmas Island it is seriously threatened by the Yellow Crazy Ant.

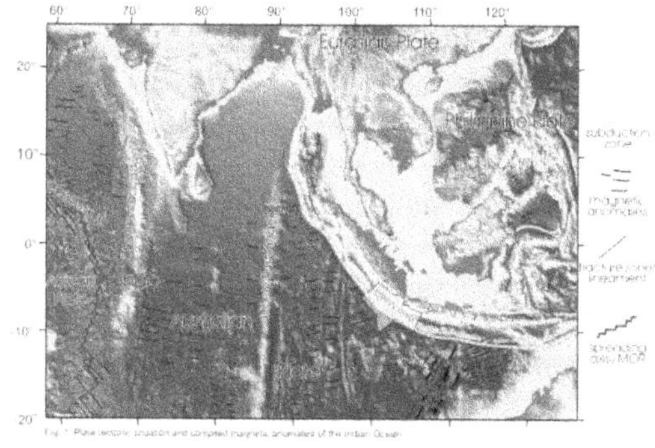

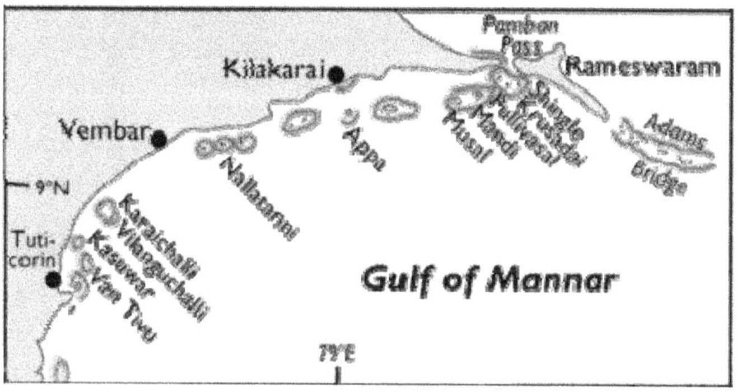

This example was photographed in 2006 on Christmas Island (Jarich / Rebecca Dominguez, Creative Commons Licence).

There are over 3,600 unique aquatic species in the Gulf of Mannar Bioreserve national parks.

Indian plate dynamically moves northwards @6 cm. per year resulting in plate tectonics (e.g Bhuj earthquake, Aceh quake).

Mannar Volcanics 100 m. old: Rama Setu an ancient submarine canyon collapse

Tectonic setting:

Plate subduction Sunda plate

Direction of inferred fault-line

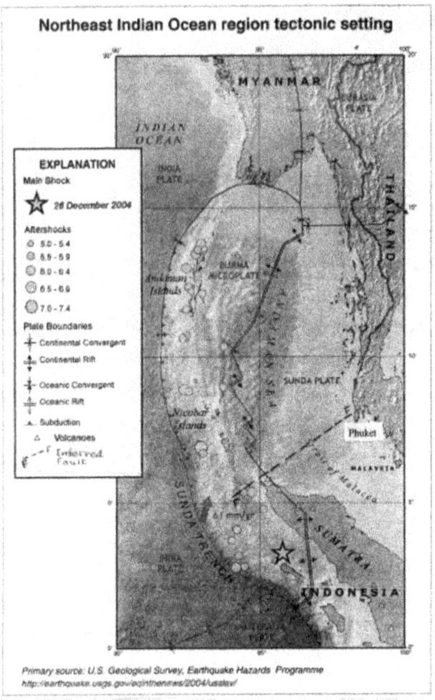

Fig. 23 - Map showing the epicenter of 26 December, 2004 Sumatra earthquake and its relation to the tectonic setting of Northeast Indian Ocean Region (after USGS Earthquake Hazards Programme, 2004)

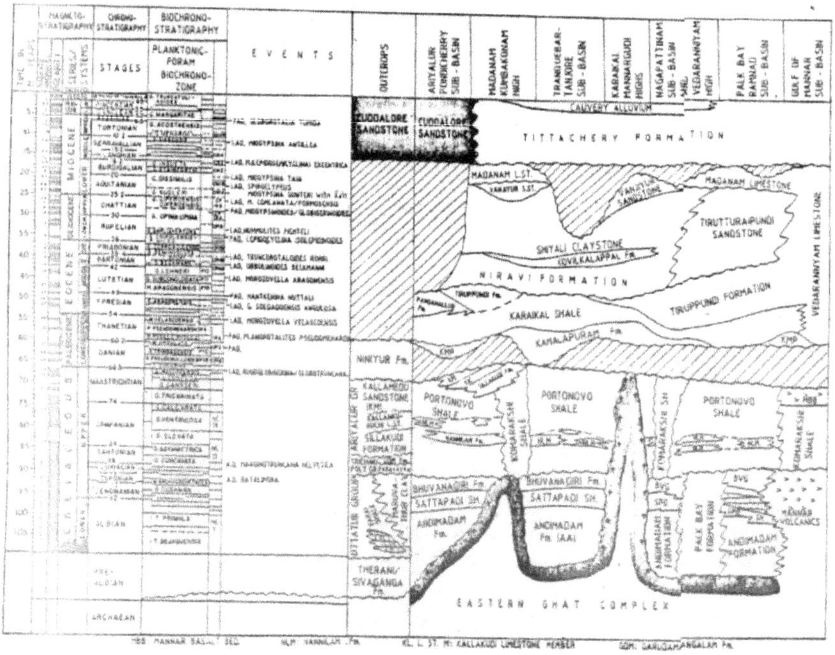

sucking in tsunami

Build tsunami protection walls as part of any canal project: example, tsunami wall in Japan

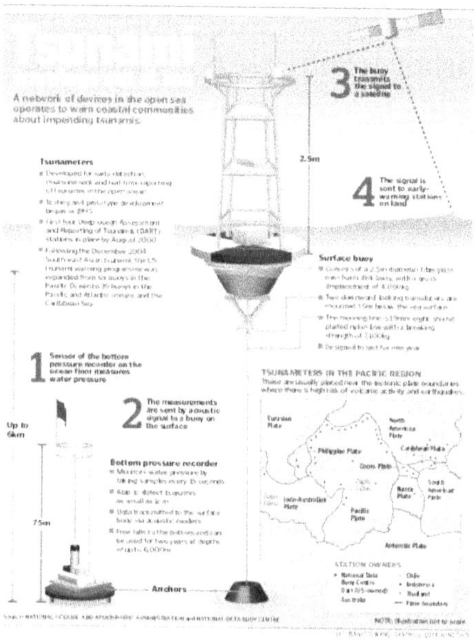

The tsunami natural hazard on the Indian Ocean can be a substantial

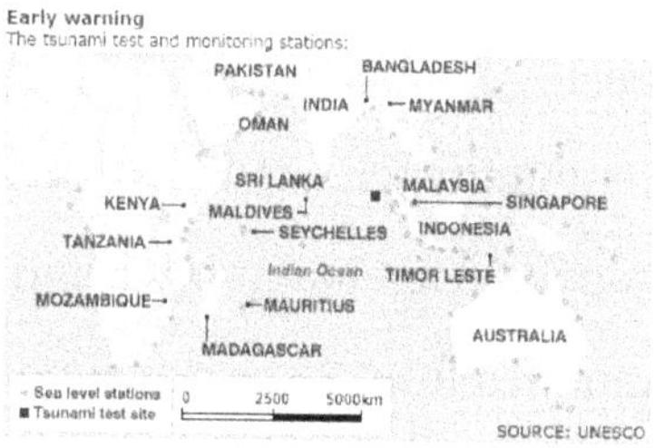

reason why the Indian Ocean Community should come into being to create cooperative institutions to harness the riches of the Indian Ocean.[92]

Many Indian Ocean Community member states are served by the Himalayan glacier waters (including the Mekong delta). Water management systems can become a major area for regional cooperation, formulation and implementation of sustainable water management projects, including development of coastal and inter-state waterways.

Many Indian Ocean Community member states are agrarian economies. Member states with proven records of development of dairy industry, achievement of green revolution by optimizing the yields from land through effective cropping patterns, seed-genetics, soil and water management systems can help in formulating regional cooperation projects in the areas of cold-storage for fisheries and related products and of establishing self-reliant dairy and agro-industry infrastructure.

There are many institutions in the member countries of Indian Ocean Community who can provide the scientific-technological framework for the developmental project and technical assistance initiatives. Some examples from India, to name a few, are: Naional Institute of Oceanography, National Institute of Ocean Technology, Indian Ocean Studies Research Group. ASEAN and APEC are regional cooperation initiatives which can be complementary to and supportive of the Asian Development Bank initiative to set up and sustain an Indian Ocean Community. As a first step, technical assistance projects can be mounted to explore the possibilities of setting up an Indian Ocean Free Trade Zone leading in due course to a common Indian Ocean Currency together with a Indian Ocean Central Bank, to provide a fiscal and financial substructure for quickening the pace of the now slow pace of development in many poor countries of the IOC.

The idea of IOC can become a reality if the lead is taken by intellectuals and a framework for coordination among collaborating institutions can be put in place.

Śreṇi dharma

For nearly 3000 years since 800 BCE and perhaps earlier, *śreṇi* has been the corporate form of varṇa system of social organization -- *varṇāśrama dharma* -- in Hindu industrial, arts, crafts, business and civic entities. This *śreṇi* corporate form pre-dates the earliest proto-Roman corporations; *śreṇi* was widespread in Ancient India in business, social and civic activities; this corporate form continues to exist even today in Independent India, despite the adoption of a written Constitution governed by principles of Roman jurisprudence and laissez-faire economic principles governing the wealth of the nation. Indian ethical pluralism is called *dharma* ; *śreṇi dharma* is *dharma* applicable to a corporation. The laws governing *śreṇi* are called *śreṇi dharma* , emphasizing social responsibility of corporations.*śreṇi dharma* provides the mechanism to embed 'social ethic' enhancing the corporate model of capitalism or socialism either of which operates within the framework of 'rational, materialistic economic ethos'. Hindu society attaches importance to ethical values, *ātman* (innate cosmic energy) as also to the creation of wealth of a nation. An ascetic is as respected in Hindu society as a just ruler of a state. This remarkable integration of materialistic ethos with the social ethic is unique in the story of human civilizations. *śreṇi dharma* as social capital can supply the missing element of trusteeship. This *śreṇi dharma* constitutes an impressive contribution of Hindu civilization to economic thought, adding spiritual value to materialistic ethos.

In Maslow's (1943) hierarchy or pyramid of human physiological needs which are at the bottom to the need of self-actualization which is at the pinnacle, the expectation is that every member of a corporation will be motivated and resolve to reach the pinnacle, up the ladder. This resolution has to be a vow, a dedication in the process of understanding the essential unity of the *ātman* (spark from the divine) with the*paramātman* (the supreme divine).

In the tradition of Indian Ocean civilizations, this unity is *dharma - dhamma*, the eternal, ethical ordering principle.

A modern *śreṇi* can evolve into a *dharma* corporation, exemplifying economic justice in a moral order.

A facet of dharma-dhamma to combat greed which is the root cause of corruption is śreṇi dharma which can be elaborated as social ethic, social insurance and social capital which

- supplies the missing element – of *dāna,*'giving, liberality'-- in the economic progress imperative,
- dramatically mitigates the deleterious effect of greed resulting in misappropriation of wealth created by economic progress,
- obviates the need for state-sponsored regulation or interventions, and
- results in a socially responsible corporate form as an economic engine.

Re-adoption of the millennial old śreṇi dharma will manadate the reform and amendment of company law by incorporation of a *śreṇi dharma* clause in the articles of association. This clause should specify a percentage, say 5 to 10 per cent of the turnover of a corporation to be accumulated into and spent as *śreṇi dharma* fund for social causes, beyond the core business of the corporation. By making the operations of the fund auditable and subject to public scrutiny through financial sentinels such as regulators of the marketplace, a legally binding process can be achieved, by adding the spiritual value of ethical responsibility to the financial balance sheet of a corporation. The Chairperson and Board of Directors of such a corporation incorporating *śreṇi dharma* will be responsible to make disclosures in their annual reports to shareholders the contributions made into and outgo from the *śreṇi dharma* fund. The fault-line of *lobha*, 'greed', will be gradually jumped with such mandated provisions of incorporation, periodical reporting to share-holders and voluntary enforcement of the provisions by the officers of a modern *śreṇi.*

Modern high-growth sectors like the Information Technology (IT) sector should include a clause of incorporation which can be called *śreṇi dharma* .Such an incorporation will help incorporate in a fast-growing technology sector of the economy of the world the ethic of social responsibility. There is evidence that many SSI clusters continue to be governed by written trust deeds (in Sanskrit, *śreṇi dharma* or in Tamil, *aṟakkaṭṭaḷai* – the *dharma* statute). This form of incorporation can be extended to large scale or global level industry or enterprise. One reason why this salutary form has not been introduced is the excessive reliance on Roman jurisprudence with emphasis on individual rights without a corresponding emphasis on social responsibility and duty of a corporate entity. The deficiency can be remedied by calling for a mandatory incorporation clause stipulating a pre-determined percentage of the turnover of an incorporated corporation to be set aside as social security and as social capital to be exclusively used for social welfare.

śreṇi dharma is a voluntary and spontaneous fulfillment of social ethic of a corporation in a polity. *śreṇi dharma* , a unique contribution to economic thought and practice, should reform corporations world-wide – to jump the fault-lines of greed, corruption and excesses of state or corporate power while adding value to materialistic ethos, upgrading the joy of material living to ecstasy of being and sharing as bliss.

The acceptance of *śreṇi dharma* in Indian Ocean Community, as one of the youngest nations on the globe (accounting for 70% of the population as less than 35 years of age), will result in a paradigm shift introducing social ethic in global economic thought and practice. Acceptance may involve reforms in Companies Act or Memoranda of Association or Incorporation of Companies, with specific, non-fuzzy ethical rules such as an agreement to set apart 5 to 10% of the income of a corporation for social causes. The enforcement of the rules has to be voluntary and by the corporation itself. The corporate tribunals will judge the deviant behavior from the agreed ethical norms and social responsibilities including specifications of punishment for disregard of the rules and procedures for legal redress by appeal against the verdict, say, of a *śreṇi* tribunal.

A rich civilizational tradition that Indian Ocean Community represents – in the comity of nations -- is destined to contribute to economic justice in a sustainable, global, moral order.

As Indian Ocean Community, free from colonial domination, emerges as a global economic power, it is time to recognize and reinstate *śreṇi dharma*, or social capital, as the missing element of economics to create, nurture and enhance the wealth of nations, while making *śreṇi dharma* an integral part of modern economic paradigm.

With dharma, yes, we can. We can be the agents of change of the world economy, reaching out to the unreached, endeavoring to achieve the ethical imperative: *sarve bhavantu sukhinah* (let all beings be happy) (āḏi śankarācārya).

Hrishikesh Vinod, who edited a Handbook of Hindu Economic Thought (which includes an article on *śreṇi dharma* by S. Kalyanaraman[93]) referred to an interesting article of Max H. Bazerman and Ann E. Tenbrunsel (2011) which discussed lapses in behavioral ethics – among regulators, prosecutors, auditors, journalists -- caused, sometimes, by their self-interest to protect reputation of corporate clients. Bazerman and Tenbrunsel make a fine distinction between such willful actions or ignorance. Maybe it is human nature to condone such lapses, but the organizational structure should provide for honest discussions within a corporation about ethical transgressions which result in excessive greed. The structure and function of Hindu corporate form has shown how a commitment can be achieved by corporate clients and regulators alike by setting up a standard percentage of *śreṇi dharma*. This overarching corporate ethic with built-in behavioral ethic expected from all corporate actors and incorporation of this mandatory social welfare contribution in the memorandum of incorporation will help mitigate the effects of excessive greed.

A monograph is presented in three sections[94]:

1. Evolution of *śreṇi dharma as* social corporate statute over 3 millennia;

2. Economics of *śreṇi* as ethical cure for *lobha*, 'greed';

3. Incorporation of Hindu *śreṇi* in economic thought and practice.

Śreṇi dharma can be operationalised by reform steps of the type suggested by the late Rajaji[95]:

"Fate of the nation is doomed if corruption poisons its life in very sphere, as most people feel and complain that it does today in our land. Administration at all levels, the economic controls which the Government exercises over those engaged in production and distribution, the transport service by road, rail and air, the elections that are held to recruit persons to the various public bodies from the villages up to Delhi, these and other public activities are poisoned with this fatal poison, and the process is so widely prevalent that people seem reconciled to it. Democracy is disclosing itself as a puppet dancing to the pull of money-strings. It is painful having to say all this about one's own country, one's own people and one's own administration. But the evil cannot be got rid of by being un-confessed and our sufferings borne in silence.

"Human nature cannot tolerate this state of affairs. The crisis will lead to revolution of some kind, communist or fascist or military. The people have to face this corruption on one side and high prices and unbearable tax-levies on the other. Oppression and corruption must lead to revolt, and passing through anarchy, democracy must turn into dictatorship. Neither can the resulting tyranny escape the total evil of the times. The dictatorship will not be a relief, for that, too, will be corrupt.

"The only hope for the nation lies in the possibility of restoring good government. The interference of ministers and others with legitimate and illegitimate powers derived from so called democracy has transformed a fairly good government (of 1950s) into an intolerably bad administrative machine. Can we retrace the steps and secure an improvement in the morale of our administrative machinery? I believe we can. Let us hope we can secure a dedicated set of young people to join the service ranks in all departments through whom we can get this revolution of character accomplished. In order to hope for this, we should make sure of a few things besides appealing to intelligent youth to dedicate them selves to a holy war against corruption.

"We must elevate the simple life to the status it had enjoyed in Gandhian and pre-independence days. It is the 'standard of life' that has corrupted and is corrupting our souls.

"We should make administration less expensive by reducing the number of people engaged in that unproductive but important work, while at the same time paying adequate salaries to those employed.

"The development of productive industries, should be unhampered by controls and bureaucratic hurdles, so that they may grow quickly and absorb more and more of intelligent young men instead of their being driven by necessity to government service.

"Less taxation and less inflation, abandonment of wholly wrong plan of finding industrial capital by oppressive taxation, and release of private capital and private initiative from the barbed wire entanglement of Central planning – these will help to a large extent in clearing the air of the poisonous fog of corruption.

"There is hope if the young men and women of our country vow to live simply, and to be honest under any circumstances and in any employment. Education is of no use if this dedicated spirit does not crown the acquisition of useful knowledge. Rectitude and rectitude only can save us. Hope thus rests on the restoration of faith in God, and even this must be given by Him. May He give us that faith in His mercy and enable us to save our dear motherland, which does not fate that over-hangs it."

Rāṣṭram -State-Panchayat structure for a dharma-dhamma constitution

Rāṣṭram is the path which led the ancestors of present-day Indians to move into Indian Ocean region to present the realization of janapadas and organization of the state, governed by dharma, the global ethic.

Within this all-enveloping framework, dharma as applied to governance, called rajadharma is explained as the facilitation of individuals of the samajam attaining the purushartha of dharma, artha and kaama without transgressing dharma, the ethical principles of conduct and inter-personal relationships. This is affirmed by Barhaspatya sutra, II-43-44: "The goal of rajaniti (polity) is the accomplishment of dharma, artha, kaama. Artha and kaama must be subject to the test of dharma. Dharma was supreme law of the state and rulers and subjects alike were subservient to this law. Dharma is the constitutional law of modern parlance, explaining the contours of the functions and responsibilities of the state, constraining the ruler by regulations which restrain the exercise of sovereignty by the ruler – a parallel to the paradigm of checks and balances enshrined in modern constitutions to prevent abuse of power while ensuring equal protection to the subjects without discrimination. "Just as the mother Earth gives an equal support to all the be living, a king must give support to all without no discrimination." (Manusmruti). "The king must furnish protection to associations following ordinances of the Veda (Naigamas) which protection should extend to all – those non-believers (paashandi) and to others as well." (*Naradasmruti, Dharmakos'a*, p. 870).

The absence of discrimination, provisions to check abuse of power and enjoining the state to promote the individual's and samajam's activities for the attainment of purushartha [achieving the goals of life -- of dharma (righteous conduct), of artha (economic well-being) and of kaama (mental well-being)] are the key facets of rajadharma. Such a rajadharma is beyond secular and is a sacred trust to be administered with diligence and commitment.

Such a rajadharma is exemplified by ramarajyam which is evoked by many rulers of Bharatam in many parts of the nation in their references to Sri Ramachandra as the ideal ruler whose example the rulers hoped to emulate in rendering social justice and in regulating the affairs of the state.

Ramarajyam is a dharma polity, governed by a dharma constitution. This is the reason why Valmiki refers to Rama in eloquent terms: Ramo vigrahavan dharmah. (Rama is the very embodiment of dharma).

The supremacy of dharma is emphasized in Brhadaranyakopanisad:

tadetat kṣatrasya kṣatram yaddharmah

tasmāddharmātparam nāsti

atho abalīyān balīyāmsamāśamsate dharmeṇa

yatha rājjā evam

The law (Dharma) is the king of kings. No one is superior to Dharma. The Dharma aided by the power of the king enables the weak to prevail over the strong.

This is further emphasised in Karṇa Parva (ch. 69, verse 58):

dhāraṇād dharma ity āhurdharmo dhārayate prajāh

yat syād dhāraṇasamyuktam sa dharma iti niścayah

Dharms sustains the society; Dharma maintains the social order; Dharma ensures well-being and progress of humanity; Dharms is surely that which fulfils these objectives.

The two great epics Ramayana and Mahabharata and the Bhagavata Purana explain dharma in action, the application of the 'ordering principles' in specific real-life situations, in moments of creative tension such as when a proponent like Arjuna had to decide to fight against his own kith and kin, members of his own kula. This moment of decision results in the delineation of the Dharmakshetra (the domain of dharma) in that Song Celestial, Bhagavad Gita. An enduring metaphor of the Bhagavatam is samudramanthanam: deva and asura apparently in conflict work together to harness the resources of the ocean by churning the ocean together. This togetherness to achieve artha and kaama is a dharmic cooperative endeavour, an example of a samajam in harmony, pulling together for a common purpose – that purpose is loka hitam, 'well-being of loka'. Loka hitam is the touchstone which determines the dharmic nature of positive action. Just as satyam is truth that is pleasing, dharma is action which is loka-hitaaya 'for the well-being of the society'. How should such action be performed or such responsibility be discharged? Governed by ethical conduct, a social ethic which respects the responsibilities being discharged by everyone in society.

Dharma is sacred because it is the divine ordering principle. Dharma is the principle which recognizes the way things are or the nature of things or phenomena. In Thai language, the compound dharmacarth (dharma carati) means 'nature'. Hence, the compound sva-dharma in the evolution of sanātana dharma in Bhāratam, means 'law and responsibility, according to one's nature'.

Rigveda notes that ṛtam 'occurrence of phenomena' or 'order' is dharma. Atharva Veda notes: Prithivim dharmaṇādhṛtam 'the world is upheld by dharma'. Sanatana Dharma in bhāratiya metaphysics (elaborated further in Buddha, Jaina, Khalsa pantha thought) is not a moral connotation. It is an inexorable organizing, creative principle which operates on the plane of the aatman and the cosmos.

Sanatana dharma is thus beyond a law regulating an individual's action. It is the very _expression of the divine. Such adherence to the divine principle is the purusharta, the purpose of life.

Let us see how an Egyptian islamist understood dharma: "It [dharma] is, so to speak, the essential nature of a being, comprising the sum of its particular qualities or characteristics, and determining, by virtue of the tendencies or dispositions it implies, the manner in which this being will conduct itself, either in a general way or in relation to each particular circumstance. The same idea may be applied, not only to a single being, but also to an organized collectivity, to a species, to all the beings included in a cosmic cycle or state of existence, or even to the whole order of the Universe; it then, at one level or another, signifies conformity with the essential nature of beings..." [Rene Guenon (aka Sheikh 'Abd Al Wahid Yahya), *Introduction to the Study of Hindu Doctrines*]

Bhishma explained to Yudhishthira: "It is very difficult to define the dharma. Dharma was explained as that which helps the elevation of the human. This is the reason, this that assures well-being is assuredly dharma. The learned rishis declared: this that supports is dharma."

Like satyam, dharma was explained with reference to the beneficial effect it generates: well-being and progress of humanity. "Dharma is this that supports and that assures the progress and the well-being of all in this world and the eternal happiness in the other world. Dharma is promulgated in the form of orders (positive and negative: Vidhi and Nishedha)." This was the elucidaton of Madhvacharya in his commentary on Parasarasmruti. This rendering of the semantics of dharma explains why dharma covered all aspects of life for the well-being of the individual and also the samajam.

The Karna Parva, Ch. 59, verse 58, praises the dharma in the following terms:

The Dharma supports the corporation, The Dharma maintains the social order, The Dharma assures well-being and the progress of humanity, The Dharma is certainly this that fills these objectives."

Jaimini, the author of the famous Purvamimamsa and uthara Mimamsa, explains that:

Dharma-dhamma is this that is indicated in the Vedas as driving to the biggest good.

> "Though the country and the people may be divided into different states (provinces) for convenience of administration, the country is one integral whole, its people a single people living under a single imperium derived from a single source." -- Dr. B.R.Ambedkar, Chairman, Drafting Committee of the Constitution of India

Justice Madan Mohan Punchhi, Former Chief Justice of India was appointed in April 2007, to head a Commission on Centre-State Relations . The Commission's Report in 7 volumes was presented to Govt. of India on 31 March 2010. An earlier Commission on Centre-State (Province)

Relations (referred to as the Sarkaria Commission after the name of its Chairman Mr. Justice R.S. Sarkaria) in its report submitted in 1988 observed:- "Decentralisation of real power to local institutions would help defuse the threat of centrifugal forces, increase popular involvement all along the line, broaden the base of our democratic polity, promote administrative efficiency and improve the health and stability of inter-governmental relations .... Unfortunately, there was not only inadequate territorial and functional decentralization in India when the country became independent, but there has also been a pervasive trend towards greater centralization of powers over the years, inter alia, due to the pressure of powerful socio- economic forces" - (Volume I, p.543).

Recognizing this democratic deficit, the Constitution was amended in 1992 (73rd and 74th Constitution Amendment Acts) to introduce a third tier system of governance at the level of Panchayats and Municipalities.

The question posed to the Punchhi Commission was: 'Are the existing arrangements governing Centre-State (Province) relations – legislative, executive and financial – envisaged in the Constitution as they have evolved over the years, working in a manner that can meet the aspirations of the Indian society as also the requirements of an increasingly globalizing world? If not, what are the impediments and how can they be remedied without violating the basic structure of the Constitution?'

The Punchhi commission notes: "The dictum of 'basic structure' of the Constitution propounded by the Supreme Court in the celebrated *Keshavananda Bharati* case also tied the hands of the Centre in important ways. The effect, *inter alia*, was that while the States (Provinces) felt handicapped in pursuing development programmes of their own for lack of adequate funds, the Centre found itself hamstrung even when there was serious breakdown in law and order in some areas." (Vol. 1, p. xxi)

Making over 200 recommendations, the Punchhi Commission also recommended amendment of Articles 355 and 356 to enable Central rule of trouble-torn areas, an internal security structure on the lines of the US Homeland Security department, making National Integration Council meaningful by making NIC meet at least once a year, and amending the Communal Violence Bill to allow deployment of Central forces without the state's (province's) consent for a short period, removal of a Governor through impeachment by the State (Province) assembly and providing for a say to the state (Province) Chief Minister in the appointment of governor, giving a right to the Governor to sanction prosecution of a minister against the advice of the council of ministers.

Overall, the recommendations of the two Commissions -- Sarkaria Commission and Punchhi Commission – have been disappointing skirting the main issue of resolving the developmental imperative of the ratram with the security imperative of the rastram.

Both the Commissions and the standing Finance Commissions which have been appointed every five years, have missed the wood for the trees, by suggesting tinkering with the system by looking at the instruments of state as instruments of violence.

These Commissions have failed to recognize the serious threats faced by the rastram on the key issues of integrity and security caused by 1) the threats of destroying the polity by criminalization and corrupt practices;

and 2) the national security threats from external and internal sources of fomenting communal tensions, by Naxalite or Maoist insurgencies and hostile neighbours seeking lebensraum. The colonial loot of unprecedented dimensions have been rivaled by the post-colonial loot by stashing away black money in tax havens abroad. (One estimate given by Director, CBI reckons this at US Dollars 500 billion, that is, Rs. 20 lakh crores). Effective remedial measures have not been suggested to undo the devastation caused to national integration efforts by the formation of Pakistan and by not commending steps to implement Article 44 of the Constitution of India which calls for a Uniform Civil Code. Article 44 is merely the first step in achieving a sense of identity among all citizens of India that they owe allegiance to the Rastram, saying no to sectarian ideologies and false denominations of secularism.

While all men are created equal, traditions of India, that is Bharat, hold that dharma-dhamma has endowed us with certain unalienable responsibilities for abhyudayam and nihshreyas (social welfare and individual unity of the atman with paramatman). The Rastram is a dharma-dhamma saapeksha rastram. This inalienable dictum, this dharma-dhamma, this foundation of the rastram which cannot be surrendered, sold or transferred for any ideology, should get enshrined in the Preamble to the Constitution by declaring a dharma-dhamma saapeksha rastram. This dharma-dhamma declaration should precede any attempt to restate the structural features of the state.

If this Constitutional Amendment is beyond the powers of the Parliament pace Keshavananda Bharati case, let there be a new Constituent Assembly to redraw the dharma constitution for the rastram. The absurd definition of secularism gets exemplified by devious attempts made to translate 'secular' in the Preamble as 'dharma nirapekshata' in Hindi official version of the Constitution kept in Rashtrapati Bhavan. Luckily, this bizarre translation was NOT approved and the word 'secular' was translated into Hindi as: 'pantha nirapekshata', that is, neutrality as to individual religious path preferences.

How should a dharma sāpekṣa Rāṣṭram be structured? Rāṣṭram is the path which enlightens. The supreme divinity is rastrii, the divine force which defines all dharmas in all walks of life and all facets of existence in a sustainable global order for wealth creation, equitable distribution and use. Such a rastram calls for a United States along the Indian Ocean Rim to create an Indian Ocean Community remembering that the largest Vishnu mandiram of the globe is in Angkor Wat, Cambodia. Such a federation of about 59 states along the Indian Indian Ocean Rim will be an economic powerhouse for abhyudayam of over 2 billion people. This organization can undo the raves of the colonial regimes which left many of these states in an impoverished state.

Such a federating union has to federate local communities, recognized as Panchayats or Municipalities or Corporations in the Indian state and comparable formations in other states of the Indian Ocean Rim.

The imperative of empowering local communities, janapadas will be consonant with the traditional forms which had evolved over millennia for involving the people of the janapadas in socio-economic activities. A good example is provided by the Uttaramerur inscription of the 12th century which described the formation of village councils after due democratic elections and after due process of selecting council members of exemplary rectitude, from within the community. Such localization of developmental activity (abhyudayam) will mean the transfer of power directly to the people. This transfer has to become meaningful by an automatic transfer of central finances directly to the panchayat raj institutions for projects such as local, small-scale industries, maintenance of roads, building and maintenance of schools, primary health-care centers and other civic responsibilities of the panchayat. The Panchayat will also have to be empowered to monitor the functioning of large industries within the geographical domain of the Panchayat, even if it means the control of, say, a nuclear power station. The present structure of central-state (province) division of responsibilities by State (Province), Central and Concurrent Lists has to be radically revamped to entrust responsibilities to the third tier, the Panchayat.

Peoples' Parliament

Inter-state transactions of trade, defense and foreign affairs can be the responsibility of the Centre. Providing for enabling legislative framework can be the responsibility of the state. The real executive has to be the Janapada, the Panchayat. This structural formation for a Rastram is a feasible proposition which can build upon the types of structures which have been proven to work effectively, for example, in Peoples' Republic of China. Decentralize for development and integrity of the state, centralize for security of the state from trans-border threats such as those from terrorism or religious conversion missions. A Peoples' Parliament can be brought into being to provide for an ideological umbrella to the

Parliamentary institutions such as the Lok Sabha or Rajya Sabha in India. The Peoples' Parliament should be composed as a Constituent Assembly .

In India, there are 640 districts. Each district should elect four representatives from among the Panchayati Raj institutions to function as members of the Peoples' Parliament which is the Constituent Assembly. This Assembly should meet at least once a year to oversee the discharge of legislative functions entrusted to the Provinces and the Panchayats Raj institutions. The Peoples' Parliament should also define the Centre-Province-Panchayati Raj institutional responsibilities using three lists: Central List, Province List, Panchayat List. These Lists should be a total revamp of the existing Union, State and Concurrent Lists defining the responsibilities of the structural components of the India polity.

The structure of the Rastram as a trans-national structure, can be regulated with the following broad allocation of responsibilities, as lists, to the three constituent institutions: Constituent Assembly, State Parliament, Panchayat Administration.

Rastram list to include: Inter-state commerce and inter-state development projects such as Trans-Asian Highway, Trans-Asian Railway, Implementation of the Law of the Sea by extending territorial waters to 200 nautical miles from the base, Interpol.

State list to include: defence, atomic energy, foreign affairs, citizenship, transport, communication, currency..

Panchayat list to include: local government, education, police, justice, agriculture, commerce, banking, insurance, control of industries, development of mines, mineral and oil resources, elections, civil code, public health and sanitation, agriculture, animal husbandry, water supplies and irrigation, land rights, forests, fisheries.

Developmental projects for Indian Ocean Community: New Law of the Sea extending Economic Zone to 200 kms. beyond territorial waters

Three developmental projects are presented: 1. Law of the Sea; 2. Trans-Asian Railway 3. Trans-Asian Highway;

Recent changes in the Law of the Sea provide an unprecedented opportunity to enter into co-operative arrangements among states of Indian Ocean Community to expand livelihood opportunities for the sea-faring and coastal people by enlarging the sustainable exploitation of the economic zone of the Indian Ocean in aquaculture and in ocean-mining by developing larger sea-going vessels and enhanced fishing-vessel berth facilities and air-conditioned storage structures to enable marine cooperatives being setup in all the 59 countries of Indian Ocean Community. India with her technological prowess in using satellite communications can provide the member countries of IOC with live satellite data on mineral and aquatic resources, while cooperating in tasks related to tsunami warning systems and protection of maritime sea-lanes through coast-guards of the 59 countries.

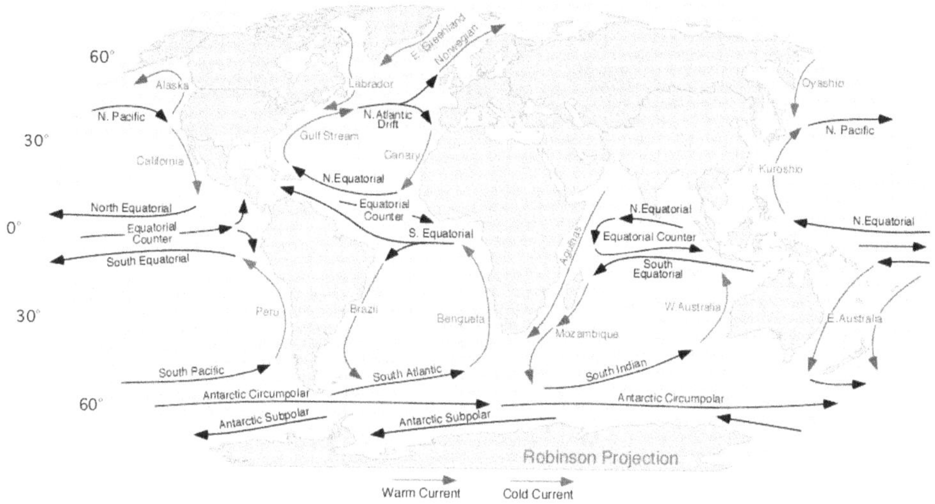

Indian Ocean has unique bi-directional (clock-wise and anti-clockwise) flows of ocean currents resulting in accumulation of placer sands with rare earths and other mineral resources along the entire Indian Ocean Rim. Heavy mineral rich Inayam Teri Sand Deposit, Kanyakumari district, Tamil Nadu

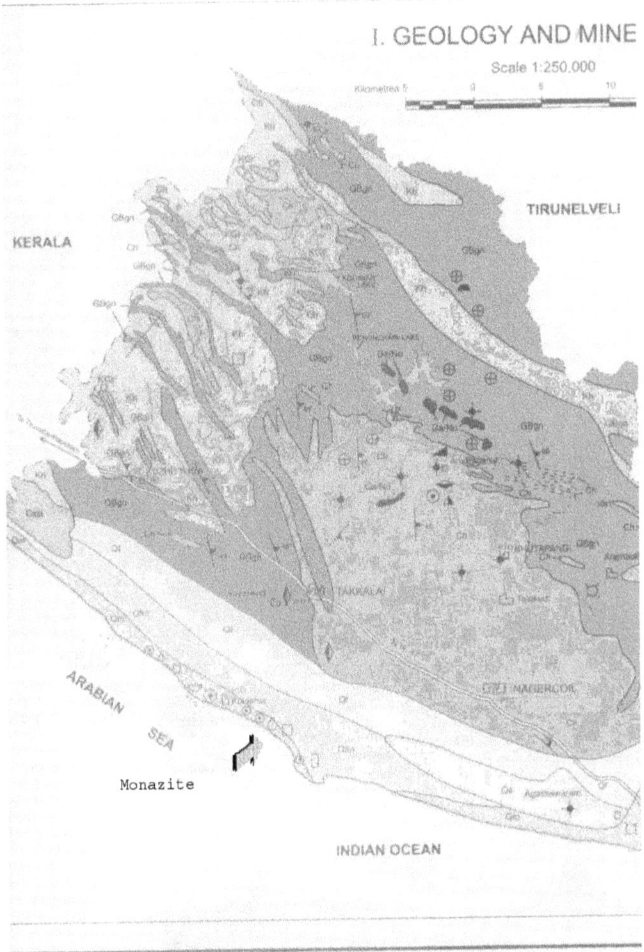

urvey of India toposheet No.58H First Edition 1969, with the permission of the Surveyor General of India.

Heavy mineral beach placers (ilmenite, rutile, garnet and monazite)

Kolachel to Kanniyakumari on 75 km.

Vattakottai and Lipuram to Manavalakurichi: 5 to 6 km. With a width of 3 to 5 m from the mouth of Valliyur River. The beach placers in Manavalakurichi, Aluva, Chavara, on an average contain 45 to 55% ilmenite, 7 to 14% garnet, 4 to 5% zircon, 3 to 4% monazite, 2 to 3% sillimanite, 2 to 3% rutile, 0.5 to 1% leucoxene and 10 to 25% others,

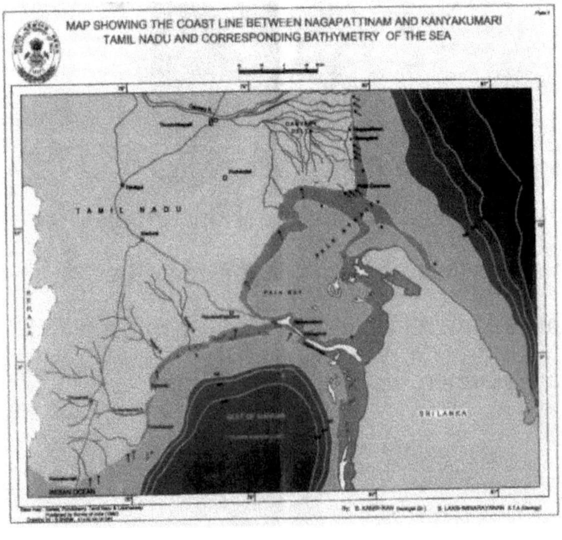

including silica.[96]

Bathymetry map of the Gulf of Mannar[97]

- Canyon below the ocean? Question of stability of any channel on this slope. "Two suites of slumps from opposite margins of the Gulf of Mannar, between Sri Lanka and southern India, have met and coalesced. The "Eastern Comorin" Slump is the more coherent of the two with a length of 70 to 100 km. The "Colombo" side slump consists of two to four blocks 15 to 35 km in length. Both slump-suites decrease to the south. A paleoslump underlies the western toe of the East Comorin Slump at a depth of some 800 meters. To the south, an enlarging and deepening submarine canyon marks the area of slump coalescence."[98]

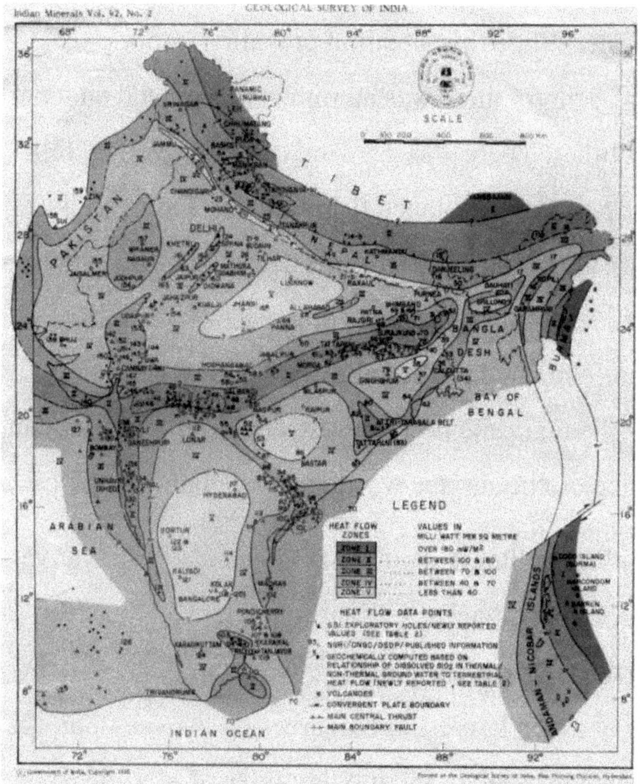

Fig. I HEAT FLOW MAP OF INDIA AND ADJOINING REGIONS

Rama's hotspot

Heatflow in Rama Setu 100 to 180 milliwatt per sq. m. comparable to Himalayan hotsprings

Law of the Sea and Freedom-of-the-seas doctrine

The oceans had long been subject to the freedom of-the-seas doctrine - a principle put forth in the seventeenth century essentially limiting national rights and jurisdiction over the oceans to a narrow belt of sea surrounding a nation's coastline. The remainder of the seas was proclaimed to be free to all and belonging to none. While this situation prevailed into the twentieth century, by mid-century there was an impetus to extend national claims over offshore resources. There was growing concern over the toll taken on coastal fish stocks by long-distance fishing fleets and over the threat of pollution and wastes from transport ships and oil tankers carrying noxious cargoes that plied sea routes across the globe. The hazard of pollution was ever present, threatening coastal resorts and all forms of ocean life. The navies of the maritime powers were competing to maintain a presence across the globe on the surface waters and even under the sea.

A tangle of claims, spreading pollution, competing demands for lucrative fish stocks in coastal waters and adjacent seas, growing tension between coastal nations' rights to these resources and those of distant-water fishermen, the prospects of a rich harvest of resources on the sea floor, the increased presence of maritime powers and the pressures of long-distance navigation and a seemingly outdated, if not inherently conflicting, freedom-of-the-seas doctrine - all these were threatening to transform the oceans into another arena for conflict and instability.[99]

The amended Law of the Sea now ratified by 162 countries (as of October 2012) offers a revolutionary new opportunity for NEW development project to harness the resources of the Exclusive Economic Zone which extends upto 200 nautical miles from the base line (modifying the present limit of territorial waters upto 12 nautical miles from the base line).

The main issues affecting the uses of the ocean and their overall governance are catalogued and described here under cross-cutting and broad topics. This section is divided into the following sub-topics:

- Climate Variability and Climate Change: origin, trends and impacts of global climate change on all sectors and possible adaptations to reduce or mitigate impacts and take advantage of opportunities. Addresses temperature changes, sea level rise, ice changes, currents, storminess, disease, algal blooms, impacts, adaptations, outlook for the future, and research and governance institutions.
- Economics: economic issues, and institutions. Includes economic yield and rent, poverty reduction, investment, profitability, economic incentives and disincentives, projections
- Emergencies: dramatic and mostly unexpected events negatively affecting ocean activities, includes harmful algal blooms, storms, hurricanes, icebergs, tsunamis, warning and aid institutions, research foci, projections, outlook for the future
- Food Security: all aspects related to access and availability of seafood from capture fisheries or aquaculture and related problems including poverty; contains information on aquaculture, fisheries

precautionary approach, catch trends & projections, institutions, enforcement, future

- Governance: contains frameworks, institutions and processes involved in Law of the Sea and other policy development and implementation (including enforcement, performance assessments, indicators) and related aspects such as information on national, regional and international policies, relating to ocean uses, laws and regulations, legislation, including legislative bodies, fishing use rights, jurisdictions, illegal fishing activities, monitoring and surveillance, CZM (Coastal Zone Management), Law of the Sea, rules & institutions, territorial waters, dispute resolution, enforcement, trends
- Human Health: includes all ocean-related phenomena issues of relevance to human health such as algal blooms, pollution, water-borne diseases, food quality and contamination, invasive species introductions, contingency planning, crowding, environmental modification, dredging, institutions, research foci, and outlook for the future
- Pollution and Degradation: describes negative modifications of the oceans environment, information on pollution and degradation, various uses and problems associated with their limitation and mitigation, ocean dumping, human-generated ocean noise, food safety, atmosphere-borne, nutrient loading, non-point source, impacts, controls, research foci, enforcement, outlook for the future
- Safety: addresses safety at sea, accidents, storms, safety standards and includes institutions, research foci and projections

- Sustainable Development: covers all issues related to sustainable and responsible conduct in using the oceans; includes legal and policy issues, indicators, status and trends, institutions, research foci, management techniques and projections.[100]

Exclusive economic zones (EEZs)

- Extends from the edge of the territorial sea out to 200 nautical miles from the baseline. Within this area, the coastal nation has sole exploitation rights over all natural resources. In casual use, the term may include the territorial sea and even the continental shelf. The EEZs were introduced to halt the increasingly heated clashes over fishing rights, although oil was also becoming important. The success of an offshore oil platform in the Gulf of Mexico in 1947 was soon repeated elsewhere in the world, and by 1970 it was technically feasible to operate in waters 4000 metres deep. Foreign nations have the freedom of navigation and overflight, subject to the regulation of the coastal states. Foreign states may also lay submarine pipes and cables.

Developmental projects for Indian Ocean Community: Trans-Asian Railway (TAR) Network[101]

The project was initiated in the 1960s, with the objective of providing a continuous 8750 mile (14,000km) rail link between Singapore and Istanbul, Turkey, with possible further connections to Europe and Africa.

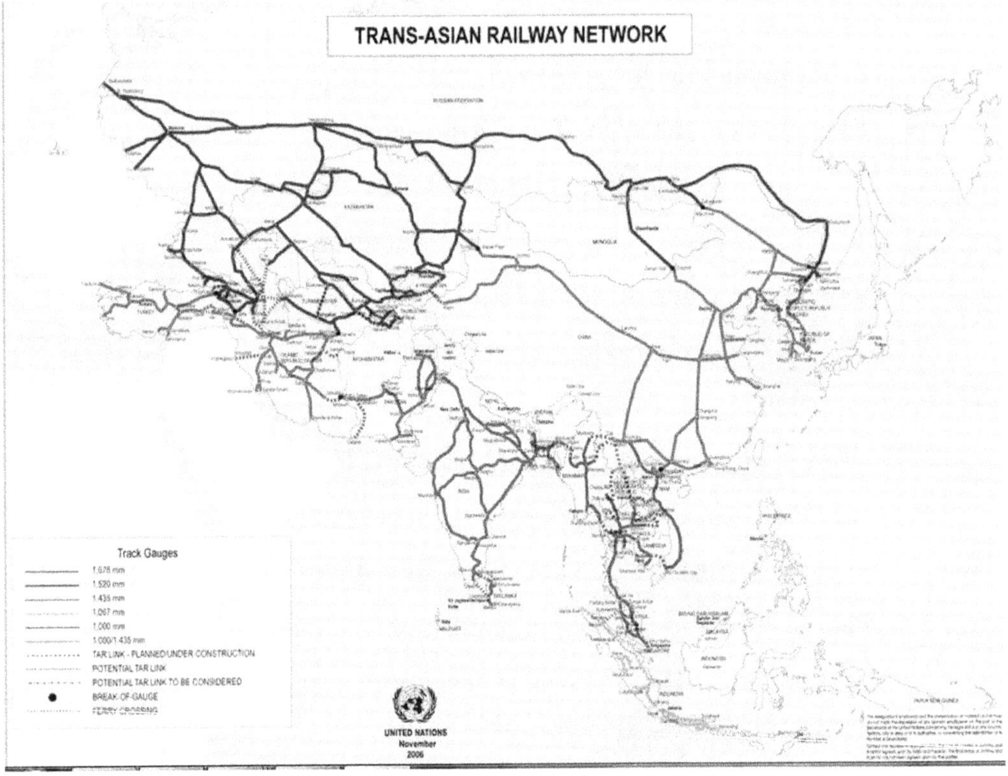

By 2001, the four corridors had been studied as part of the plan:

The Northern Corridor will link Europe and the Pacific, via Germany, Poland, Belarus, Russia, Kazakhstan, Mongolia, China, and the Koreas, with breaks of gauge at the Polish-Belarusian border (1435 mm to 1520 mm), the Kazakhstan-Chinese border (1520 mm to 1435 mm), and the Mongolian-Chinese border (1520 mm to 1435 mm). The 5750 miles (9,200km) Trans-Siberian Railway covers much of this route and currently carries large amounts of freight from East-Asia to Moscow and on to the rest of Europe. Due to political problems with North Korea, freight from

South Korea must currently be shipped by sea to the port of Vladivostok to access the route.

TAR routes in operation cover a distance of almost 81,000 km in 26 countries distributed as follows:

South-East Asia:	Cambodia, Indonesia, Malaysia, Myanmar, Singapore, Thailand, Viet Nam	12,600 km
North-East Asia:	China, Democratic People's Republic of Korea, Mongolia, Republic of Korea, Russian Federation	32,500 km
Central Asia and Caucasus:	Armenia, Azerbaijan, Georgia, Kazakhstan, Kyrgyzstan, Tajikistan, Turkmenistan, Uzbekistan	13,200 km
South Asia + Islamic Republic of Iran and Turkey:	Bangladesh, India, Islamic Republic of Iran, Pakistan, Sri Lanka, Turkey	22,600 km
Total:		**80,900 km**

The Southern Corridor will go from Europe to Southeast Asia, connecting Turkey, Iran, Pakistan, India, Bangladesh, Myanmar, and Thailand, with links to China's Yunnan Province and, via Malaysia, to Singapore. Gaps exist in eastern Iran, between India and Myanmar, between Myanmar and Thailand, between Thailand and Cambodia, between Cambodia and

Vietnam and between Thailand and Yunnan. Breaks of gauge occur, or will occur, at the Iran-Pakistan border (1435 mm to 1676 mm), the India-Myanmar border (1676 mm to 1000 mm), and to China (1000 mm to 1435 mm).

A Southeast Asian network[102]

The North-South Corridor will link Northern Europe to the Persian Gulf. The main route starts in Helsinki, Finland, and continues through Russia to the Caspian Sea, where it splits into three routes: a western route through Azerbaijan, Armenia, and western Iran; a central route across the Caspian Sea to Iran via ferry; and an eastern route through Kazakhstan, Uzbekistan and Turkmenia to eastern Iran. The routes converge in the Iranian capital of Tehran and continue to the Iranian port of Bandar Abbas.

The Trans-Asian Railway system will consist of four main railway routes. The existing Trans-Siberian railway, which connects Moscow to Vladivostok, will be used for a portion of the network in Russia. Another corridor to be included will connect China to Korea, Mongolia, Russia and Kazakhstan. **Developmental projects for Indian Ocean Community: Trans-Asian Highway Network[103]**

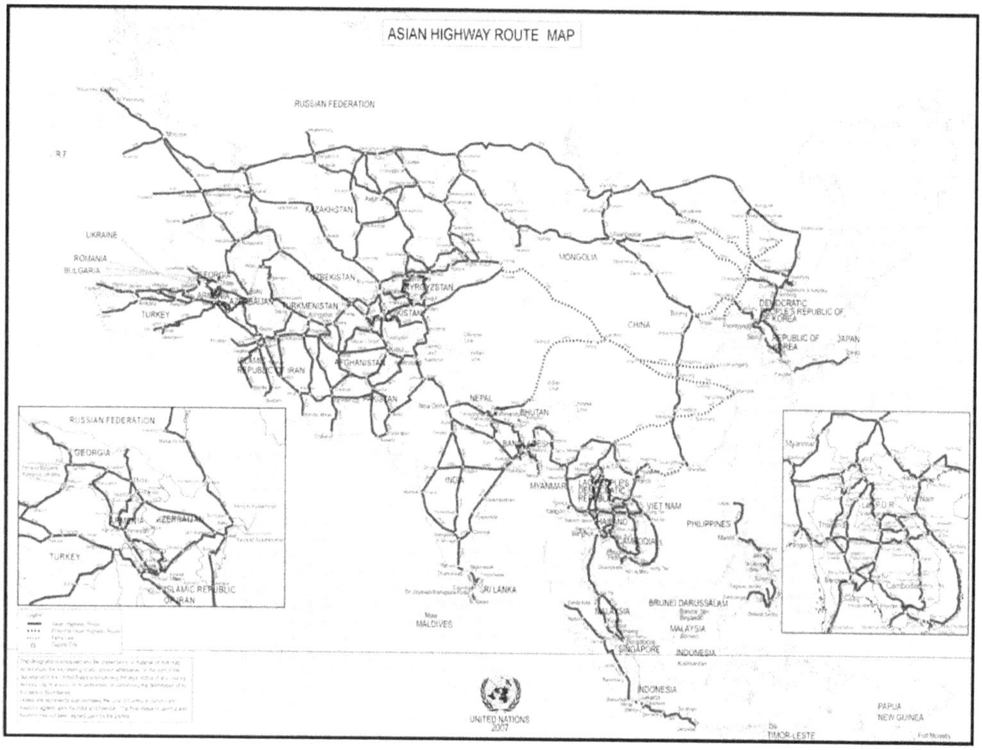

The Asian Highway network Project of UNESCAP is a network of 141,000 kilometers of standardized roadways crisscrossing 32 Asian countries with linkages to Europe.

The Asian Highway project was initiated in 1959 with the aim of promoting the development of international road transport in the region. During the first phase of the project (1960-1970) considerable progress was achieved, however, progress slowed down when financial assistance was suspended in 1975.

Entering into the 1980s and 1990s, regional political and economic changes spurred new momentum for the Asian Highway Project.

It became one of the three pillars of Asian Land Transport Infrastructure

Development (ALTID) project, endorsed by ESCAP Commission at its forty-eight session in 1992, comprising Asian Highway, Trans-Asian Railway and facilitation of land transport projects.

The Intergovernmental Agreement on the Asian Highway Network was adopted on 18 November 2003 by an intergovernmental meeting held in Bangkok, was open for signature in April 2004 in Shanghai and entered into force on 4 July 2005. A total of US$26 billion has already been invested in the improvement and upgrading of the Asian Highway network. However, there is still a shortfall of US$18 billion.

UNESCAP secretariat is now working with its member countries to identify financial sources for the development of the network to improve their road transport capacity and efficiency.

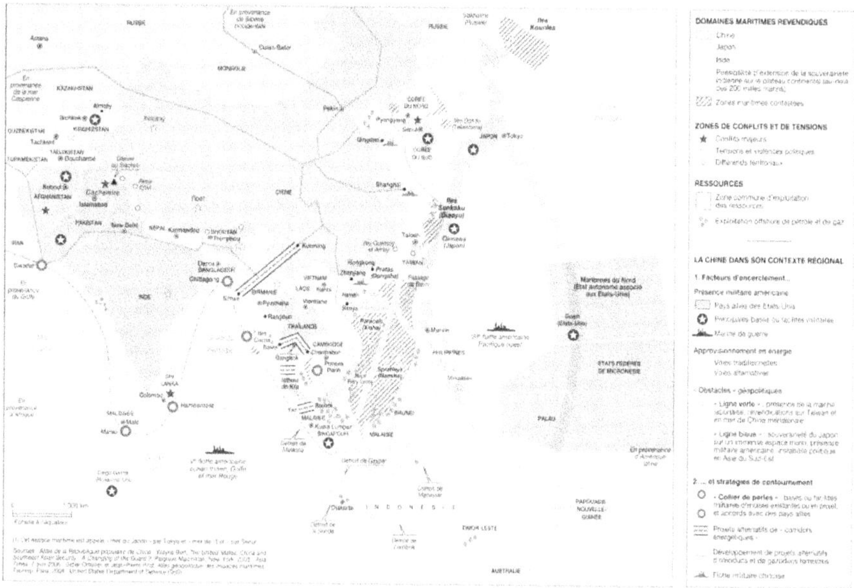

Maritime claims among nations and conflict zones

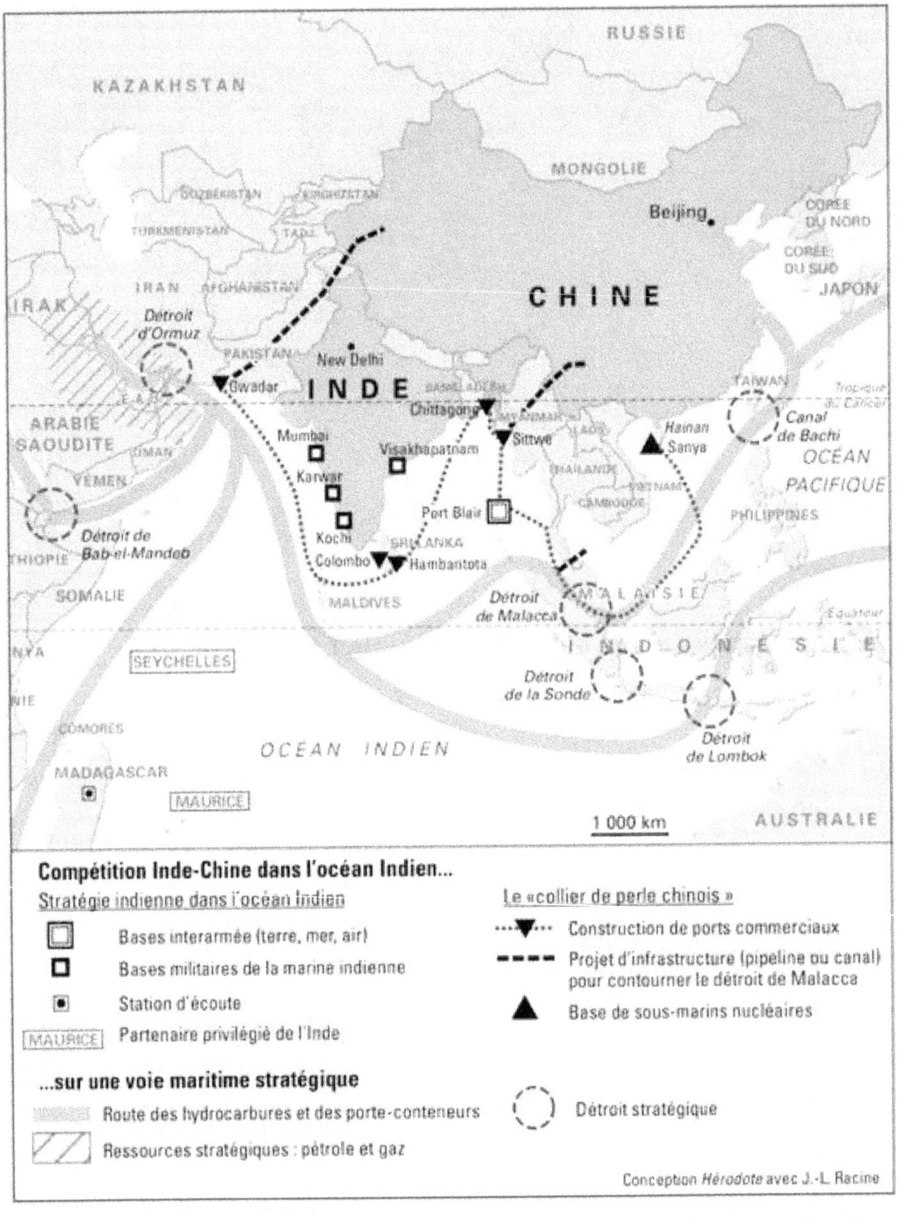

Powerplay vs. Regional cooperation

One view is that next geopolitical power play will be at sea, including the

Indian Ocean.[104]

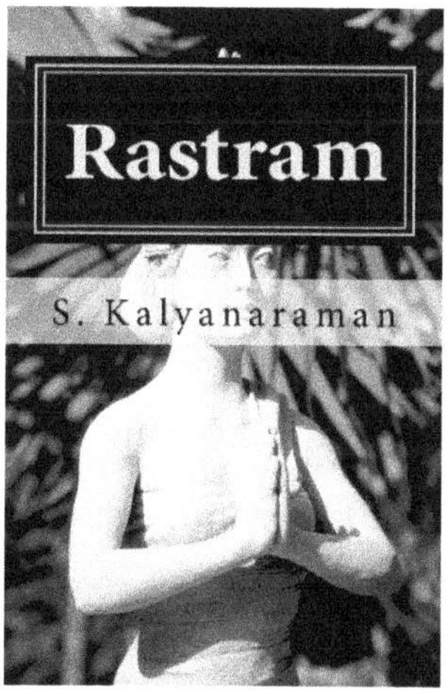

The Indian Ocean is set to be the central theatre of conflict and rivalry for the US, China and India

"Dr.Kalyanaraman has elaborated the strategic calculus in his book bearing the unusual title Rastram which is not amenable to any precise translation. Its attributes transcend those of a state ((which is mainly composed of institutions of governance) or a nation (which is a conglomerate of people with self-identity living in harmony). In his view, if only the countries of the Indian Ocean Rim constitute themselves into a collective entity, the tremendous financial and economic leverage that it will exercise will make it play a phenomenal role which will redress the balance of the present, largely skewed, world economic order. The idea has great appeal as well as relevance. The Indian Ocean Community (IOC), as expounded in Dr.Kalyanaraman's book, is predicated on the same rationale as the supra-national European Community which was initially conceived as a mechanism for joint policy making with reference to production and marketing of coal and steel but got expanded to full-fledged and integrated economic organisation with Euro as a common currency and a European Central Bank as a provider of banking services based on homogenous norms and criteria to all the members. This happened as an economic imperative despite the two world wars fought among the European nations. "[105]

INS Sudarshini, set sail from Kochi for a Historical Odyssey of Six Month Voyage to Commemorate Indian Association with ASEAN Countries[106]

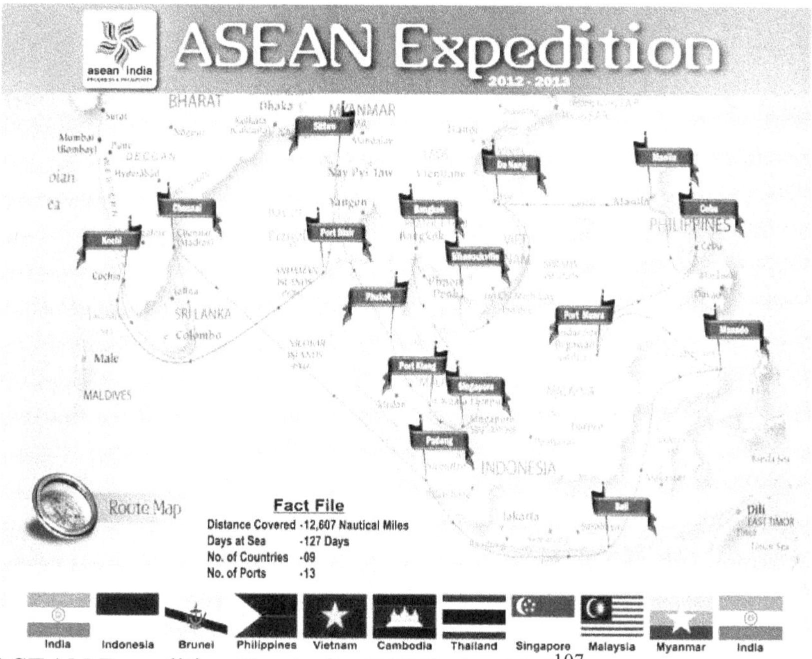

ASEAN Expedition Route for INS Sudarshini[107]

Bali Yatra, a remarkable cultural memory of history

[quote] Bali Yatra Festival[108] in Orissa marks the culmination of all the religious festivities held in the month of Karthik, which is considered the most auspicious month of the 12 months in a calendar year. Held on the full moon day in November - December that is celebrated all over Orissa as Karthik Purnima, Bali Yatra commemorates Orissa's ancient maritime legacy.

Karthik Purnima was considered the most auspicious day by the traders (sadhabas) of Orissa to venture on a journey to distant lands namely the islands of Bali, Java, Sumatra, Borneo and Ceylon (Sri Lanka). Tourism of Orissa offers tours to Orissa during the Bali Yatra fair and festival so that you can get a glimpse of Orissa's rich cultural history and colorfully vibrant present on your tour of Festivals in Orissa.

Bali Yatra is a hugely popular fair held on the banks of Mahanadi River in the fort area of Cuttack city from where the traders of Orissa (sadhabas) undertook voyages, along the sea trade route, on huge boats called Boita. To celebrate the glory of the ancient times, the people in Cuttack as well as in the rest of Orissa float small boats made of cork, colored paper and banana tree barks in the river and water tanks.

The ritual of launching tiny paper boats lit by lamps placed within its hollow is known as Boita Bandana. You too can marvel at the spectacle of thousand lamps afloat in the rivers and tanks on your tour of Festivals in Orissa with Tourism of Orissa tour packages.

As images of Karthikeswar are worshipped and immersed in the waters of river Mahanadi, near the Shiva Temple, to mark the end of the month of Karthik; the banks of the river in Cuttack come alive with chants and rejoicing people. Suddenly Bali Yatra takes a life of its own.

Held over 3-4 days till the full moon day, the fair of Bali Yatra is attended by thousands of enthusiasts and is marked with fun and frolic at the riverbanks where countless shops selling food, clothes, curios and miscellaneous items and swings come up during the evenings. You can indulge your shopaholic side or go on boat rides under the full moon on your tour to the Bali Yatra festival in Orissa with Tourism of Orissa tour packages. [unquote]

Indian Ocean Community as Rāṣṭram governed by Dharma-Dhamma

Indian Ocean Rim Association for Regional Cooperation (IOR-ARC)[109] was. established in 1957. The Association comprises 20 member states:

- Australia
- Bangladesh
- Comoros
- India
- Indonesia
- Iran
- Kenya
- Madagascar
- Malaysia
- Mauritius
- Yemen
- Mozambique
- Oman
- Seychelles
- Singapore
- South Africa
- Sri Lanka
- Tanzania
- Thailand
- United Arab Emirates

Dialogue Partners

- China
- Egypt
- France
- Japan
- United Kingdom
- United States

Turkey has applied for dialogue partner status. The Indian Ocean Tourism Organisation has observer status.

IOR-ARC is characterised by consensus decision making and minimal institutionalisation. At the IOR-ARC Ministerial Meeting in August 2010, a new Charter was endorsed.

Indian Ocean Area

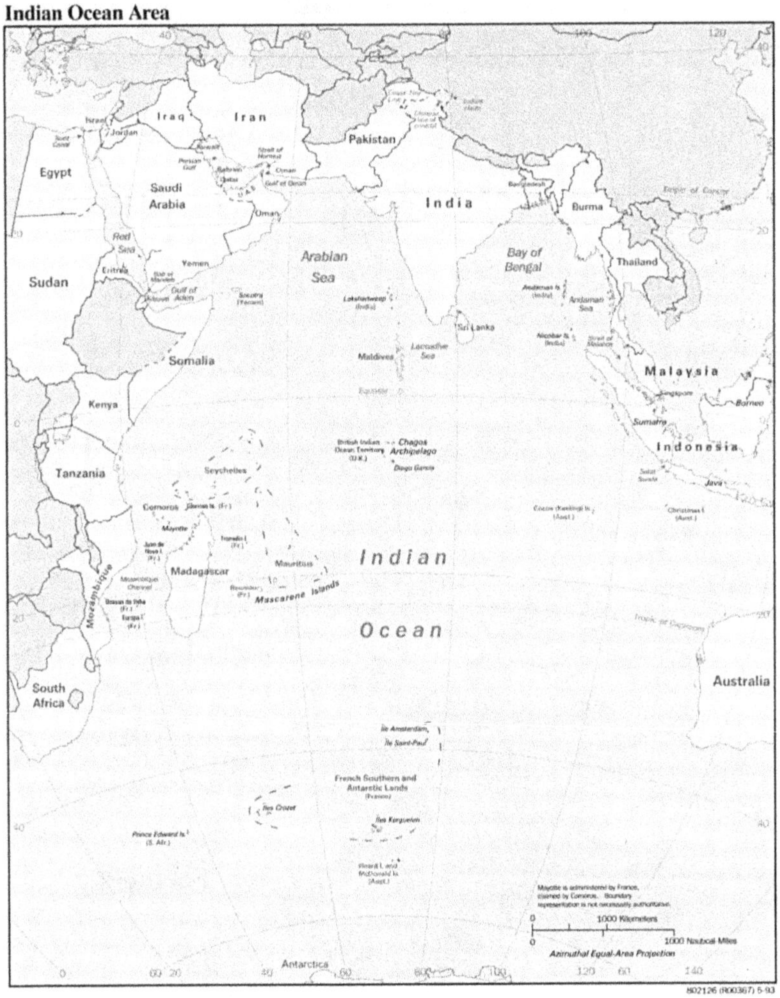

802126 (R00367) 5-93

The 2010 IOR-ARC Charter states that the organisation's primary objective is to promote the sustained growth and balanced development of the region and of member states, and to create common ground for regional economic cooperation.

The IOR-ARC Charter lists areas of cooperation including trade facilitation and liberalisation, promotion of foreign investment, scientific and technological exchanges, tourism, movement of natural persons and service providers on a non-discriminatory basis; and the development of infrastructure and human resources inter-alia poverty alleviation, promotion of maritime transport and related matters, cooperation in the fields of fisheries trade, research and management, aquaculture, education and training, energy, IT, health, protection of the environment, agriculture, and disaster management.

In 2011 six priority areas of cooperation were identified for IOR-ARC. These include: Maritime Safety and Security, Trade and Investment Facilitation, Fisheries Management, Disaster Risk Management, Academic and Science & Technology Cooperation, and Tourism and Cultural Exchanges.

At the November 2011 Council of Ministers' (COM) meeting in Bengaluru, India, Australia was appointed as Vice Chair of IOR-ARC for the first time for a two-year period. Australia will assume the Chair after India for a two-year period from late 2013 to late 2015. Location: body of water between Africa, the Southern Ocean, Asia, and Australia

Coastline: 66,526 km

Area total: 68.556 million sq km This is about about 5.5 times the size of the US

N*ote:* includes Andaman Sea, Arabian Sea, Bay of Bengal, Flores Sea, Great Australian Bight, Gulf of Aden, Gulf of Oman, Java Sea,

Mozambique Channel, Persian Gulf, Red Sea, Savu Sea, Strait of Malacca, Timor Sea, and other tributary water bodies

Natural resources: oil and gas fields, fish, shrimp, sand and gravel aggregates, placer deposits, polymetallic nodules.[110]

Indian Ocean World (IOW) - from China to Southeast and South Asia, the Middle East and Africa. This macro-region witnessed the early emergence of major centres of production and a monsoon-based system of trans-oceanic trade that led to the emergence by at least the tenth century of a sophisticated and durable system of long-distance exchange of commodities, monies, technology, ideas and people. The IOW was thus home to the first 'global' economy, one that dominated the macro-region until at least the mid eighteenth century – some would argue the nineteenth century, and which is again resurgent. Today the IOW comprises 50% of the planet's population and is forecast to become the leading world economy by 2020.[111]

Founded in 1982 and institutionalized by the Victoria Agreement in 1984, the Indian Ocean Commission is an intergovernmental organization of regional cooperation that groups five member states [Union of Comoros, France / Reunion, Madagascar, Mauritius, Seychelles], thus constituting of four ACP countries and, for the French side, an outermost region of Europe.[112] ISLANDS is a project of the Indian Ocean Commission (IOC) financed by The European Union. The official name of the project is 'Implementation of the SIDS Mauritius Strategy in the Eastern Southern African-Indian Ocean Region'

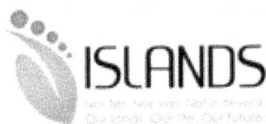

(ISIDSMS). However, a brand has been chosen to have a more generic name to the project and to be able to communicate more easily.

Indian Ocean Community: Desalination plant on a barge supplying waters for Rāṣṭram

The Indian Ocean Community has to be founded on the declaration with which this odyssey started and to create an economic community beyong the sporadic initiatives of IOR-ARC or IOC – two initiatives which have provided a good start clearing the air for understanding among the IOC nations. The foundations on a firm footing will emerge once three projects are launched: 1. Trans-Asian Railway; 2. Trans-Asian Highway and 3. Projects related to the amended Law of the Sea extending Special Marine Economic Zone to 200 nautical miles from the present range of only 20 nautical miles as territorial waters, to create marine cooperatives with enhanced facilities of sea-faring vessels and fishery-berths for larger vessels which will enable the fisherfolk to be out on the Indian Ocean for 3 days and nights harnessing the aquatic resources of the Indian Ocean. A short-term goal should be set and accomplished to create Indian Ocean Community as a Free Trade Zone working towards the emergence of a common currency, the Mudra to offer a global financial platform to work with Euro, the American Dollar and other world convertible currencies to provide for the finance engine the global financial system is searching for to overcome the present crises of the world's banking systems and trading communities trading in puts and calls as options obstructing the creation of real and lasting wealth of nations. There has to be a clarion call, the resonating OM sound of the conch-shell, the sankhanaada to restore the world GDP to the equitable world order which existed prior to the colonial era which began over 400 years ago, in 1700 CE. Just as the European Steel and Coal Community resulted in the formation of the European Community, these economic initiatives among Indin Ocean nations will result in the formation of the Indian Ocean Community as Rāṣṭram.

Desalination plant on a barge supplying waters for Rāṣṭram

Nolan Hertel, a professor of nuclear and radiological engineering at Georgia Tech, wrote, "... nuclear reactors can be used ... to produce large amounts of potable water. The process is already in use in a number of places around the world, from India to Japan and Russia. Eight nuclear reactors coupled to desalination plants are operating in Japan alone ... nuclear desalination plants could be a source of large amounts of potable water transported by pipelines hundreds of miles inland..."[113] An aircraft carrier in the US military uses nuclear power to desalinate 400,000 US gallons (1,500,000 l; 330,000 imp gal) of water per day.[114]

Shevchenko BN350 desalination unit.[115] Indicative costs are US$ 70-90 cents per cubic metre. India has been engaged in desalination research since the 1970s. In 2002 a demonstration plant coupled to twin 170 MWe nuclear power reactors (PHWR) was set up at the Madras Atomic Power Station, Kalpakkam, in southeast India. This hybrid Nuclear Desalination Demonstration Project (NDDP) comprises a reverse osmosis (RO) unit with 1800 m^3/day capacity and a multi-stage flash (MSF) plant unit of 4500 m^3/day costing about 25% more, plus a recently-added barge-mounted RO unit.

This is the largest nuclear desalination plant based on hybrid MSF-RO technology using low-pressure steam and seawater from a nuclear power station. They incur a 4 MWe loss in power from the plant. In 2009 a 10,200 m^3/day MVC (mechanical vapour compression) plant was set up at Kudankulam to supply fresh water for the new plant. It has four stages in each of four streams. An RO plant there supplied the plant's township initially. The full MVC plant is being commissioned in mid 2012, with quoted capacity of 7200 m^3/day to supply the plant's primary and secondary coolant and the local town. Cost is quoted at INR 0.05 per litre (USD 0.9/m^3).[116]

The barges mounted with a desalination plants supplying safe drinking water, should be stationed on every major port in every one of the nations of the Indian Ocean Community and moved along the Indian Ocean Rim of 63,000 miles to supply water to the communities, as the symbol of the Rāṣṭram with bountiful waters heralding a veritable blue revolution to resolve the problems of global financial crisis.

Rāṣṭram is the path of dharma-dhamma -- *philosophia perennis et universalis* -- for the Indian Ocean Community in her destined pilgrims' progress -- *aham rashtrī samgamanī vasūnām* (RV 10.125)—I, *vākdevi, divinity of wisdom,* am the Rāṣṭram leading the people to the wealth-and-welfare-yielding treasures…

dhármāṇi prathamāni āsan

Dhammapada:

nahi verena verani—aammanti dha kudacancam- averenacca sammanti—esa dhammo sanantano - The Buddha

Trans. Hatred never ceases through hatred, but through love alone they cease.

Rigveda 1.164.50-51:

yajñéna yajñám ayajanta devā́s tā́ni dhármāṇi prathamā́ni āsan
té ha nā́kam mahimā́naḥ sacanta yátra pū́rve sā́dhiyāḥ sánti devā́ḥ

samānám etád udakámúc caíti áva cā́habhiḥ
bhū́mim parjányā jínvantidívaṃ jinvanti agnáyaḥ

Trans. The uniform water passes upwards and downwards in the course of days; clouds give joy to the earth; fires rejoice the heaven.

I invoke for our protection the celestial, well-winged, swift-moving, majestic (Sun); who is the germ of the waters; the displayer of herbs; the cherisher of lakes replenishing the ponds with rain.

Rigveda 10.90.16:

yajñéna yajñám ayajanta devāstāni dhármāṇi prathamāni āsanté ha nākam mahimānaḥ sacantayátra pūrve sādhiyāḥ sánti devāḥ

Trans. By prayer the divinities worshipped (him who is also) the yajna; those were the first duties. Those great ones became partakers of the heaven where the ancient divinities the Sādhyas[117] abide.

Index

A

angle 129
archer 52, 109
arrow 101, 109
Atharva Veda 59
Australia 5, 7, 10, 18, 135, 139, 142, 146, 161, 165, 166, 212, 214

B

Bangladesh 10, 60, 203, 212
Bharata 52
bird 77
boat 18, 19, 26, 210
body 19, 35, 41, 51, 69, 82, 125, 214
branch 70, 77, 124
Buddha 121
Burma 10, 24, 68, 70, 71, 72, 73, 84, 85, 93, 95, 102, 104, 106, 120, 121, 131, 163

C

Cambodia 65, 70, 73, 85, 88, 95, 103, 105, 116, 117, 120, 121, 151, 152, 163, 191, 203
canal 25, 173
carpenters 26
Caspian Sea 204
catamaran 23
cattle 57
Central Asia 121
China 86, 95, 116, 117, 118, 123, 124, 135, 143, 146, 153, 161, 165, 192, 202, 203, 204, 206, 212, 215
community 24, 38, 59, 60, 61, 62, 63, 68, 73, 74, 121, 139, 150, 192, 216
conch 37, 216
corner 108, 122
crab 171

D

dance 100, 105, 115, 152
dharma 27, 37, 55, 75, 76, 83, 99, 100

E

Egypt 8, 9, 10, 212
Egyptian 186

F

fish 4, 76, 140, 198, 214

G

gold 8, 19
guild 88

H

Hajar 113
Hindu 75, 82, 100, 121

I

Indian Ocean Commission 215
Indonesia 5, 7, 10, 24, 30, 65, 87, 89, 90, 91, 94, 95, 96, 99, 100, 105, 107, 108, 109, 110, 112, 114, 118, 121, 132, 134, 135, 163, 203, 212
Indus script 15, 19
intercourse 60
IOR-ARC 140, 164, 212, 213, 214, 216
Iran 7, 10, 106, 203, 204, 212
iron 4

J

joined 57, 133
jump 178

K

Kalyanaraman 1, 3, 179, 208
Kish 16

L

ladder 175
language 63
Laos 70, 73, 85, 95, 102, 105, 121, 123, 163
lead 100
linga 14

M

Madagascar 5, 6, 8, 9, 33, 135, 212, 215
Mahābhārata 27, 75
Malaysia 10, 19, 24, 65, 96, 103, 104, 121, 141, 163, 164, 203, 212
Mediterranean 7, 15
Mesopotamia 8, 17
mineral 4, 193, 194, 195, 196
monkey 91
mountain 128, 131

N

nation 49, 52, 75, 101
neck 51, 115
Nippur 16, 17
numerals 108

O

offering 58, 102, 115

P

pace 152, 156, 162, 165, 174, 190
Pacific 9, 121, 144, 146, 164, 171, 202
Pakistan 10, 60, 106, 190, 203
Persian Gulf 5, 6, 7, 9, 15, 19, 204, 214
Philippines 9, 105, 122, 144, 149
plants 42, 47, 52
platform 201, 216
Possehl 224

R

Rāmāyaṇa 14, 75, 76, 101
rashtram 53, 54, 55, 57, 59, 83, 99
ratha 55
Rigveda 185, 219
road 152, 180, 205, 206

S

Sarasvati 1, 2, 3, 8, 15, 19, 36, 55, 137
saw 54
seal 18
silver 19
Singapore 7, 19, 92, 94, 96, 123, 202, 203, 212
slope 197
Somalia 8, 10
South Africa 9, 96, 126, 149, 212
spear 42
śreṇi 175, 176, 177, 178, 179, 180
star 8, 9, 33, 42, 126, 165
state 53, 63
steel 29, 42, 209
step 18, 32, 174, 190
stone 32, 102, 110
summit 110, 128
Susa 16

T

Taiwan 143
Tello 16
Thailand 10, 68, 70, 71, 72, 73, 85, 93, 95, 96, 102, 106, 118, 121, 123, 132, 151, 163, 203, 212
Tibet 121, 137

tin 4
tree 32, 57, 68, 77, 114, 124, 210
Turkmenistan 203

U

Ur 16

V

Veda 34, 59, 79, 183, 185
Vedic 12, 28, 34, 37, 38, 42, 55, 75, 81
vessel 19, 24, 194
Vietnam 73, 85, 97, 120, 121, 151, 152, 163, 204

W

war 102
wheel 57, 88, 92
workshop 15
worship 37

[1] http://www.britannica.com/EBchecked/topic/285876/Indian-Ocean/22782/Biological-resources

[2] http://iri.columbia.edu/~lareef/tsunami/

[3] "Propagation of the Southwest Indian Ridge at the Rodrigues Triple Junction", *Journal Marine Geophysical Researches*, Dec. 1997

[4] Source: NOAA, ETOPO2

[5] http://en.wikipedia.org/wiki/List_of_ports_and_harbours_of_the_Indian_Ocean http://en.wikipedia.org/wiki/Culture_of_the_Indian_Ocean_Islands

[6] https://www.cia.gov/library/publications/the-world-factbook/geos/xo.html

[7] http://en.wikipedia.org/wiki/Indian_Ocean#cite_ref-12

[8] Blocked by the Ottoman Empire in ca. 1453 with the fall of the Byzantine Empire, new sea route around Africa was found.

[9] http://en.wikipedia.org/wiki/Indian_Ocean#cite_ref-12

[10] From Greek ἐπιστήμη (epistēmē), meaning "knowledge, understanding", and λόγος (logos), meaning "study of". The word *veda* itself means 'that which is know-able', derived from the root: *vid* 'to know'.

[11] English word 'bund' comes from Bharatiya word: bandha

[12] Gregory L. Possehl, 2002, *The Indus civilization: a contemporary perspective*, Rowman Altamira, p.225

[13] Ibid., After Fig. 12.1: Areas of the Middle Asian Interaction Sphere, p. 215

[14] Ibid. p. 228. The figures of seals are also from the work of Gregory L. Possehl, p.225.

[15] http://www.newsbriefsoman.info/item/2006/04/seafaring-in-the-days-of-magan-historical-oman

[16]http://www.khaleejtimes.com/DisplayArticleNew.asp?xfile=/data/middleeast/2010/July/middleeast_July343.xml&section=middleeast

[17] Image source: *India Through the ages* - By K. M. Panikkar and *Transoceanic Contacts between the Old and the New World.*

[18]http://www.newworldencyclopedia.org/entry/File:Priests_traveling_across_kealakekua_bay_for_first_contact_rituals.jpg

[19] http://www.bibliotecapleyades.net/vimanas/esp_vimanas_11c.htm

[20] Law, NN, 1921, *Aspects of ancient Indian Polity*, OUP.

[21] European Community (EC), the pillar of the European Union, since 1967, connotes a supranational entity comprising three, shared international governing institutions: European Coal and Steel Community (ECSC), European Economic Community (EEC) and European Atomic Energy Community (EURATOM). The treaty of ECSC expired in 2002 and its activities were absorbed into EC which came into force on 1st November 1993..

[22]http://articles.timesofindia.indiatimes.com/2012-09-24/bhopal/34061009_1_buddhism-murli-manohar-joshi-sanatan-dharma
'Dharma, Dhamma have similar roots'

[23] A visionary is defined as "one who is given to novel ideas or schemes which are not immediately practicable" (*Macquarie Dictionary*, p. 1939).

[24] Horsch, Paul, 1967, 'vom schopfungsmythos zum weltgesetz', in Asiatische studien: zeitschrift dder schweizerischen gesellschaft fur aslankunde, vol. 21 (Francke: 1967), pp. 31-61; English tr. By Whitaker, J.L., 'From creation myth to world law: the early history of dharma', in: Olivelle, Patrick, ed., 2009, 'Dharma, studies in its semantic, cultural and religious history', *Journal of Indian Philosophy*, Vol. 32, Number 5-6.

[25] Dhaatup. Xix, 74.

[26] Bauddham. (2009). In *Encyclopædia Britannica*. Retrieved May 29, 2009, from Encyclopædia Britannica Online: http://www.britannica.com/EBchecked/topic/83184/Bauddham

[27] http://en.wikipedia.org/wiki/Greater_India "**Greater India** was the historical extent of the culture of Indiabeyond the Indian subcontinent. This particularly concerns the spread of Hinduism in Southeast Asia, introduced by the Indianized kingdoms of the 5th to 15th centuries, but may also refer to the spread of Buddhism from India to Central Asia and China by the Silk Road during the early centuries of the Common Era. To the west, Greater India overlaps with Greater Persia in the Hindu Kush and Pamir mountains. The term is tied to the geographic uncertainties surrounding the "Indies" during the Age of Exploration."

[28] **gR**cl. 1. P. %{garati} , to sprinkle , moisten Dhatup. xxii , 39 (cf. %{ghR}.)

[29] **व्रज** *m.* a way , road; a fold , stall , cow-pen , cattle-shed , enclosure or station of herdsmen

[30] índra bráhma kriyámāṇā juṣasva yā te śaviṣṭha náviyā ákarma
vástreva bhadrā súkṛtā vasūyū rátham ná dhīraḥ suápā atakṣam

[31] **सेना** an army , armament , battle-array , armed force (also personified as wife ofकार्त्तिकेय ; ifc. also *n*(सेन).)

[32] **अर्थ** substance , wealth , property , opulence , money; affair , concern (Ved. often acc. /अर्थम् with √ इ , or गम् , to go to one's business , take up one's work)

[33] **ओजस्** *n.* (√वज् , or उज् ; cf. उग्र) , bodily strength , vigour , energy , ability , power; water; light , splendour , luster

[34] **भृत्** *mfn.* bearing , carrying , bringing , procuring , possessing , wearing , having , nourishing , supporting , maintaining (only ifc. ; cf. इषु- , क्षिति- , धर्म- , वंश-भृत् &c)

[35] **स्व--राज्** self-resplendent , self-luminous; *m.* N. of ब्रह्मा; *m.* of one of the 7 principal rays of the sun; एका*ह (day)

[36] **दध्** (redupl. of √ धा) , *cl.1.* °धते , to hold Dhatup. ii , 7

मधु—मती *f.* a partic. supernatural faculty belonging to a योगिन्; pleasant , agreeable; *m.* N. of a country g. कच्छा*दि and सिन्ध्व्-ादि

पृच्यन्ताम् to give lavishly , grant bountifully , bestow anything (acc. or gen.) richly upon (dat.) unite , join; to mix , mingle , put together with

महि great, the earth

क्षत्र wealth, water (RV 1.12); sg. and pl. dominion , supremacy , power , might (whether human or supernatural , especially applied to the power of वरुण-मित्र and इन्द्र); the military or reigning order (the members of which in the earliest times , as represented by the Vedic hymns , were generally called राजन्य , not क्षत्रिय ; afterwards , when the difference between ब्रह्मन् and क्षत्र or the priestly and civil authorities became more distinct , applied to the second or reigning or military; the rank of a member of the reigning or military order

क्षत्रिया *f.* (Pan. 4-1 , 49 Vartt. 7) a woman of the military

---

क्षत्रिय *mfn.* (Pan. 4-1 , 38 ; g. श्रेण्यादि) governing , endowed with sovereignty (RV 4.22.1); *m.* a member of the military or reigning order

वन् to like , love , wish , desire; to gain , acquire , procure (for one's self or others) RV. AV. S3Br. ; to conquer , win , become master of , possess; to prepare , make ready for , aim at ; Intens. (only वाव्/अनः and वावन्ध्/इ ; but cf. वनीवन्) to love , like

अधृष्टाँ unsubdued

सद् p. सीदति to sit down before , besiege , lie in wait for , watch; sitting or dwelling in

सहौजस् **ojas-saha, with ojas; ओजस्** *n.* (√वज् , or उज् ; cf. उग्र) , bodily strength , vigour , energy , ability , power; water; light , splendour , luster

[37] Bhadram: n. blessed, auspicious , fortunate, prosperous, happy; good, gracious, friendly, kind; excellent, fair, beautiful, lovely, pleasant, dear; good i.e. skilful in (loc.).

[38] From Greek ἐπιστήμη (epistēmē), meaning "knowledge, understanding", and λόγος (logos), meaning "study of". The word *veda* itself means 'that which is know-able', derived from the root: *vid* 'to know'.

[39] http://orwell.ru/library/essays/nationalism/english/e_nat

[40] *Saptahik Hindustan* (May 1, 1977) reported a remarkable event. Shahi Imam of Jama Masjid, Delhi, was in Mecca for pilgrimage. A local resident asked the Imam, Are you a Hindu? Imam was startled and replied: No, I am a Muslim. Why do you ask? The answer given by the local resident is instructive: In Mecca, all Hindusthanis are called Hindu? The historian Arnold Toynbee calls the nationality of people of India as Hindu.

So do US President George Bush and many other western leaders and scholars.

[41] Loc. Cit. Arvind Sharma, 2002, An Indic Contribution Towards an Understanding of the Word "Religion" and the Concept of Religious Freedom http://www.infinityfoundation.com/indic_colloq/papers/paper_sharma2.pdf Wilfred Cantwell Smith, *The Meaning and End of Religion* (New York: The Macmillan Company, 1963). Arvind Sharma questions the use of the word 'religion' itself in the context of comparative studies of cultures. [quote] … what we are dealing with at the moment is not so much the Christian West as the secular West, and it is on account of this difference that for the organising category of "Christianity," one now substitutes the word "religion… Wilfred Cantwell Smith (1916-2000) is well known for pointing out how the word "religion" became reified in the course of the intellectual evolution of the modern West.1 It is not as often recognised that he also connects this development with the rise of secularism… In place of the Christian religion we are now, in fact, operating with a Christian conception of religion… A subtle fact needs to be noted here—that Christianity and Islam first deny one salvation because one is not in them and then offer it to all who would join them. This is one kind of universalism. But according to the Hindu position salvation is yours as your are—and without having to become a Hindu. Thus it too offers universal salvation— without making itself the intermediary of it. So I ask you: Which of these two universalisms is more universal—the conditional one ("join us") or the unconditional one? Now contrast this with two conceptions of rights—human rights and citizen's right. Which of the two are more universal? You have citizen's right if you are a citizen of a state, but even a stateless human being possesses human rights—merely by virtue of being a human being. This is the whole point in calling them universal. It is worth noting that up to a point in the deliberations at the U.N.O. the document which ultimately became the Universal Declaration of Human Rights was referred to as the International Declaration of Human Rights. The significance of ultimately designating them as universal rather than international should not be overlooked.1 The

situation is analogous to the Indic position on religious salvation—that a human being has access to it not by virtue of belonging to this or that religion—but by the mere fact of being a human being. This, I submit to you, is also the dharmic position—the position of much of Asia and of the indigenous world. It is also the more universal of the two. It is therefore ironical that the Universal Declaration of Human Rights does not accord explicit recognition to this position. In advocating the dharmic position the Indic tradition is perhaps poised to make a crucial contribution to both contemporary religious discourse and contemporary human rights discourse." [unquote]

[42] . M. Hiriyanna, 1975, *Indian Conception of Values*, Mysore, Kavyalaya Publishers, p. 154.

[43] http://www.dhamma.it/jsps/portal/introduzione/cronologia.jsp

[44] Geiger, Wilhelm (1912). *The Mahawamsa or Great Chronicle of Ceylon*. Oxford: Oxford University Press (for the Pali Text Society). pp. 300.http://lakdiva.org/culavamsa/vol_0.html.

[45] T.W. Rhys Davids, 1902, *Buddhist India*, repr. Delhi, Munshiram Manoharlal, p. 167; Edict citations, pp. 295-297.

[46] http://www.vridhamma.org/Qualities-of-the-Triple-Gem.aspx

[47] In this context, it will be useful to refer to what the Constitution Bench of the Supreme Court, headed by the former Chief Justice of India, Shri Gajendragadkar, observed in Shastri Versus Muldas, 1966 SCC 1119, and SCR 1966(3) 263:

"Beneath the diversity of philosophic thoughts, concepts and ideas expressed by Hindu philosophers who started different philosophical schools, lay certain broad concepts which can be treated as basic. The first among these basic concepts is the acceptance of the Vedas as the highest authority in religious and philosophical matters. This concept necessarily implies that all the systems claim to have drawn their principles from a reservoir of thoughts enshrined in the Vedas… The other basic concept, which is common to six systems of Hindu philosophy, is that all of them accept this view of the great world rhythm. Vast periods of creation, maintenance and dissolution follow each other in endless succession… It may also be said that all the systems of Hindu philosophy believe in rebirth and pre-existence".

48 http://blogs.nd.edu/contendingmodernities/ Scott Appelby

49 Mahabharata Santi Parva, Section CCXLI Tr. Kisari Mohan Ganguli

50 Adi S'ankara (Gita Bhashyam)

51 http://en.wikipedia.org/wiki/Hinduism_in_Southeast_Asia

52 Sources cited at https://sites.google.com/site/indianoceancommunity1/

53 http://www.indonesianhistory.info/pages/chapter-3.html Mirrored at: https://sites.google.com/site/indianoceancommunity1/

54 http://exhibitions.nlb.gov.sg/kaalachakra/about.htm

55 http://exhibitions.nlb.gov.sg/kaalachakra/alliances_and_rivalries.htm

56 http://bharatkalyan97.blogspot.in/2011/08/pancaratra-and-angkor-wat-temple.html

57 http://exhibitions.nlb.gov.sg/kaalachakra/alliances_and_rivalries.htm

58 http://www.learnnc.org/lp/multimedia/2616

59 Frits Staal, 2005, The sound pattern of Sanskrit in Asia – an unheralded contribution by Indian Brahmans and Buddhist monks: lecture given during the inaugural session of the International Conference on 'Sanskrit in Asia' at Silpakorn University, Bangkok, June 23, 2005, subsequently published in Sanskrit Studies Central Journal, *Journal of the Sanskrit Studies Centre,* Silpakorn University, 2 (2006) 193-207 http://fritsstaal.googlepages.com/soundbook

60 Courtesy: Phasook Indrawooth

[61] Source: http://www.jnicc.com/ Jawaharlal Nehru Indian Cultural Centre, Jakarta (Embassy of India)

[62] http://www.thejakartapost.com/news/2001/05/19/indian-noted-writer-tagore-makes-return-java-jis.html?1

[63] http://en.wikipedia.org/wiki/Gangaikonda_Cholapuram

[64] http://en.wikipedia.org/wiki/Mekong_Delta

[65] http://en.wikipedia.org/wiki/Angkor_wat

[66] Sastri, K.A. Nilakanta (1949). South Indian Influences in the Far East. Bombay: Hind Kitabs Ltd.. pp. 82 & 84.

[67] George Coedes, *Les etats hindouises d'Indochine et d'Indonesie*, Paris: Editions E. de Boccard, 1964.

[68] Bayley, Susan (2004), "Imagining 'Greater India': French and Indian Visions of Colonialism in the Indic Mode",*Modern Asian Studies* **38** (3): 703-744.

[69] Wheatley, Paul, 1982, "Presidential Address: India Beyond the Ganges--Desultory Reflections on the Origins of Civilization in Southeast Asia", *The Journal of Asian Studies* **42** (1), pp. 27-28.

[70] http://www.news.wisc.edu/6138
http://www.nature.com/nature/journal/v411/n6833/abs/411062a0.html
Evolution of Asian monsoons and phased uplift of the Himalaya–Tibetan plateau since Late Miocene times by An Zhisheng et al.

[71] http://en.wikipedia.org/wiki/Angkor_wat

[72] http://www.buddhanet.net/e-learning/buddhistworld/lanka-txt.htm

http://www.theravada.gr/srilanka.html

[73] Dorian Q. Fuller et al., 2009, Crops, cattle and commensals across the Indian Ocean

[74] http://www.bradshawfoundation.com/stephenoppenheimer/

[75] http://en.wikipedia.org/wiki/Milankovitch_cycles

[76]http://www.indiana.edu/~geol105/images/gaia_chapter_4/milankovitch.htm

[77] http://www.ausairpower.net/APA-2012-01.html

[78] http://en.wikipedia.org/wiki/Krakatoa#cite_ref-12

[79] http://www.columbia.edu/cu/pr/95/18688.html Geologists Find: An Earth Plate Is Breaking in Two

[80] The Collision of India and Asia (90 mya - Present) Deformation of Asia and the formation of the Himalayas and Tibetan Plateau http://www.scotese.com/indianim.htm

[81] http://www.iotc.org/English/

[82] See: http://en.wikipedia.org/wiki/European_Coal_and_Steel_Community

[83] http://sedac.ciesin.columbia.edu/entri/texts/acrc/IndianO.txt.html

[84] http://www.fao.org/docrep/s5280T/s5280t0s.htm

[85] http://www.ausairpower.net/APA-2012-01.html

[86] http://www.financialexpress.com/news/Connecting-Mekong-region-with-India-through-infrastructure-linkages/269478/

[87]http://www.ggdc.net/Maddison/other_books/Contours_World_Economy.pdf

[88] http://aric.adb.org/pdf/aeim/AEIM_2012July_FullReport.pdf Asian Economic Integration Monitor, July 2012, Asian Development Bank, Manila.

[89] http://www.asiaone.com/News/AsiaOne%2BNews/Asia/Story/A1Story20121022-378928.html

[90] http://www.dailynews.lk/2007/10/06/fea05.asp

[91] http://dsal.uchicago.edu/reference/schwartzberg/pager.html?object=071 *Schwartzberg Atlas*, p. 34.

[92] http://www.noaanews.noaa.gov/stories2009/20091217_tsunami.html

[93] http://bharatkalyan97.blogspot.in/2012/10/hindu-social-corporate-form-and-sreni.html

Hindu Economics: Caste as Social capital - R. Vaidyanathan. Hindu social corporate form and śreṇi dharma: -- S. Kalyanaraman ***Expected to be chapters in a forth coming book on the –Hindu Economics
[94] http://bharatkalyan97.blogspot.in/2012/10/one-nation-one-indian-ocean-community.html

[95] Dedicated service, the only hope [written by Rajaji – May 4, 1963, *Swarajya*]

[96] Data base, Geological Survey of India

[97] cf. Murty et al., 1994
http://www.Setusamudram.in/htmdocs/Articles/cp_rajendran_2.htm

[98] See William Vestal and Allen Lowrie, Geology and Geophysics Branch-Code 7220, U.S. Naval Oceanographic Office NSTL Station, 39522, MS http://www.springerlink.com /content/m602j3k746342lnl

[99] http://www.un.org/Depts/los/convention_agreements/convention_historical_perspective.htm

[100] https://sites.google.com/site/indianoceancommunity1/law-of-the-sea

[101] Source: http://en.wikipedia.org/wiki/Northern_East_West_Freight_Corridor

[102] http://www.railpage.com.au/f-t11311667-s15.htm

[103] Source: http://en.wikipedia.org/wiki/Asian_Highway_Network

[104] http://www.theaustralian.com.au/opinion/next-geopolitical-power-play-will-be-all-at-sea/story-e6frg6zo-1225952487003

[105] B.S. Raghavan, A union of Indian Ocean Nations, July 18, 2011 http://www.thehindubusinessline.com/opinion/columns/b-s-raghavan/article2235882.ece?homepage=true

[106] http://indiannavy.nic.in/press-release/ins-sudarshini-set-sail-historical-odyssey-asean-countries Admiral DK Joshi, Chief of the Naval Staff Flag off IN Sail Training Ship '"Sudarshini" on her historic Voyage to the ASEAN countries.

[107] https://sites.google.com/site/indianoceancommunity1/ S. Kalyanaraman, National President, Rameshwaram Eamasetu Protection Movement; Director, Sarasvati Research Centre; Former Sr. Executive, Asian Development Bank (October 2012)

[108] http://www.tourismoforissa.com/festivals-in-orissa/bali-yatra.html

[109] http://www.dfat.gov.au/geo/indian_ocean/regional_orgs/ior-arc.html

[110] http://geography.about.com/library/cia/blcindian.htm

[111] http://indianoceanworldcentre.com/about

[112] http://ioconline.org/

[113] Opinion column in the *The Atlanta Journal-Constitution*, Dec. 26, 2007 http://www.world-nuclear.org/info/inf71.html

[114] Harris, Tom. (2002-08-29) How Aircraft Carriers Work. http://science.howstuffworks.com/aircraft-carrier2.htm

[115] View of the only shore based nuclear-heated desalination unit in the world. Image and description from Argonne National Laboratory Website http://en.wikipedia.org/wiki/File:Shevchenko_BN350_desalinati.jpg

[116] http://www.world-nuclear.org/info/inf71.html

[117] "*n.* Accomplishment, perfection…*m.* A class of celestial beings belonging to the गण-देवता… according to यास्क [Nir. xii , 41] their locality is theभुवर्लोक or middle region between the earth and sun ; in Mn. i , 22 , the साध्यs are described as created after the gods with natures exquisitely refined , and in iii , 195 , as children of the सोम-सद्s , sons of विराज् ; in the पुराणs they are sons of साध्या , and their number is variously twelve or seventeen ; in the later mythology they seem to be superseded by the सिद्धs » सिद्ध; and their names are मनस् , मन्तृ , प्राण , नर , पान , विनिर्भय , नय , दंश , नारायण , वृष , प्रभु)." (Monier Williams lexicon, p. 1202).

www.ingramcontent.com/pod-product-compliance
Lightning Source LLC
Chambersburg PA
CBHW081646270326
41933CB00018B/3364
* 9 7 8 0 9 8 2 8 9 7 1 5 7 *